Perspectives on Consumer Choice

Gordon R. Foxall

Perspectives on Consumer Choice

From Behavior to Action, from Action to Agency

Gordon R. Foxall
Business Department
Cardiff University
Cardiff, United Kingdom

ISBN 978-1-137-50119-6   ISBN 978-1-137-50121-9   (eBook)
DOI 10.1057/978-1-137-50121-9

Library of Congress Control Number: 2016948384

Printed on acid-free paper

This Palgrave Macmillan imprint is published by Springer Nature
The registered company is Macmillan Publishers Ltd.
The registered company address is: The Campus, 4 Crinan Street, London, N1 9XW, United Kingdom

Acknowledgments

I am grateful to Maddie Holder and Liz Barlow at Palgrave Macmillan for the opportunity to write this book and for their help in bringing it to publication. I would also like to record my debt to Sally Osborne, my secretary at Cardiff Business School, for her willing and able assistance.

I am grateful for discussions on the nature of behavioral economics, economic psychology, and the philosophy of explanation to Professors Erik Arntzen, Asle Fagerstrøm, Donald Hantula, Patrícia Luque, Vishnu Menon, Peter Morgan, Jorge Oliveira-Castro, Valdimar Sigurdsson, and Mirella Yani-de-Soriano.

I am especially grateful, as always, to my wife Jean for her reading and discussing of various drafts, for help with the diagrams, and for her unfailing good cheer and encouragement.

Contents

List of Figures and Tables

List of Boxes

1

Introduction

This book suggests how we might approach the explanation of the central pattern of behavior in affluent, marketing-oriented societies. The task is well worth the effort since it is a central component of both social scientific endeavor and the need to comprehend ourselves in the twenty-first century. While our parents and grandparents were primarily producers, we are more likely to define ourselves as consumers. Parts of our very identities are bound up with something as superficially trivial as our shopping behavior. There is, of course, much more than this to consumer choice: so much so that seriously seeking to understand ourselves as consumers ought surely to assume a dominant position in our epistemological landscape.

But this is an intellectual task and we cannot seek to approach it at the level of either popular cultural studies or managerial marketing in the expectation that we shall thereby gain real understanding. The social and behavioral sciences need to be brought to bear on the task of elucidating consumer choice. The disciplines of economic psychology, philosophy, behavioral economics, and neuropsychology are required as well, of course, as the insight that comes from knowledge of cultural awareness

© The Editor(s) (if applicable) and The Author(s) 2016
G.R. Foxall, *Perspectives on Consumer Choice*,
DOI 10.1057/978-1-137-50121-9_1

and the technological possibilities—and limitations—of contemporary marketing.[1]

In approaching the nature of humans as consumers, we are forced to acknowledge the depth of their personal involvement in the behaviors in which we are interested. Consumers invest their most intimate resources—their desires, beliefs, emotions, and perceptions—in the choices that create their economic and social welfare. The difficulty is that it is not obvious which beliefs and desires, let alone which emotions and perceptions, to attribute to them as we seek to explain and interpret their choices. It is easy to speculate and romanticize about, deconstruct, and overinterpret consumer behavior and there are many examples in both consumer research and cultural studies that exhibit this tendency only too well. Avoiding these admittedly imaginative avenues, that are ultimately not germane to the present task, we must tread a more mundane but finally more illuminating path. In particular, if we are to ascribe intentionality in a responsible manner to consumers, we must first establish the boundaries of the behaviorist explanation of what they do.

This initial pursuit of consumption as behavior is beneficial in its own right since there emerge aspects of consumer choice that are only amenable to such treatment, things we can learn about the behavior of consumers that depend on this parsimonious methodology. Many aspects of brand, product, and store choice, for example, are yielded through the pursuit of this procedure. The true nature of what it is that consumers maximize is also revealed in this conceptually frugal enterprise. Equally, there are aspects of consumer choice that cannot be understood in this

---

[1] Academic marketing is not a discipline in its own right, but an application area that relies on the perspectives, theories, methodologies, and techniques provided by disciplines such as economics and psychology. At a theoretical level, therefore, it generally incorporates rather than creates. As a result, it frequently makes philosophical and methodological assumptions that stem directly from the deliberations of other scientists pursuing other ends. Whatever discipline forms the predominant underlying intellectual basis of marketing science at the moment—it was once economics, has been and continues to be economic psychology, but sociology and anthropology have had their days too—tends to provide a philosophical and theoretical foundation of a sort, somewhat ad hoc, and necessarily temporary. There may not be an easy alternative to this, given the nature of marketing inquiry, but it raises certain difficulties of explanation. For the methodological imperatives imported into marketing are, inevitably, not constructs that are in some way absolutely characteristic of the discipline involved but only those that are currently acceptable to the exponents of that discipline or a subdisciplinary section of it.

way: we can only appreciate what they are when we have exhausted the insights we can obtain from the behaviorist approach. Then the nature and scope of an intentional account of behavior become apparent.

We cannot account, for instance, for some aspects of the continuity and discontinuity of consumer behavior without recourse to intentional idioms, desires, and beliefs, as explanatory devices. We cannot account for the personal level of the consumers' experience, its meaning, unless we make reference to their desires and beliefs, emotions and perceptions, as well as to the rewards and costs that consumption brings. Finally, it would be impossible to delimit behavioral interpretations of choice were it not for our ability to attribute the thoughts and feelings appropriate to their history and current situation. These things we learn only from the pursuit of the behaviorist methodology, pushing to its limits the model of consumer choice derived within such confines. This in turn opens up the sure route to a responsible Intentional Interpretation of consumer choice, but it is only the beginning of our social scientific quest.

For it remains all too easy to invent fanciful desires and beliefs that consumers might be embodying in their behavior. The point is to explain, not to embellish. So how are we to discipline our intentional account? One way, following the lead of philosopher Daniel Dennett, is to start with an idealized view of the consumer as a utility maximizer and work out what manner of desires and beliefs he or she ought to have given their history and circumstances. We can be bolder in our prescription of intentionality than Dennett's scheme permits, however, for the very reason that we begin our intellectual task with the behavioral account of consumer choice. So we can elaborate the notion of utility by remembering that consumers maximize a bundle of utilitarian and informational reinforcements rather than just a vague quantity called utility. We know from our empirical research how to conceptualize and operationally measure these sources of reward and how to relate them to the emotional reactions that are the ultimate evolutionarily sanctioned rewards that contribute to biological fitness and personal survival. These insights from the behavioral perspective place the ensuing intentional account of consumer choice on a much firmer footing than any strategy which proceeds directly to psychological explanation in its absence.

This idealized intentional view must be cashed out in what we know about the actual functioning of consumers, principally their cognitive and metacognitive processing. We need to consult the theories that have been advanced in these areas in order to see whether they are consistent with our Intentional Interpretations and whether the cognitive functioning they proposed has generated the intentionality required for our first approximation of their behavior and its mainsprings. It is essential to keep our feet on the ground here by ensuring that our Intentional Interpretations and Cognitive Interpretations are consistent with what we know of the extensional sciences that investigate economic and social behavior: neurophysiology and behavioral science. The resulting use we make of the cognitive psychology of consumer choice ought then to constrain our interpretations as well as ground our account of consumer behavior in what we know of rational human decision making—and its shortcomings.

These intellectual concerns provide the subject matter of this book. Given that the aim is to propose a metatheoretical framework for the cognitive explanation of consumer choice, rather than an exposition of consumer behavior per se, psychology and philosophy figure strongly. Consumer choice is a part of the pattern of human activity and its explanation therefore is that of human choice in general. The framework of conceptualization and analysis that elucidates how we are to understand consumer choice must apply more generally than just to the particular typology of behavior with which we are primarily concerned. It is inevitable in view of this that it draw upon and respond to the theories of human behavior, action, and agency that have been advanced by psychologists and philosophers. To this extent, the book is not about consumer choice per se; it is about how we can speak about consumer choice.

Earlier chapters set the scene by introducing behaviorist and cognitive approaches to consumer choice and showing how their interaction leads to richer explanations, and describe an extensional model of consumer choice which portrays consumer *behavior* as the outcome of the consumer's history of reinforcement and the opportunities for purchase and consumption offered by the current consumer behavior setting. Hence, Chapter 2 introduces the philosophy of Intentional Behaviorism and describes radical behaviorism as a psychological methodology. Chapter 3 projects this understanding into the explanation of consumer choice from a behaviorist standpoint, notably in terms of the Behavioral Perspective Model and the evidence for its capacity to elucidate consumption as behavior. This approach has yielded a basic understanding of the nature of consumption that allows the prediction of such aspects of consumer behavior as brand, product, and store choice; the sensitivity of consumption to changes in price; and the types of reinforcement that consumers seek in the course of utility maximization. It also permits the interpretation of swathes of more complex consumer choice such as saving and investment, the adoption and diffusion of innovations, and environmental despoliation and protection. Even though such interpretations are not in themselves amenable to a behaviorist analysis, they are evaluable by means of data generated by other researchers in marketing, economic psychology, and behavioral economics on the basis of which they can be understood in terms of the extensional model which suggests hypotheses for further empirical research.

Several succeeding chapters derive and elaborate the methodology of Intentional Behaviorism by identifying aspects of consumer choice that are not amenable to empirical analysis in behaviorist terms because the stimuli necessary for such an investigation are not available. Accounting for the continuity/discontinuity of behavior, for instance, as well as the personal level of consumer experience, and formulating suitably constrained behaviorist interpretations, all fall short of the usual canons of behaviorist practice because it is not feasible to identify clearly the antecedent and consequential stimuli that would normally form the stimulus field through which the behavior is explained. In identifying these limitations, these chapters establish the *bounds of behaviorism* which demarcate the points at which it becomes necessary to turn to an intentional account of the behavior for which no stimulus field is obvious. Each of the bounds of behaviorism finds a counterpart in the *imperatives of intentionality* which indicate the direction a psychological explanation should take: the principles of ensuring an intentional account of the behavior, of taking first-person experience into consideration, and of maintaining stimulus proximity in proffering behaviorist interpretations. The investment in the philosophy of economic psychology that is made in Chapters 4, 5, and 6, is necessary to the overall project of the book which aims to place the psychological explanation of consumer choice on a secure epistemological footing.

Pursuit of the imperatives of intentionality enjoins a rigorous methodology. We have seen that this psychological explanation of consumer choice has two stages, suggested by but differing from Dennett's (1987) approach to intentional psychology. The first stage involves the creation of an *Intentional Interpretation* of behavior which treats the consumer as an idealized (utility maximizing) system whose intentionality (desires and beliefs) can be deduced from knowledge of its learning history and current circumstances. This Intentional Interpretation must be critically examined in terms of the extent to which the consumers' cognitive processes would be capable of generating the desires, beliefs, emotions, and perceptions by reference to which the Intentional Interpretation proceeds. This process, the construction and deployment of a *Cognitive Interpretation*, is the second stage of psychological explanation.

This methodology is elaborated in the context of intentionality and cognition. In the first stage of psychological explanation, based, as I have said, on an intentional perspective of consumer choice, the consumer situation and the patterns of reinforcement which explain behavior are delineated in intentional terms and the relationships among them are drawn out. This permits the idealized projection of the intentionality of a consumer with a particular consumption history in a specified setting which promises reinforcing and punishing outcomes for further consumption behaviors. This framework of conceptualization and analysis can then be employed to elucidate the behavior of consumers more generally, ranging from the routine—everyday consumer behavior such as brand choice for familiar food products—to the extreme—such as addiction to slot machine gambling. The resulting Intentional Interpretation must also be consistent with what is known of consumer choice via the extensional sciences of neurophysiology and behaviorology.

The second stage of psychological explanation, again as has been noted, seeks to establish the degree to which the Intentional Interpretation is consistent with cognitive psychology. How far does our knowledge of the structure and functioning of cognitive processes justify the view that consumer choice that is not amenable to a behaviorist explanation can be interpreted intentionally? Two sources of cognitive psychology are employed for this purpose, reflecting the need to link the personal level of exposition first with the sub-personal (via neurophysiology) and second with the super-personal (via operancy).[2] These explanations, respectively termed micro-cognitive psychology (MiCP) and macro-cognitive psychology (MaCP), are represented, in turn, by dual and triprocess models of metacognitive functioning (e.g., Stanovich 2009a), and theories of collective intentionality and the construction of social reality (e.g., Searle 1995, 2010a, b). The account of MiCP illustrates not only the capacity of unchecked neurophysiological responses to environmental stimuli to dominate consumer choice but also the abilities instantiated by cortical and subcortical brain regions to perform the executive functions that potentially forestall these impulses and make considered responding a possibility. The account of MaCP discusses the ability of humans, acting collectively, to fashion for themselves the contingencies of reinforcement and punishment that will influence their actions, something that is a far cry from the behaviorist notion that locates agency in the controlling environment rather than the person. In order to bridge the gap between these micro- and macro-perspectives on consumer choice, we require a meso-cognitive level of theorizing and the possibility that this role is fulfilled by picoeconomics (Ainslie 1992) is explored. At this level of cognitive functioning, it is the individual who determines for himself or herself which pattern of contingencies will influence choice.

Therefore, while Chapters 3 and 4 are primarily concerned with the exposition of consumer choice as behavior and the consequences of this perspective for explanation, Chapters 5 and 6 are concerned with the nature of intentionality and the criteria for its ascription, and Chapters 7, 8, 9, 10, and 11 successively treat consumer choice as action, decision, and agency. Consumer choice, once it is perceived as action as well as behavior, lends itself to additional interpretation in cognitive and agential terms. This inexorable progression entails a multiperspectival vision. Only the attempt to confine understanding to a single standpoint can inhibit our quest to comprehend not just our "getting and spending" but our very selves.

---

[2] By *operancy* I mean the processes described by operant *behaviorology* or operant psychology in terms of the linkages between behavior and its contingent environmental consequences. See the discussion of radical behaviorism in Chapter 2.

Bibliography

Ainslie, G. (1992). *Picoeconomics: The strategic interaction of successive motivational states within the person.* Cambridge: Cambridge University Press.

Dennett, D. C. (1987). *The intentional stance.* Cambridge, MA: MIT Press.

Searle, J. R. (1995). *The construction of social reality.* New York: Free Press.

Searle, J. R. (2010a). *Making the social world: The structure of human civilization.* Oxford: Oxford University Press.

Searle, J. R. (2010b). Consciousness and the problem of free will. In R. F. Baumeister, A. R. Mele, & K. D. Vohs (Eds.), *Free will and consciousness: How might they work?* (pp. 121–134). Oxford: Oxford University Press.

Stanovich, K. E. (2009a). Distinguishing the reflective, algorithmic, and autonomous minds: Is it time for a tri-process theory? In J. S. B. T. Evans & K. Frankish (Eds.), *In two minds: Dual processes and beyond* (pp. 55–88). Oxford: Oxford University Press.

2

Explaining Consumer Choice

Introduction

How can we responsibly ascribe beliefs, attitudes, intentions, and other apparently intra-psychic concepts in the explanation of consumer behavior? It is necessary to specify that we do this "responsibly" because it is so tempting to invent a mental account of behavior that purports to explain it. Our first task is to discover whether an intentional account of behavior is even necessary.

On the logic of intentional explanation, if I repeatedly buy a particular brand it must be because I believe it is good for me or have a positive attitude toward it; or perhaps it fits my personality better than other brands, conforms to my self-image, or facilitates my processing of information in a particular way. I do not think that consumer researchers are so naïve as to invent mentalistic explanations of this kind at will in order to account for choice but there is an automatic tendency to ascribe understandings of consumer behavior on the assumption that it is rationally governed by our pre-behavioral cognitive processes. After all, since the Enlightenment we have had an image of humans as governed by reason rather than whim, and much social and behavioral science would be impossible unless we

© The Editor(s) (if applicable) and The Author(s) 2016
G.R. Foxall, *Perspectives on Consumer Choice*,
DOI 10.1057/978-1-137-50121-9_2

entertained some suppositions about the continuity of human choice. But we should guard against the attribution of cognitive processes to consumers in the absence of a sound theoretical basis for their ascription.

In order to consider the implications of behaviorism for the explanation of consumer choice, the second part of the chapter sets out its major tenets. Particular attention is accorded the radical behaviorist treatment of verbal behavior since in this we discover its orientation toward the phenomena that most psychologists portray as cognition. The beginnings of strategy for the analysis of consumer choice in behaviorist terms can now be laid down. This is the contextual stance which presents the consumer as an operant system which can be predicted and influenced via the contingencies of reinforcement.

Consumer Choice

Few things are more familiar to members of affluent, marketing-oriented societies than consumer choice. Confronted by a plethora of competing brands and products, services, and e-tailed opportunities that are but a click away, we naturally wonder how we choose among them to achieve the particular array of goods that suit our lifestyle. There are numerous explanations of consumer behavior, some of which put us at the mercy of relentlessly persuasive advertising, some of which emphasize the ways our minds work in formulating beliefs, attitudes, and intentions that guide our marketplace selections, and some of which lay stress on the situational determinants of choice—the store layouts, price promotions, and distribution systems that apparently make buying and consuming so easy. Some standpoints portray the consumer as sovereign, exercising freewill; for others, our choices are strictly determined. In a nutshell, consumer choice can be understood from several perspectives: as consumer *behavior*, as consumer *action*, and as consumer *agency*.

First, there is a sense in which choice just connotes behavior: selecting tea rather than coffee, buying brand A rather than brand B. A more sophisticated but still behavioral view of choice casts it as the relative frequency with which the consumer buys a specific product or brand. Most consumers of a product category (say, butter) buy not one but several versions of it, that is, brands, over a period of time. A small proportion of buyers are exclusive purchasers of one or other brand but the vast majority of buyers are multibrand purchasers. This is true not only of fast-moving consumer goods but also of durables and even industrial products. Behavior of this sort is often predictable, at least at the aggregate level, from no more than knowledge of the situational or environmental circumstances in which it occurs. Although the behavior may seem random, it closely reflects the pattern of costs and benefits associated with each brand.

Behavior is, therefore, activity viewed from an etic perspective, that is, by means of categories that seem important from the standpoint of the investigator. Its causation is a matter of selection by consequences, whether by the operation of phylogenetic or ontogenetic contingencies (Skinner 1981). Within this framework we may distinguish *inborn behavior* (responses produced by innate releasing mechanisms); *reflexive behavior* (responses produced in classical conditioning); and *operant behavior* (which consists in movements that can be predicted from the situation). Even here there is the possibility of responses being modified to an extent through experience, as in the course of stimulus and response generalization, for instance. But when we seek principally to predict and perhaps influence consumer activity, we understand consumer behavior, viewed as relative consumer choice, as falling into this category.

Action, by contrast, is activity viewed from an emic perspective, that is, from the standpoint of the actor, in terms of the meaning the activity has for him or her: it is said to be *voluntary* or *intended*, the result of the individual's acting rather than his or her being acted upon. It is activity that is explained not in terms of the contingencies of reinforcement but as the outcome of mental deliberation requiring the formulation of desires and beliefs.

Between the extremes of behaviorism, in which the environment is a kind of agent in the sense of the initiator or cause of activity, and the view that the person is the agent, lies the viewpoint of cognitive psychology in which desires, beliefs, emotions, and perceptions are considered causes of behavior which themselves form deterministic chain of events. There is no sense of conceding autonomy to the individual in ascribing these intentional terms in the explanation of his or her behavior. Rather the use of intentional language which these concepts require is understood as a purely materialistic approach to the explication of choice. The reason for adopting this cognitive stance is that the language of extensional behavioral science has ceased to account for behavior. The sole resort is then to intentional language. I mention this particularly because otherwise it may seem that the sole alternative to behaviorism is agent causation. Cognitive psychology provides another possibility, though it entails considerations of where agency lies since the implication is that beliefs, attitudes, and intentions are the result of intra-personal information processing. The theme of this volume, the role of cognition in the explanation of consumer choice, draws upon all three of these aspects of consumer activity. In it, I suggest a methodology for arriving at a responsible intentional and cognitive understanding of consumer choice: *Intentional Behaviorism*. While behavior (or, better, activity) is all we have to study, there is more than one language in which we may speak of it, even within a scientific purview. There is more than one perspective, more than one language of explanation that we can adopt in order to arrive at a comprehensive understanding.

Intentional Behaviorism

Methodologies of Explanation

Just because cognitive inference is a central part of the cultural sea in which we currently swim, it does not follow that we can leave its methodological basis unexamined. There does not appear to be a straightforward means of ascribing intentionality and cognition that does not rest uncritically on the ideological assumption that behavior is impossible in the absence of prior mentation. My research program over many years has been concerned with establishing the point at which cognitive explanation becomes inevitable because its alternative, the behavioristic endeavor to explain consumer choice entirely in terms of its environmental consequences, reinforcers, and punishers, has been exhausted. In the process of seeking to explain consumer choice in a strictly behaviorist manner we may, first, discover the positive benefits of taking this contextual stance by demarcating the way in which consumption is well-described in terms of the rewards and sanctions it produces. There is always the possibility that, given our research objectives, this will suffice. The work of Andrew Ehrenberg and his colleagues (Ehrenberg 1988; Romaniuk and Sharp 2016; Sharp 2010) has shown that many facets of consumer choice that are useful to practitioners and instructive to theoretical researchers can be accessed without an elaborate cognitive framework of conceptualization and analysis. In this case an intentional or cognitive explanation may be unnecessary. However, the empirical component of the research program to which this monograph belongs leads to the conclusion that while a behaviorist perspective is indeed useful in important respects, the need to progress to psychological explanation is inevitable if we are to do more than predict and, possibly influence, consumer choice.

The cognitive explanation of behavior is problematic, however, insofar as it refers to theoretical unobservables for its explicatory power, entities that have to be inferred from behavioral and neurophysiological measures rather than apprehended directly. It is all too easy to assume that a pattern of behavior must be a function of some underlying attitudinal or personality variable rather than of environmental stimulation or neurophysiological inputs. Only when these have been eliminated from inquiry can we safely turn to intentional explanations. The consequent strategy of *Intentional Behaviorism*, which is the research philosophy on which this quest for the responsible incorporation of cognition into the explanation of consumer choice rests, entails developing models of consumer behavior in accordance with a strictly descriptive behaviorism, and testing them to destruction, before incorporating intentional and cognitive variables as and when they are required.

Intentional Behaviorism uses radical behaviorism and intentional psychology to understand the role of cognition in the explanation of consumer choice. This chapter is principally concerned to examine the distinct explanatory mode presented by radical behaviorism, while later chapters examine the nature of psychological explanation and develop a unique methodology for its deployment in the process of making consumer choice intelligible. The distinct accounts of human choice offered these two approaches are reflected in their respective uses of extensional and intentional languages to make sense of their subject matter. A cardinal tenet of this multidisciplinary approach is that the personal level of exposition, that which is concerned with the individual's behavior, desires, and beliefs, must be kept distinct in the course of explanation from both the sub-personal level of exposition, represented by neurophysiology, and the super-personal level of exposition, represented by behaviorology. The early part of this chapter expands on this theme by describing how Intentional Behaviorism draws upon these approaches to knowledge in establishing what we know of consumer choice and how a psychological explanation contributes to its understanding. In particular, Intentional Behaviorism entails a definite sequence of exposition, in which psychological explanation becomes necessary only when the behaviorist account has become exhausted in terms of its contribution to understanding consumer choice. At that point, we must turn to Intentional Interpretation and cognitive psychology.

The need for an initial approach that depends on a parsimonious, behaviorist model of consumer choice and, where it has been shown to be empirically necessary, a cognitive stage of explanation, is apparent from the nature of these distinct methodologies.

The essential explanatory feature of cognitivism is the pre-behavioral representation of the environment, ranging from relatively simple perceptual to complex symbolic processing, as required by linguistic comprehension (de Gelder 1996). These representations may relate to the organism's internal as well as its external world. This is an entirely distinct manner of explanation from that of behaviorism in which the effect of the environment is direct, unmediated by representations; behavior is a function of the external reinforcing and punishing stimuli that have followed it in the past. Compiani (1996, pp. 46–7) remarks that

> Behaviourism recognizes the environment as playing a determinative role in directing and conditioning the actions of the subject whose internal state can be completely characterized using externally controllable parameters. Consistently, the conditioning of the system can also be obtained through an external supervision mechanism based on gratification or frustration as a function of the response to stimuli.

Crucially,

> This reasoning exclusively in terms of external parameters (stimulus and response) assumes that the processing by the system does not add anything at all to the information content of the input; that is, the performance of the system can be completely characterized externally without recourse to the internal properties of the system.

Although he has Pavlovian conditioning in view, what he says is equally true of operant conditioning.

The emphasis on internal representation and the computational operations performed on them as the essential feature of cognitive explanation is central to modern accounts (e.g., Braisby and Gellatly 2012; Eysenck 2012). The fundamental difference between behaviorism and cognitivism is that the variables of which behaviorists claim behavior to be a function are empirically available for the direct testing of their influence on responding. It is possible to demonstrate with intersubjective agreement that behavior is a function of these independent variables by experimental analyses. By contrast, the variables proposed by cognitive psychology are theoretical, existing only in the mind of the investigator. Variables understood to embody, underlay, or correlate closely with cognitive states can be deduced from neurophysiology and behavioral science and tested empirically but this is not the same as having direct access to them. They are inferences rather than concrete, manipulable entities. This does not mean they are not real; nor does it exclude the fashioning of causal accounts of behavior in terms of cognitive variables. But it does require that we distinguish carefully the kind of knowledge that psychological explanation provides from that which direct experimentation makes available. And therein lies the significance of the insistence on a behaviorist substrate for the theory of consumer choice.

Languages of Explanation

Consumer researchers frequently account for choice by arguing that the customer buys this or that brand because she *prefers* it, *likes* it, *wants* it or *needs* it, *has a positive attitude* toward it, or *intends* to purchase it, and despite the increased complexity of social cognitive psychology in recent decades, this level of understanding suffices for much semi-popular marketing writing and as the foundation of more serious research. The ubiquity of this intentional language is clear from both standard textbook treatments and the research reported in leading journals. Consumer behavior is ascribed generally to mental processing and its outcomes in the form of brand beliefs, brand attitudes, and brand-related purchase and discontinuance intentions. But what justifies this cognitive stance? Although there is no shortage of discussion of the most appropriate methods by which this assumption can be demonstrated, it is seldom questioned that the cognition-behavior approach is a legitimate source of explanation. It is also rare among consumer researchers to go beyond the formalism of social cognitive psychology in order to examine the philosophical basis of the explanation that is being offered. Usually in empirical work it is sufficient that coefficients reach a conventional level of significance for hypotheses to be accepted, for knowledge of the phenomena under investigation to be assumed. And critical theoretical work is rare enough to constitute no threat to the prevailing order.

Nevertheless, scientific explanation is verbal behavior and the linguistic mode we adopt in accounting for consumer behavior has implications for the explanation we propose. Theories and metatheories are concerned to establish the syntactical rules that govern explanation. Any attempt to comprehend behaviorism as a philosophy of psychology, therefore, requires an appreciation of how its practitioners use language. It also requires some familiarity with the ways in which competing systems of explanation use language. For this reason alone, we cannot avoid intentionality. Some behaviorist rebuttals of intentional explanation do not even mention that it inheres above all in a particular form of linguistic usage, even before any ontological questions have been settled (see Foxall 2004, for an extended treatment of radical behaviorism as an approach to psychology that is committed to an extensional linguistic mode). It seems essential, therefore, to understand the nature of intentionality and to contrast it with the extensional explanation toward which behaviorism has traditionally striven. For, whatever our aims, if we use intentional language, we are using intentional explanation.

Intentionality is the property that some things have of being *about* something other than themselves. Mental states such as *believes, desires,* and *intends* are all intentional terms. It is impossible just to *know*: we know about something; or just to *believe*: we believe that this or that is the case; or just to *desire*: again we desire some thing or other (see, for instance, Chisholm 1957; Dennett 1969; Quine 1960; Searle 1983). Let us start with the definitions given by Searle (1983). Mental states are intentional in that they refer to or represent something outside themselves. Behavior can also be intentional in this sense: the waggle dance of the honey bee is intentional because it is about the position and distance of new nesting sites, water, and the flowers that provide nectar and pollen for other members of the nest. Some manmade artifacts also exhibit intentionality. Turner's *Fighting Temeraire* is not simply oil paint and canvas, not even just a picture: to a sentient onlooker, it symbolizes the fate of a once-distinguished sailing ship superseded by steam vessels like the tug that is towing it away to be broken up.

Searle (2007) distinguishes the original or intrinsic intentionality just described from the "derived intentionality" possessed by, say, a shopping list. Whereas a shopping list displays intrinsic intentionality when it exists in my mind, when it is written down the marks on the paper derive their intentionality, their aboutness, from the original intentionality of my mental list. Dennett (1996, pp. 50–55) goes further than Searle by claiming that *all* intentionality is derived intentionality, that even a mental shopping list is secondarily intentional. This need not detain us in the present context since the use I shall make of derived intentionality does not depend on its uniquely comprising intentionality per se.

Theoretical accounts of behavior are differentiated by the kind of language they employ and the logic on which it is based. This logic sets out, for example, the criteria by which the truth of the sentences these accounts employ is to be judged. The essence of radical behaviorism, in common with most natural sciences, is its use of *extensional language*, that is, sentences that have the following characteristics. First, coextensive terms are interchangeable without altering the truth value of the statement. "*Titus Andronicus* was written by Shakespeare" can be rendered "*Titus Andronicus* was written by the Bard of Avon" without its meaning being altered. "Shakespeare" and "Bard of Avon" are said to be coextensive because they share a single extension, namely the man who wrote the play. Extensional sentences are said to be referentially transparent because of this substitutability. Second, an extensional object must have actual existence: my statement "I have just returned from Rome" is true only if there is an actual place, Rome, from which I have recently come. Compare this with "I have just eaten ambrosia." How would one establish the truth value of this statement, given that ambrosia is the mythical food of the (equally mythical) gods? Third, extensional objects are not contained within the language in which they are expressed but are to be found in the environment; hence, the extension of "Titus Andronicus" is the play itself.

Intensionality (with an *s*) is also specifically a linguistic matter, a property of sentences that contain particular kinds of verb such as "thinks," "desires," or "believes." Words like *believes, desires, perceives*, and *feels* are known as "attitudes" by philosophers and their meaning or content is given by the proposition following them: for example, "that *p*." A statement such as "Adele believes that watching television is addictive" comprises an attitude (believes) and a proposition (that watching television is addictive) and is thus known as a propositional attitude. Propositional attitudes are often used in intentional explanations and they differ markedly from those generally employed in scientific discourse. Propositional sentences do not conform to the rules of the extensional sentences that we have considered; rather, they have a logic of their own that affects their truth value. Whereas extensional language permits the substitution of codesignative terms while retaining the truth value of the sentence (Quine 1960), intentional sentences do not. First, the statement "Jones *believes* that *Titus Andronicus* was written by Shakespeare" cannot be rendered "Jones *believes* that *Titus Andronicus* was written by the Swan of Avon" since Jones may not be aware that Shakespeare is the Swan of Avon (even the worst clichés are, thankfully, not always ubiquitous). "Shakespeare" and "the Swan of Avon" are both intensions (or meanings): their extension (that to which they refer) is, as I have said, the man who wrote the play in question. The principle of the substitutability of coextensives does not apply to intensional terms since they do not share the same extension. Intensional expressions are therefore sometimes said to be referentially opaque. Second, intensional objects need not exist in the external world. "Jones is seeking the elixir of youth" might actually be the case: that Jones is looking for something does not imply that it is real. Third, intensional sentences *contain* their objects which exist within the sentence. The elixir of youth exists *in* the sentence about what Jones is doing: the sentence is said to exhibit *intentional inexistence*. It does not matter whether the intensional object actually exists (e.g., the play *Titus Andronicus*) or is fictitious (the food of gods known as ambrosia).[1]

---

[1] McGinn (1996) distinguishes two kinds of mental phenomenon: sensations and propositional attitudes. (See the figure below.) The former, which are first-personal, and subjective (private) if felt directly, but objective if ascribed to another, are divisible into bodily sensations and perceptions. While bodily sensations do not have an intentional object, perceptions do. One is conscious of a bodily sensation such as itching but it is not about anything; a perception, by contrast, is always *of* something or other. Adele does not just perceive; she perceives the mountain or whatever. To perceive is a transitive verb. (Note that this is different from perceiving *that* p, as in "I perceive that you mean to kill me," which is a cognitive propositional attitude.) Propositional attitudes are third-personal, and subjective (i.e., private) if ascribed to oneself; objective, if ascribed to another.

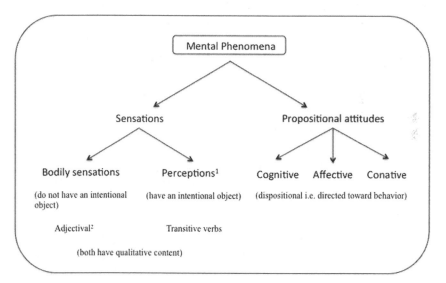

Mental Phenomena

Notes:
1. However, to perceive *that* p is a cognitive propositional attitude
2. Adjectival according to McGinn but also, I would add, nounal

For Searle (1983, pp. 20–26), there is a world of difference between intentionality and intensionality. Whereas intentionality refers to the capacity of mental states, states of the human mind like desires and beliefs to be about something other than themselves, intensionality is entirely a property of sentences, those that do not conform to the rules set out for extensional sentences. Their truth value differs from that of extensional sentences and, therefore, their use necessarily involves the adoption of an alternative mode of explanation.

But, while Searle draws a sharp distinction between intentionality and intensionality, Dennett (1996) sees the two terms as denoting essentially the same thing. Dennett (1969) is, following Chisholm (1957), a strong advocate of the idea that intentionality (with a *t*) is a linguistic phenomenon anyway and in *Kinds of Minds* (Dennett 1996) he defends the view that intentionality and intensionality are essentially not worth distinguishing for most purposes. I think we have to steer a clear course between these views.

It is useful and proper to distinguish *extensional* sentences from *intensional* sentences, on the grounds that they have peculiar properties that affect their truth value (their referential opacity or transparency, for instance). However, it remains the case that attitudes such as *desires* and *believes* are intentional insofar as they refer to some part of the world. It is also the case that the very sentences that are intensional are those that contain such intentional verbs; hence, there is a connection between intentionality and intensionality. Extensional sentences and the radical behaviorist explanation that relies on them emphatically eschew both intentional words and intentional explanation. Intentional Behaviorism argues that there are some behaviors that cannot be explained in extensional terms; these behaviors require the use of intentional attitudes and these give rise, in turn, to explanations that proceed intensionally. Intentional Behaviorism raises such questions as: How do both behaviorism and intentionality elucidate consumer choice? Are their contributions competitive or complementary? Can we have one without the other?

As a strategy for research in psychology, Intentional Behaviorism involves both a parsimonious approach to the explanation of behavior (such as radical behaviorism) and a psychological explanation based on

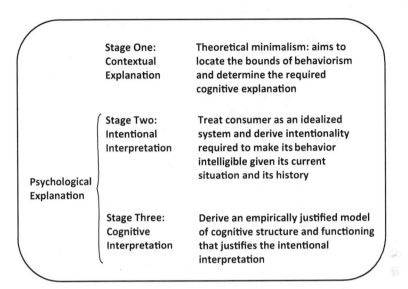

Fig. 2.1 Intentional Behaviorism: The methodological sequence

cognitive psychology. The principal aim in presenting these schools of thought is to show how cognitive terms can be legitimately employed in the explanation of consumer behavior. Why is this an issue? Surely it is obvious that any act we undertake muse be preceded by a belief, attitude, or intention? Unfortunately, it is so obvious that we can all too easily fall into the habit of attributing every behavior to a psychological cause that is not empirically available for further investigation. In addition, there are many aspects of behavior that are understandable without resort to this kind of psychological reductionism. The fascinating intellectual problem that remains therefore has two aspects: first, to identify those facets of consumer behavior which can be illuminated by a noncognitive analysis; and, second, to propose what form the cognitive analysis of consumer behavior should take (Fig. 2.1).

The first stage seeks to understand behavior as determined by its context, the environment of rewards and punishers that have followed it in the past and which will shape and maintain it in the future. Its objectives are (i) to demonstrate the contribution that this parsimonious approach to behavioral science, shorn of any reference to intra-personal cognitive or neurophysiological influences can make to consumer research, and (ii) to delineate the bounds of behaviorism, the points at which this school of psychology can no longer explain behavior, generally because the stimuli necessary to account for behavior are not identifiable. In short, we construct a behaviorist model of choice and test it to destruction in order to identify both its positive contribution to understanding consumer choice and the point at which it can go no further. This is the *theoretical minimalism* stage of Intentional Behaviorism, that which consists in the production of a contextual explanation of choice.

The second stage entails formulating an *Intentional Interpretation* of that behavior for which a behaviorist explanation evades us, treating it as explicable in terms of the actor's desires, beliefs, emotions, and perceptions. This account, if it is to be consistent with what we have learned of consumer choice by means of the behaviorist model, is obtained at the price of treating the consumer as a rational system that maximizes utility. By treating the system as rational in this way, we can ascribe to it the desires and beliefs that it "ought" to have given its history and current circumstances. The aim is to explain or interpret but not necessarily to predict the behavior of the system. This stage draws to an extent on Dennett's (1987) Intentional Systems Theory (IST) formulation for dealing with an intentional system by idealizing its objective function and deriving its appropriate intentionality (though in his case in order to predict the system's behavior). It is not our aim to predict the behavior of the system on the basis of information available at this basic level of interpretation; rather it is to establish the likely intentional consumer situation that would explain its behavior as a rational system. In this way, the contribution of an intentional account of consumer behavior can be assessed through judgment of the extent to which it provides an intelligible explanation of activity for which the behaviorist depiction proved inadequate.

The third stage seeks to ascertain how far this idealized interpretation of consumer behavior can be justified on the basis of our understanding of cognitive decision processes. We constructed the Intentional Interpretation on the basis of certain assumptions about the motivation of the consumer and we must now establish the extent to which we think this is borne out by what we know of the psychology of cognitive functioning. While the initial, theoretically minimalist, stage provided a contextual explanation of behavior, the two following stages, the Intentional Interpretation and the Cognitive Interpretation, provide a psychological explanation. This psychological explanation is evaluated in part by reference to its consonance with the findings and theories of neuroscience and behavioral science, which are leading constraints on cognitive theorizing. The third stage, *Cognitive Interpretation*, does not include variables that can enter directly into an empirical analysis: cognition by its very nature is a theoretical source of explanation. The empirical testing of cognitive hypotheses and models remains, therefore, the business of the extensional sciences of behavior and neurophysiology.[2]

Imperatives of Intentional Explanation

This methodological procedure, this appeal to representation in order to explain, is necessitated by the failure to find the stimulus-response correlations on which operant explanation depends (Skinner 1931, 1935a, b). Such explanatory deficits take two forms, both of them instances of *misrepresentation* that distinguish behavior that requires a psychological explanation from that which does not (Bermúdez 2003).

First, the response may occur in the absence of the requisite discriminative or reinforcing stimulus, a state of affairs which encourages the assumption that the creature has a representation of the stimulus which occasions the production of the behavior. This is relevant to the persistence of behavior in the absence of reinforcement. The operant paradigm stipulates that in order to control the rate of a behavior, a reinforcer must be presented *immediately* after the response has been performed. However, when an animal or person has been trained to perform a behavior on a variable ratio (VR) schedule[3] which provides a reinforcement on

---

[2] This conclusion about the impossibility of directly testing cognitive accounts means that the second stage of psychological explanation is the production or application of a *competence* rather than a *performance* theory. This marks further deviations from Dennett's approach, which are discussed in Chapter 6.

[3] Schedules of reinforcement relate rate of responding to the arrangement of the reinforcers that maintain it. This programming of reinforcement may be temporal or cumulative. A fixed interval (FI) schedule is one "of intermittent reinforcement in which the first response occurring after a

average for every 50 responses, only 2 % of the responses are reinforced by the immediate presentation of a reward (Bandura 1986). The behavior continues unabated, however, and may be strengthened by further "stretching" of the schedule (so that, for instance, only 1 % of responses are followed by immediate reinforcement). This situation nicely illustrates how an operant and a psychological interpretation of behavior may coexist.

The operant paradigm is concerned only with the prediction and control of behavior: the observation of the relationship between responding and the presentation of reinforcers may be sufficient for this purpose. Such a mechanistic or technological understanding of behavior has indeed been elaborated into a sophisticated understanding of schedule effects (Ferster and Skinner 1957). However, this success does not remove the observation that very few responses need be reinforced in order to shape and maintain robust patterns of behavior, nor the quest for an explanation. The explanation is psychological and adverts to the necessity of the creature representing in some way the relationship between its behavior and reward. It is legitimate for the radical behaviorist to suggest that the behavior of the animal is the result of its learning history and, where this history is known, for the investigator to be able to predict and control responding. But, if we are to explain the behavior, the history of reinforcement that is held to control responding has to be assumed to be internally represented by the animal. The use of the notion of learning history to "explain" the behavior of adult humans, say in complex situations of purchasing and consuming, is an explanatory fiction and must be replaced by cognitive assumption. Clearly, the topography of the behavior is identical when it is accounted for in operant terms and when it is explained psychologically. The difference is one of perspective

---

given interval of time, measured from the preceding reinforcement, is reinforced," while a fixed ratio (FR) schedule is one "in which a response is reinforced upon completion of a fixed number of responses counted from the preceding reinforcement." A variable interval (VI) schedule programs reinforcements "according to a random series of intervals having a given mean and lying between arbitrary extreme values," while a variable ratio (VR) schedule programs reinforcements "according to a random series of ratios and having a given mean and lying between arbitrary extreme values" (Ferster and Skinner 1957, p. 727, p. 734). The concurrent schedules employed in matching experiments involve "Two or more schedules independently arranged but operating at the same time, reinforcements being set up by both" (ibid., p. 724).

and depends on the question, technological or explanatory, posed by the investigator.

Second, the presence of the stimulus may not generate the response, leading to the assumption that the stimulus is not satisfactorily represented for it to bring about the appropriate response. This possibility is illustrated by the well-known phenomenon of schedule insensitivity, exhibited by human adults (though not by nonhuman animals) taking part in matching tasks. Experiments of this kind require responding on two concurrent schedules of reinforcement. The apparatus consists of two keys, A and B, each of which produces a reinforcer after a different interval of time has elapsed provided that at least one response has been made on that key during the period (concurrent variable ratio schedules). If pressing key A is reinforced every 10 seconds as long as at least one press has been made and pressing key B once every 20 seconds as long as at least one press has been made, then the matching law predicts that the participant will allocate two-thirds of responses to key A and one-third to B. It turns out that the participant obtains the same ratio of reward from the two keys to the ratio of responses allocated to them: hence, the term *matching* (Herrnstein 1997). But if the schedules are now modified so that different periods of time must elapse before responding receives reinforcement, human participants often do not adjust quickly to the new contingencies, but retain their former response pattern. This insensitivity to the new schedules is not explicable by reference to the discriminative and reinforcing stimuli now in operation since the behavior is clearly not influenced by them. An explanatory factor that seems compatible with radical behaviorism is the private events (thoughts and feelings) that are a central, even defining, element in this philosophy of psychology (Skinner 1969a, b). The rules that participants devise for themselves in order to comply with the schedules in force during phase 1 of the experiment and that are enshrined in their thoughts, are held to be carried over to the new situation and to lead the individual to continue the behavior pattern that was reinforced in the first part of the experiment but not the second. An alternative radical behaviorist explanation might assume that the individual's learning history carries over, that he or she is constrained by previous reinforcement patterns to repeat the behavior under the new stimulus conditions (Foxall and Oliveira-Castro 2009).

On closer consideration, however, each of these putative behavioral explanations includes unobservables that cannot enter directly into either an experimental or correlational analysis. Statements regarding the verbal rule-formulations that influenced the decision making of a participant are mere fabrications, untestable conjectures, explanatory fictions. The fact that the participant alluded to these verbal processes in the course of debriefing does not alter the ontological status of the statements. Nor can a learning history that is not empirically available be part of a scientific explanation. Both are speculations the purpose of which is to save the theory and are precisely the sorts of explanatory fiction that behaviorists such as Skinner sought to eliminate from scientific inquiry. The fact that they proceed in the terminology of behavior analysis may seduce the reader into thinking that they do not "appeal to events taking place somewhere else, at some other level of observation, described in different terms, and measured, if at all, in different dimensions" (Skinner 1950, p. 193). Resort to private verbal behavior or to an unobserved learning history is an appeal to extraneous events, perhaps reportedly observed at best but unreplicable in a third-personal science, and discriminable only in different dimensions from those of public behavior. It would be intellectually dishonest to provide accounts of this kind simply in order to prop up the radical behaviorist ideology of explanation or to appeal to some form of "action-at-a-distance" to fill in the gaps that scientific observation is unable to fill. The fact of the matter is that the behavior cannot be explained in terms of the extensional language that is the hallmark of behaviorist psychology and perhaps its very raison d'être (Foxall 2004). More satisfactory is to acknowledge the explanatory gap that arises when the stimuli responsible for a behavior pattern cannot be identified and to employ intentional language to account for the behavior.

Our next task in elucidating this methodology is to gain an increased understanding of the nature and implications of both radical behaviorism and intentional psychology.

Why Radical Behaviorism?

It seems unusual to incorporate radical behaviorism within a contemporary account of consumer choice, especially one that accords a central explanatory position to cognitive psychology. However, there is good reason to do so. Radical behaviorism is a philosophy of psychology which seeks to explain behavior in extensional language that describes the environmental consequences which influence the future rate at which the behavior is emitted (Skinner 1945, 1974; see also Foxall 2004). Although this is sufficient to predict and control much behavior, especially that occurring in the operant laboratory and similarly relatively closed settings, some aspects of behavior are not amenable to an operant account. These include characteristics of the continuity/discontinuity of behavior, the personal level of exposition which involves private events, and the scope of radical behaviorist interpretation. When this is the case, it is necessary, for reasons of clarity and intellectual honesty, to employ the intentional language of desiring, believing, perceiving, and feeling. But the ascription of intentionality must be circumscribed to conform to the principle of "selection by consequences" including evolution by natural selection and the ontogenetic selection of behavior by the environment. This means that the aspects of behavior that are interpreted intentionally must be consistent with neurophysiological-behavioral patterns and molar environmental-behavioral sequences. Like radical behaviorist explanation, the interpretation of behavior in intentional language so-circumscribed is governed by pragmatism and constitutes a linguistic rather than an ontological procedure.

Operant conditioning provides a means of predicting and controlling the behavior of organisms in relatively closed settings such as the operant chamber ("Skinner box"), and in other experimental and quasi-experimental situations where environmental control can be unambiguously observed (Skinner 1938).[4] The principles of behavior established in these "favorable" contexts may also be employed to "plausibly" interpret

---

[4] Skinner disarmingly points out that he does "not write as *the* behaviorist" (Skinner 1974, p. 3), even as *the* radical behaviorist, but I have taken what I understand his view of radical behaviorism to be as my starting point because it is one of the most extensively articulated accounts, developed over decades, and is familiar to specialist scholars and others as forming a definite school of psycho-

patterns of behavior that cannot be studied in this way because they are simply not amenable to an experimental analysis (Skinner 1957, p. 13, 1969a, b, p. 100, 1988, p. 207). The experimental and interpretational analyses of these phenomena comprise one aspect of the school of psychology known as behavior analysis. The philosophical dimension of behavior analysis is radical behaviorism (Skinner 1974). The essence of radical behaviorist explanation is that behavior is followed by consequences that affect its subsequent rate of performance. Some consequences are followed by an increase in the rate at which this and similar behaviors are emitted, while other consequences are followed by a reduction in the rate at which behaviors of the type that precede them are emitted. The first class of consequences is known as "reinforcers" since, metaphorically, they strengthen the behavior; the second, as "punishers." The relationship between behavioral responses and the reinforcing and aversive consequences that are said to predict and control them is correlational (Skinner 1931). Stimuli in the presence of which these behavior-consequence correlations are established may also come to exert control over responding; such "discriminative stimuli" do not *elicit* behavior in the way in which a unconditioned stimulus (UCS) generates a unconditioned response (UR) in Pavlovian or respondent conditioning. Rather, in the case of operant conditioning (so-called because it concerns behavior that "operates on the environment to produce consequences": Skinner 1971, p. 18), the organism *emits* responses, originally in a somewhat random fashion, some of which through reinforcement come to be included in its behavioral repertoire. When the stimulus conditions that predict and control behavior have been identified, and can be experimentally manipulated to modify the behavior in predictable ways, the behavior has been explained.

Attempts to criticize radical behaviorism often attack the adequacy of its explanatory strategy to encompass an explanation of complex behavior. The claim that one or other element of the "contingencies of reinforcement" is empirically unavailable or superfluous is encountered in critical comments from Tolman (1932) to Bandura (1986), Gardner and Gardner (1988), Foxall (2004), and beyond. The manifest aim is usu-

---

logical theory. However, not all who describe themselves as radical behaviorists would wish to be uncritically associated with Skinner's views.

ally to eliminate operant conditioning from psychology and replace it with other systems which to varying degrees admit cognitive accounts of behavior. However, this fails to consider the contribution made by operant psychology where it is able to demonstrate that behavior is predictable from and controlled by its consequences. The contexts in which such demonstration is possible are confined: this delimits the scope of radical behaviorism but does not undermine it. Such delimitation may indeed safeguard its future.

In view of this it is inappropriate to seek to replace radical behaviorism. Recent contributions of operant psychology to behavioral economics and applied behavior analysis attest to the discipline's intellectual and practical value. This is not to say that radical behaviorism has no limitations, however. Although extensional language is well suited to an approach which confines itself to the prediction and control of behavior, it is inadequate to capture some aspects of observed behavior: first, it fails to deal with some aspects of the continuity or discontinuity of behavior; second, it does not come to terms with the personal level of explanation; and, third, it has no means of delimiting the extra-laboratorial interpretation of behavior. In these instances, intentional language is the only intellectually honest means by which to account for behavior. To speak of consumer choice as behavior, therefore, is to understand it as activity that is under the causal control of the environment in contrast to consumer *action* which carries the implication of activity that is controlled by the consumer himself or herself.

Extensional Behavioral Science

Behaviorist explanation has as its goals the prediction and control of behavior and it achieves these by monitoring the influence of environmental stimuli on behavior (usually in the tightly controlled circumstances of the experimental space) and by manipulating these stimuli in order to maintain or change the behavior.

Radical behaviorism, or at least Skinner's system of explanation, has been distinguished from other behaviorist schools and from cognitivism by its repudiation of the "explanatory fictions" that masquerade as theoretical terms (Skinner 1950, 1963) and by its acknowledgment of thinking and feeling, that is "private events," as part of its subject matter (Skinner 1974). But the dimension that actually demarcates radical behaviorism from these other approaches to behavioral explanation is more subtle. Radical behaviorism does not actually avoid theoretical terms (Zuriff 1980; see also Foxall 2004); nor is its treatment of private events, viewed originally by Skinner as responses but subsequently and necessarily construed by other radical behaviorists as (causal) consequences, definitive. Rather, its distinctiveness inheres in its attempt to base a methodology of behavioral explanation on a particular linguistic usage, namely the exclusive employment of extensional language to describe responses, the stimulus elements held to be responsible for their rate of emission, and their relationships. The truth criterion of this explanatory device (the three-term contingency consisting of a discriminative stimulus, a response, and a reinforcing stimulus) is a pattern of intersubjectively observed relationships among events in the laboratory or other closed setting. Skinner strove to maintain this linguistic usage throughout his career. His request that his doctoral dissertation consist of a series of linguistic clarifications based on operational definitions of psychological terms was denied (Skinner 1984) but his early papers attest to his meticulousness in the use of language to define stimulus-response relationships and ultimately a novel psychology (Skinner 1931, 1935a, 1938). He was preoccupied with the meaning of psychological terms and its implications for the nature of psychology (Skinner 1945) and some of his last works were still concerned with discriminating radical behaviorism from cognitive psychology on the basis of the meanings of words (Skinner 1989a, b). An example of the care he took in defining expressions so that they excluded intentional explanations of behavior is found in his depiction of the meaning of "in order to" as when we speak of a fisherman spreading his nets in order to catch fish. For Skinner, the order is to be understood purely in terms of the temporal sequencing of spreading and catching, not in any mentally held purpose or plan to snare fish (Skinner 1969a, b). A statement with respect to the temporal ordering of activities is extensional, whereas the implication of an intention to catch fish is that intentional explanation is being offered.[5]

It follows from this that the bounds of behaviorism can be located where the possibility of employing extensional language runs out, when it is no longer possible to identify the stimuli of which behavior is a function. At this point, an intentional account becomes necessary.

Radical behaviorism as a philosophy of psychology is strictly extensional: it strives to account for its subject matter, behavior, in sentences that are referentially transparent, in which codesignatives are substitutable because they have the same extension. It is thus distinguished from cognitivism by its rigorous avoidance of intentional language, and from both cognitivism and other neo-behaviorisms by its inclusion of thinking and feeling ("private events") as phenomena that require explanation on the same terms as public responding. Its focus is the prediction and control of behavior by reference to its environmental consequences and the antecedent stimuli that set the scene for reinforcement or punishment; in its adherence to Machian positivism, it holds that when the environmental stimuli that control behavior have been identified the behavior has been explained. The truth criterion it applies to this endeavor is pragmatism, which asks how we can use the world, rather than realism, which asks how and what the world actually is (Foxall 2004, 2010a).

This philosophy, behavior analysis, seeks to prediction and control behavior by reference to environmental–behavioral relationships as denoted by the familiar "three-term contingency." In saying that behavior analysis proceeds extensionally, I mean that it seeks to confine its explanations to verbal behavior that avoids propositional content, describing

---

[5] As the founder of radical behaviorism, Skinner (1945) strove to avoid intentional terms in scientific discourse. His already-noted meticulous standards of linguistic expression inhere in his writing later that, "We say that spiders spin webs in order to catch flies and that men set nets in order to catch fish. The 'order' is temporal" (Skinner 1969a, b, p. 193). That is, we are saying simply that *first* the spider spins and *then* it catches flies, that men *first* set their nets and *then* catch fish. Neither the spider nor the men pursue a purpose or seek to fulfill an intention when spinning or setting. Skinner (1971, p. 18) is also scrupulously careful to avoid intentional language in defining operant behavior, as we have seen, as "behavior that *operates* on the environment to produce consequences." There is no suggestion that the operation is performed "with the intention" of producing consequences, emphasizing that the order implied is just that of temporal sequence. Extensional linguistic convention is the heart of radical behaviorism, the locutionary style that defines it as a philosophy of psychology (Foxall 2004).

its observation in language that is referentially transparent. It has two components or modes: the experimental analysis of behavior which is a laboratory-based investigation, and radical behaviorist interpretation which uses the principles of behavior gained in that analysis to provide an account in operant-contingency terms of the complex behaviors that are not amenable to direct experimental examination. Radical behaviorist interpretation frequently involves the use of mediating events, something ostensibly ruled out by Skinner's avoidance of "theoretical terms" but which appears necessary at this level of explanation. However, these mediating events are not intentionalistic: they remain part of an extensional account whose explanatory terms are extrapolated from the experimental to the nonexperimental sphere.

Radical behaviorist explanation thus proceeds on the basis of the *contextual stance* (Foxall 1999b) which states that behavior is predictable insofar as it is assumed to be environmentally determined; specifically, insofar as it is under the control of a learning history that represents the reinforcing and punishing consequences of similar behavior previously enacted in settings similar to that currently encountered. The contextual stance thus portrays behavior as taking place at the temporal and spatial intersection defined by learning history and behavior setting. It is this intersection that defines the situation (precisely as it is defined in the Behavioral Perspective Model [BPM]).

While there is no doubting the capacity of behavior analysis within the framework of radical behaviorism to predict and control behavior, at least in the relatively closed setting of the operant laboratory, there is a need for further conceptualization if we wish to account further for certain aspects of that behavior. Explanation of this kind is optional for behavior analysts, who may wish to remain within the philosophy of science set by Machian positivism, as did Skinner (Smith 1986; see Foxall 2010a, 2015c, for a detailed account of the nature of radical behaviorism). But there is no compelling reason to confine inquiry to this extensional level of analysis. In seeking to extend the conceptual framework here, I am concerned with methodology, with instances in which it is impossible to proceed with inquiry in the absence of intentional language, rather than with ontological questions. I should like to pursue three areas in which I believe explanation that goes beyond the *n*-term contingency can yield answers to questions that would be asked as a matter of course in most scientific endeavors but which have not usually found a place within radical behaviorism. These concern the treatment of the personal level of analysis, accounting for the continuity of behavior, and delimiting behavioral interpretations of behavior by delineating the scope of behavioral consequences that can be called upon to provide a causal explanation thereof.

The "three-term contingency" is a theoretical construal which proposes that

---

Box 1.1 Summary of the Contextual Stance

Philosophy of explanation:
Explains and interprets behavior as environmentally determined. Behavior is to be explained in terms of the *consumer situation;* the interaction of the individual's learning history and the stimuli that compose the current behavior setting. The consumer situation is coterminous with the scope of the consumer behavior setting.

Method:
Proceeds by identifying elements of the environment as stimuli and responses (highly theoretical terms) on the basis of their demonstrated functional interrelatedness. The demonstration may be by (i) experimentation, (ii) correlation/regression, (iii) interpretation as understood by Skinner.

Epistemology:
The relationships between stimuli and responses are described in extensional language.

Success criterion:
The prediction and control of responses on the basis of the location and manipulation of antecedent and consequential stimuli.

Scope:
Human and non-human animal behaviour which is predictable by its treatment as a contextual system.

Agency:
Agency is invested in the environment.

---

where S^D is a cue or *discriminative stimulus*, R is a response, and S^r is a reward or *reinforcing stimulus*. The discriminative stimulus (S^D) sets the occasion for (:), but does not elicit (as does the unconditioned stimulus of classical conditioning) a response (R) which is followed by ($\rightarrow$) a reinforcing consequence (S^r), that is, on which makes the future enactment of this or a similar response in similar circumstances more probable (Staddon and Cerutti 2003). The behavior in question is *operant* behavior, that which by operating on the environment generates the consequences that control its future rate of emission. It is said to have been explained when the environmental variables of which it is a function (S^r and by implication S^D) have been identified. The three-term device summarizes what behaviorists refer to as the *contingencies of reinforcement*.

Sidman (1994) proposes that n-term contingences can be invoked to explain increasingly complex behavior. In the four-term contingency, for instance, the presence of an initial stimulus controls the subsequent $S^D \rightarrow R \rightarrow S^r$ relationship. Michael (1982, 1993) has drawn attention to the possibility that motivating stimuli can fill the role of this initial stimulus, making the reinforcer that completes the sequence more desirable. An additional pre-behavioral stimulus or a social rule might enhance the reinforcing capacity of the S^r or even transform a neutral consequence into a reinforcer or punisher. Such *motivating operations* extend the range of explanation of the contingencies (Fagerstrøm et al. 2010).

Each element of the three- or n-term contingency is described in extensional language: its operation is not dependent upon wants or beliefs, desires or intentions (Smith 1994). Radical behaviorism describes both contingency-shaped and rule-governed behaviors in terms of "a system of functional relationships between the organism and the environment" (Smith 1994, pp. 127–8). Hence, an *operant response* "is not simply a response that the organism thinks will have a certain effect, it does have that effect." Further, a *reinforcer* "is not simply a stimulus that the organism desires to occur. It is a stimulus that will alter the rate of behavior upon which its occurrence is contingent." And a *discriminative stimulus* "is not simply a stimulus that has been correlated with a certain contingency in the organism's experience. It is one that successfully alters the organism's operant behavior with respect to that contingency." Descriptions of contingent behavior do not take propositions as their object; rather their object is relationships between an organism's behavior, its environmental consequences, and the elements that set the occasion for those contingent consequences. So behavior analysis does not attribute propositional content to any of the elements of the three-term contingency. "Instead of accepting a proposition as its object, the concept of reinforcement accepts an event or a state of affairs – such as access to pellets – as its object" (Smith 1994, p. 128). Hence, there is no place for a mentalistic description, such as "The animal desires that a pellet should become available" in the behavioral explanation of choice. The behavior analytic description is not "The animal's lever presses are reinforced [in order] that a pellet becomes available." It is: "The animal's lever presses are reinforced by access to pellets." A discriminative stimulus would not be described as a signal *that* something will happen but simply that a contingency exists. "It attributes an effect to the stimulus, but not a content." Whereas the substitutability of identicals fails in mentalistic statements (such statements are said to be logically opaque), behavioral categories are logically transparent, suggesting that "behavioral categories are not a subspecies of mentalistic categories" (Smith 1994, p. 129).

Neither is the proposition that "reinforcer" merely denotes "desire" feasible: desires are not equivalent to reinforcers, nor reinforcers to desires. Common-sense notions imply that if a stimulus is (positively) reinforcing it is desired, and if it is desired it is because it is a (positive) reinforcer but in fact neither holds. Objects of desire may not be attainable (the fountain of youth, perpetual motion) and so cannot be (linked to) reinforcers. Nor are reinforcers necessarily desired: on fixed interval (FI) schedules, electric shock maintains responding for monkeys, pigeons, and rats. The shocks are easily avoidable, but are not avoided. They cannot be "desired," yet they reinforce behavior.

Verbal Behavior

Verbal Behavior of the Speaker

An important breakthrough in radical behaviorist theory came with Skinner's (1969a, b) paper on problem solving in which he distinguished "contingency-shaped behavior" from "rule-governed behavior," the former being shaped directly by environmental stimuli, the latter by the verbal behavior of other people. This elaboration on Skinner's (1957) treatment of verbal behavior simply in terms of the contingencies of reinforcement observed in experiments with animals marked progress in at least three ways. First, it brought peculiarly human variables to bear on the way in which language is used to present contingencies and thereby to control behavior. Only humans seem to make rules which they express linguistically and to base inducements to act in particular ways and sanctions for behaving differently on verbal statements of what is required. Second, it allowed radical behaviorism to deal with many of the phenomena that cognitive psychologists had previously claimed as their sovereign territory: notably problem solving, decision making, and other forms of thinking. Third, it eventually opened up analysis of the behavior of the listener. Skinner's (1957) *Verbal Behavior* concentrated on the verbal behavior of the speaker which is only half of the story. Although it provided a theoretical (Skinner would say "interpretive") account of verbal behavior, its generation of empirical research was very limited. By the end of the 1980s, however, the experimental analysis of the verbal behavior of the listener was in full swing (e.g., Hayes 1989).[6]

The functional units of the speaker's behavior identified by Skinner (1957) are defined to exclude propositional content (see also Foxall 1999b; Smith 1994); they are simply statements of contingencies that account for an individual's behavior in the absence of his or her direct exposure to those contingencies. Among them, *mands* and *tacts* are the best known. A mand (a term derived from a com*mand* or a de*mand*) is verbal behavior that specifies what will reinforce it: for example, "Give me a drink" plus the unspoken, "You owe me a favor" or "Else I shall ignore your requests in future." Even if this is expressed as "I desire that you give me a drink..." it is actually no more than a description of contingencies. A tact is a description of the environment that allows the listener to discriminate or delineate some aspect of it: "Here is the bank." Even if this were expressed as, "Look at the bank," its function would be confined to establishing the stimulus control of the word "bank," as when the listener replies, "Oh, yes, the bank." More technically, the *mand* denotes the consequences contingent upon following the instructions of the speaker or of imitating his or her example. Much advertising consists of mands—"Buy three and get one free!" "Don't forget the fruit gums, mum"—which indicate contingencies that are under the control

---

[6] To be fair, Skinner did not always ignore this (see Skinner 1989a, b). But he downplayed it as early as his William James lectures on verbal behavior (1948), and his *Verbal Behavior* (1957) concentrates almost entirely on the verbal behavior of the speaker.

of the speaker. *Tacts* present a con*tact* with part of the environment and, depending on learning history, a potential for behavior on the part of the recipient. A trade mark or logo may be followed by making a purchase or entering a store. The definitive source is Skinner's *Verbal Behavior* (1957).

Other functional units of speaker behavior identified by Skinner include *intraverbals, autoclitics,* and *echoics.* An intraverbal is verbal behavior under the control of other verbal behavior: having said "W, X, Y," the speaker is likely to continue with "Z." Each letter following the others is an example of an intraverbal. An autoclitic is a verbal expression that modifies the effect of the rest of the statement: in the sentence, "I believe the train is due," "I believe" functions as an autoclitic. An echoic is simply a repetition of what has been said. My telling someone that I have won a million dollars is likely to meet the response, "*A million dollars?*" This imitative verbal behavior is an echoic.[7]

Verbal Behavior of the Listener

The functional units of the listener's verbal behavior, as proposed by Zettle and Hayes (1982) similarly attempt to describe contingencies rather than express propositional content. *Pliance,* for instance, is the behavior of the listener who complies with a verbal request or instruction: hence, "Pliance is rule-governed behavior under the control of apparent socially mediated consequences for a correspondence between the rule and relevant behavior" (Hayes et al. 1989, p. 201). If a customer asks the bookstore assistant to show her where the newly published novels are kept, the assistant responds by pointing to the relevant display. The customer's manding verbal behavior, amounts to the presentation of a rule in the form of a *ply*: "If you show me the books I want to see, I will

---

[7] Note that the structure and logical meaning of sentences is not altered by their being parsed functionally rather than structurally. Hence, the problem of the irreducibility of intentional sentences to extensional sentences is not overcome by Schnaitter's (1999) suggestion that we parse the sentence, "He said that it was raining" functionally. A structural parsing would be: He (pronoun); said (verb); that it was raining (noun clause object). A functional parsing of the sentence would be: He said that (autoclitic); it was raining (tact). But this does not alter the meaning of the sentence. If we parse the sentence according to its construction in terms of propositional attitudes, it exhibits the phenomenon of referential opacity whether we construe it structurally or functionally. If we use intentional language, we are using intentional explanation.

reward you by making a purchase or at least by thanking you." Note that this behavior of the assistant is verbal too since it is under the control of what the customer has said (and is therefore socially mediated); it will be reinforced if it corresponds to the requirements of the rule. It is the assistant's behavior that is described as pliance and it is rule-governed behavior which is a variety of verbal behavior. Pliance can, therefore, be understood as the behavior involved in responding positively to a mand.

Tracking is "rule-governed behavior under the control of the apparent correspondence between the rule and the way the world is arranged" (Hayes et al. 1989, p. 206). It involves tracking the physical environment as when following instructions how to get to the supermarket. Once again, its form—for example, "Turn left at the traffic light" plus the unspoken "And you'll get to Sainsbury's"—is a basic description of contingencies rather than an expression of propositional attitudes. The person providing the instructions is *tacting*; the follower of the instructions is evincing a particular kind of rule-governed behavior known as *tracking*. Both are verbal behaviors. Precisely as Smith (1994) concludes with respect to contingency-shaped behavior, we may conclude with respect to rule-governance: "Beliefs and desires have propositional content. ... Designations of discriminative stimuli and reinforcing stimuli, by contrast, do not accept *that*-clauses" (Smith 1994, p. 128).

A third functional unit of listener behavior has no corresponding unit for the speaker: the *augmental* (Zettle and Hayes 1982) is a highly motivating rule that states emphatically how a particular behavior will be reinforced or avoid punishment. "Just one more packet top and I can claim my free watch!" "Think positively and you will achieve all you desire!"

Catania et al. (1989) point out that two sets of contingencies enter into rule- governed behavior: the nonverbal relationships that govern the contingency-shaped aspects of the behavior and the verbal relationships that govern its rule-governed aspects.

Private Events

The private events which distinguish radical behaviorism are not "cognitive" or "mental" rather than material or physical. They are essentially private, collateral responses under the influence of the same environmental stimuli that control overt—or, better, public—responding. As such their ontological status is fixed by their place in the three-term contingency: they are responses in need of operant explanation by means of an account that causally links them with antecedent and reinforcing stimuli occurring in the extra-personal environment, rather than discriminative or reinforcing stimuli which are capable of determining the frequency of a response. They are dependent variables. Radical behaviorism explains verbal behavior in similar terms to nonverbal: that of the speaker as a series of functionally defined speech (and quasi-speech) units—tacts, mands, autoclitics, echoics, intraverbals; that of the listener as a series of functionally defined verbal units that prescribe the consequences of rule-following—tracks, plys, and augmentals.

Behaviorists have themselves shown differing attitudes toward private events. Some allow them directly to bear on accounts of behavior, especially that for which a preexisting stimulus field is not apparent (e.g., Lowe 1983; see also Foxall and Oliveira-Castro 2009). Others find little if any place for them even in novel theories of radical behaviorism (e.g., Rachlin 1994). The traditional view, reflecting Skinner's own assessment, is evinced by Baum and Heath (1992, p. 1313) for whom

> Private events are observable, even if only by an audience of one. They are just as real as public events... Mental (fictional) events, in contrast, are unobservable because they are nonphysical.

A more recent view, perhaps reflecting the growing interest in the verbal behavior of the listener among behaviorists is suggested by Schnaitter (1999, p. 239)

> At the very least behaviorists should consider the problem of intentionality to be a most interesting case of verbal behavior, not to be dismissed but to be explored and understood. The standard behavioristic line that the mental is the fictional is just not good enough.

Indeed, it is not.

Structure and Function of Extensional Explanation

Adopt the Contextual Stance

The quest for the bounds of behaviorism which is at the heart of Consumer Behavior Analysis (Foxall 2001, 2002) requires another kind of evaluation of the BPM, an assessment of the kind of model it is, the kinds of knowledge it generates, and the significance of the theoretical and empirical work just described to the acceptance or rejection of a cognitive component to our understanding of consumer choice. The BPM, as presented in the next chapter, is an extensional model. It rejects, *ex hypothesi*, the intentional idioms of desires, beliefs, emotions, and perceptions in favor of the description of patterns of behavior made intelligible by means of the concepts of, inter alia, reinforcement, discrimination, and generalization. Though these concepts involve theorization, the pursuit of radical behaviorist explanation assiduously avoids the language of intentionality and thus intentional explanation.

Rather, it adopts a particular philosophical position on the explanation of behavior, the *contextual stance* (Foxall 1999b). This is the philosophical position that portrays behavior as the result of contingencies of reinforcement and punishment, more particularly in terms of the three-term contingency in which a discriminative stimulus sets the occasion for particular behavioral consequences contingent on the performance of a given response. Some consequences of responding have the effect of increasing the probability of the emission of a similar response in similar circumstances in future; these consequences are known as reinforcers and the procedure described is positive reinforcement. An aversive consequence, when received by the individual reduces the rate of the behavior and is known as a punisher. Behavior that serves to avert an aversive consequence is said to be negatively reinforced: it is still reinforced because it is strengthened (repeated) but negatively because it has the effect of avoiding or escaping from the aversive consequence. The sequence seems superficially contradictory since the variable of which behavior is a function follows the response but the point is that it is the individual's history of reinforcement that determines his or her current behavior. *The contextual stance*, then, is the view that the behavior of an organism can be predicted and controlled by relating it to its prior consequences; the behavior is predictable from the consumer situation in which it is located, that is, the interaction of its learning history, and the reinforcing and punishing consequences of future behavior as indicated by the discriminative stimuli and motivating operations that comprise the current behavior setting. This stance adopts as its central explanatory device the consumer situation, in which the probability of a response is decided by the intersection of that learning history and the current stimulus setting. In essence, the context stance states that a "contextual system" or "operant system" is an entity that is predictable from its learning history and the behavioral outcomes made possible by its current situation (Foxall 1999b).

Box 2.1 summarizes the components of the contextual stance. Note, in particular, that it is impossible to conceive of a radical behaviorist

---

Box 2.1 Summary of the Contextual Stance

Philosophy of explanation:

Explains and interprets behavior as environmentally determined. Behavior is to be explained in terms of the consumer situation; the interaction of the individual's learning history and the stimuli that compose the current behavior setting. The consumer situation is coterminous with the scope of the consumer behavior setting.

Method:

Proceeds by identifying elements of the environment as stimuli and responses (highly theoretical terms) on the basis of their demonstrated functional interrelatedness. The demonstration may be by (i) experimentation, (ii) correlation/regression, (iii) interpretation as understood by Skinner.

Epistemology:

The relationships between stimuli and responses are described in extensional language.

Success criterion:

The prediction and control of responses on the basis of the location and manipulation of antecedent and consequential stimuli.

Scope:

Human and nonhuman animal behavior which is predictable by its treatment as a contextual system.

Agency:

Agency is invested in the environment.

methodology, on which the contextual stance is modeled, that did not insist on (a) the three-term contingency as the basis of behavioral explanation and (b) the empirical demonstration of the relationships it embodies. As we have seen, the consumer behavior analysis research program is an attempt to find the limits of the contextual stance, that is, the bounds of behaviorism.

Understanding the kind of explanation offered by the contextual stance requires that we fix the level of exposition at which it explains. Dennett's (1969) distinction of the *personal level* from the *sub-personal level* has become well-entrenched in the explanation of behavior. The personal level of exposition is that of whole persons, their behavior and their intentionality, principally their desires and beliefs. It encompasses, therefore, whatever the individual does, be it behaviorally or mentally. This is the domain of the cognitive psychologist, who is concerned with explaining behavior is terms of mental processes or reports thereof. The sub-personal level is that of the nervous system, principally the central nervous system of neuronal activity. It is the domain of the neuroscientist and the biological psychologist who are concerned to account for behavior, including verbal reports of cognitive and emotional activity, by reference to neurophysiological events and processes. I should like to add to Dennett's dichotomy a third level, the *super-personal level* of exposition which links behavior with the environmental stimuli that control it (Foxall 2004, 2007a). This is the domain of the behaviorologist or behavior analyst, who is concerned with the analysis of observed behavior in terms of environmental stimuli, whether in terms of classical conditioning or operant conditioning. In the context of consumer behavior, we are predominantly interested in operant behavior since this is behavior that is under the control of its consequences, the rewards (reinforcers) and punishers that alter the probability of the behavior's being reenacted. Economic behavior is instrumental in this sense. The behaviorologist seeks, therefore, to understand the forms assumed by behavior (at the personal level) in terms of the regularity of environmental stimuli as they impact that behavior (at the super-personal level of exposition).

The sub-personal and super-personal levels provide the subject matters of the extensional sciences of neurophysiology and behaviorology which accrue knowledge by means of experimental investigations which enable the manipulation of independent variables in order to ascertain their influence on the dependent variable. They also employ statistical analyses, based on correlational techniques for the same purpose. The explanations provided in terms of intentionality cannot be directly evaluated in the same way since the mental entities which form their independent variables are theoretically rather than directly available. It is necessary to employ surrogate variables which belong to either neurophysiology or extensional behavioral science in order to provide indirect tests of hypotheses that refer to desires and beliefs, for instance. We might refer to their accounts as interpretations rather than explanations for this reason.

Treat the Consumer as a Contextual System

A contextual or operant system is an entity, the behavior of which can be predicted by means of the empirically observed relationships between a sequence of such behavior and a sequence of its consequences such that the behavior can be described as a function of its prior consequences. This relationship can be described in entirely extensional language without recourse to intentional language such as those of desires, beliefs, emotions, and perceptions. The limited goal of the analysis that leads to the formulation of such relationships is the prediction and possibly control of the behavior in question.

Understand Behavior as Environmentally Determined

Extensional explanation in this case entails the demonstration that a behavior (the dependent variable) is functionally related to particular aspects of the environment or neurophysiology (the independent variables). This can be achieved most satisfactorily via an experimental analysis since this increases the chances of intersubjective agreement on whether the rules of behavioral syntax have been met. It can also, however, be met where this is appropriate by inferential statistics such as regression analysis. It is least of all possible in the case of behavioral interpretation, which requires rigorous rules of correspondence to be established. In the case of consumer behavior, an extensional explanation consists in the construction of a consumer situation (defined as the intersection of the consumer's learning history and the stimulus conditions of the social and physical setting in which he or she is located) with the objective of predicting his or her consumption choices.

Extensional syntax (meaning the syntax of an extensional explanation) is a means of encapsulating the basic explanatory system of science in terms of causation. It is the language of explanation adopted by sciences that adopt the physical and design stances (Dennett 1978, 1987), and the contextual stance (Foxall 1999b). The physical stance is appropriate for understanding material artifacts, enabling the comprehension of elements of the natural and manmade worlds as purely physical entities. The design stance applies to aspects of human interaction with physical entities, whether natural or manmade. Based on a kind of reverse engineering, it leads to an explanation of the behavior of entities that deconstructs the intentionality of their inventors: a computer can thus be understood in terms of what it is intended by its creator to achieve, while entities that evolved in the course of natural selection can be explained from this stance in terms of "Mother Nature's" intentions. In the case of behavioral science, based on the contextual stance (Foxall 1999b), *behavioral syntax* requires that we identify the three paradigmatic elements S^D, R, and $S^{r/a}$ and the relationships among them such that the rate of R increases when it has been previously followed by S^r, decreases when it has been previously followed by S^a. In the first case R is said to be reinforced by S^r; in the second it has been punished by S^a. If these operations have been carried out in the presence of S^D, then in the first instance, R may be enacted in its continued presence even if S^r is not forthcoming; and, in the second, R may be suppressed in the presence of S^D even though S^a no longer ensues. We have seen that the syntax for attributing operant conditioning is summarized as the three-term contingency. That syntax may be extended, as we have also noted, by the inclusion of motivating operations and it is possible in principle to extend the contingency further than this—the "n-term contingency."

Chapter 3 takes these features of the contextual stance and applies them to the investigation of consumer choice through the development of the Behavioral Perspective Model.

Attitudes, Behavior, Decision: A Behavioral Interpretation of Consumer Choice

Psychologists and consumer researchers cannot measure attitudes directly; they measure behavior, generally verbal behavior, and use the results to predict other, generally nonattitudinal, behavior. Despite the success of attitude psychology over the last two or three decades (Fishbein and Ajzen 2010), its findings substantiate a behavioral model of human choice as much as they do a cognitive account (Foxall 1983, 1997a, 2005). Recent research on attitude-behavior relationships supports this in two ways. First, attitude research has sought to make measures of attitude, intention, and behavior far more situation-specific than has traditionally been the case. As a result of the emphasis on such tight situational correspondence among the measures it employs, attitude research has actually pointed up the situational or contextual determinants of behavior rather than having shown that behavior is caused (or is most accurately predicted) by cognitive precursors. Second, attitude researchers increasingly measure respondents' behavioral histories in order to predict their behavior. The variable most predictive of current and future behavior is past behavior in similar contexts. However, because of the fixed adherence of the investigators to the social cognitive metatheory, the findings are cast in the language of information processing. The challenge for attitude researchers is to appreciate the environmental influences responsible for both the verbal and nonverbal responses and for any continuity between them. The need is not for a paradigm shift, of the kind documented by Kuhn (1972), so much as an "active interplay of competing theories" (Feyerabend 1975).

Behavior analysts have surmised that behavior is rule-governed only on its initial emission; thereafter, it comes under contingency control. The analysis undertaken in this paper suggests a more elongated process. At first the consumer has no specific learning history with respect to the consumption behavior in question. Perhaps presented with a new brand in a new product class, there is no accumulated experience or knowledge of buying and using the item and the consequences of doing so. However, in proportion to the consumer's having a learning history for rule-following, other-rules may be sought out for guidance and action. These might take the form of the advertising claims which first created awareness of the innovation; alternatively, they might come from significant others, acquaintances, and opinion leaders. Whatever their source, these rules are not passively accepted by the consumer but used as the basis of a sequence of deliberation and evaluation, first of the claims themselves, and their comparison with similar claims for other products and brands, then of accumulated consumption experience. The consumer's actions involved in the trial and repeat purchase/consumption of the product develops a learning history. Moreover, reasoning with respect to personal experience of the item, and the evaluation of this experience, will lead to the formation of self-rules which henceforth guide action without constant deliberation. The consumer has moved from the central route to the peripheral, from deliberation to spontaneity, from systematic reasoning to the application of heuristics. The initial lack of a relevant learning history prompted a search for other-rules; the acquisition of such a history means that self-rules can be extracted from experience. Only the acquisition of such an extensive history can transform the behavior finally from rule-governed to contingency-shaped and even then the distinction between self-rule governance and contingency shaping is not empirically available. The import of this analysis lies not in its reiterating the sequence of consumer decision making found in cognitive models of initial and subsequent information processing but in its capacity to account for these phenomena without extensive reliance on theoretical entities posited at a metabehavioral level.

Bibliography

Bandura, A. (1986). *Social foundations of thought and action: A social cognitive theory*. Englewood Cliffs: Prentice Hall.

Baum, W. M., & Heath, J. L. (1992). Behavioral explanations and intentional explanations in psychology. *American Psychologist, 47*, 1312–1317.

Bermúdez, J. L. (2003). *Thinking without words*. Oxford: Oxford University Press.

Braisby, N., & Gellatly, A. (2012). *Cognitive psychology* (2nd ed.). Oxford: Oxford University Press.

Campiani, M. (1996). Remarks on the paradigms of connectionism. In A. Clark & P. Millican (Eds.), *The legacy of Alan Turing* (Connectionism, concepts, and folk psychology, Vol. II, pp. 45–66). Oxford: Oxford University Press.

Catania, A. C., Shimoff, E., & Matthews, B. A. (1989). An experimental analysis of rule-governed behavior. In S. C. Hayes (Ed.), *Rule-governed behavior: Cognition, contingencies, and instructional control* (pp. 119–150). New York: Plenum.

Chisholm, R. M. (1957). *Perceiving: A philosophical study*. Ithaca: Cornell University Press.

De Gelder, B. (1996). Modularity and logical cognitivism. In A. Clark & P. Millican (Eds.), *The legacy of Alan Turing* (Connectionism, concepts, and folk psychology, Vol. II, pp. 147–168). Oxford: Oxford University Press.

Dennett, D. C. (1969). *Content and consciousness*. London: Routledge and Kegan Paul.

Dennett, D. C. (1978). *Brainstorms*. Montgomery: Bradford.

Dennett, D. C. (1987). *The intentional stance*. Cambridge, MA: MIT Press.

Dennett, D. C. (1996). *Kinds of minds: Towards an understanding of consciousness*. London: Weidenfeld and Nicholson.

Ehrenberg, A. S. C. (1988). *Repeat buying* (2nd ed.). London: Griffin.

Eysenck, M. (2012). *Fundamentals of cognition* (2nd ed.). Hove/New York: Psychology Press.

Fagerstrøm, A., Foxall, G. R., & Arntzen, E. (2010). Implications of motivating operations for the functional analysis of consumer behavior. *Journal of Organizational Behavior Management, 30*(2), 110–126.

Ferster, C. & Skinner, B. F. (1957). *Schedules of reinforcement*. Englewood Cliffs: Prentice-Hall. (Republished, 1997, with additional Forewords by Copley Publishing, Acton, MA.)

Feyerabend, P. (1975). *Against method*. London: Verso.

Fishbein, M., & Ajzen, I. (2010). *Predicting and changing behavior*. New York: Psychology Press.

Foxall, G. R. (1983). *Consumer choice*. London: Macmillan; New York: St. Martin's Press.

Foxall, G. R. (1997a). *Marketing psychology: The paradigm in the wings*. London: Macmillan; New York: St. Martin's Press.

Foxall, G. R. (1999b). The contextual stance. *Philosophical Psychology, 12,* 25–46.

Foxall, G. R. (2001). Foundations of consumer behaviour analysis. *Marketing Theory, 1,* 165–199.

Foxall, G. R. (2002). *Consumer behaviour analysis: Critical perspectives in business and management.* London/New York: Routledge.

Foxall, G. R. (2004). *Context and cognition: Interpreting complex behavior.* Reno: Context Press.

Foxall, G. R. (2005). *Understanding consumer choice.* London/New York: Palgrave Macmillan.

Foxall, G. R. (2007a). *Explaining consumer choice.* London/New York: Macmillan.

Foxall, G. R. (2010a). *Interpreting consumer choice: The behavioral perspective model.* New York: Routledge.

Foxall, G. R. (2015c). Consumers in context: The BPM research program. London/New York: Routledge

Foxall, G. R., & Oliveira-Castro, J. M. (2009). Intentional consequences of self-instruction. *Behavior and Philosophy, 37,* 87–104.

Gardner, R. A., & Gardner, B. T. (1988). Feedforward versus feedbackward: An ethological alternative to the law of effect. *Behavioral and Brain Sciences, 11,* 429–493.

Hayes, S. C. (Ed.). (1989). *Rule-governed behavior: Cognition, contingencies, and instructional control.* New York: Plenum.

Hayes, S. C., Zettle, R. D., & Rosenfarb, I. (1989). Rule-following. In S. C. Hayes (Ed.), *Rule-governed behavior: Cognition, contingencies, and instructional control* (pp. 191–220). New York: Plenum.

Herrnstein, R. J. (1997). *The matching law: Papers in psychology and economics.* In H. Rachlin & D. I. Laibson(Eds.). Cambridge, MA/New York: Harvard University Press/Russell Sage Foundation.

Kuhn, T. (1972). *The structure of scientific revolutions* (2nd ed.). Chicago: Chicago University Press.

Lowe, C. F. (1983). Radical behaviorism and human psychology. In G. C. L. Davey (Ed.), *Animal models of human behavior* (pp. 71–93). Chichester: Wiley.

McGinn, C. (1996). *The character of mind.* Oxford: Oxford University Press.

Michael, J. (1982). Distinguishing between discriminative and motivational functions of stimuli. *Journal of the Experimental Analysis of Behavior, 37,* 149–155.

Michael, J. (1993). Establishing operations. *The Behavior Analyst, 16,* 191–206.

Quine, W. V. O. (1960). *Word and object.* Cambridge, MA: MIT Press.

Rachlin, H. (1994). *Behavior and mind: The roots of modern psychology.* Oxford: Oxford University Press.

Romaniuk, J., & Sharp, B. (2016). *How brands grow. Part 2: Including emerging products, services, durables, new and luxury brands.* Oxford: Oxford University Press.

Schnaitter, R. (1999). Some criticisms of behaviorism. In B. A. Thyer (Ed.), *The philosophical legacy of behaviorism* (pp. 209–249). Dordrecht: Kluwer.

Searle, J. R. (1983). *Intentionality: An essay in the philosophy of mind.* Cambridge: Cambridge University Press.

Searle, J. R. (2007). *Freedom and neurobiology.* New York: Columbia University Press.

Sharp, B. (2010). *How brands grow: What marketers don't know.* Oxford: Oxford University Press.

Sidman, M. (1994). *Equivalence relations and behavior: A research story.* Boston: Authors Cooperative.

Skinner, B. F. (1931). The concept of the reflex in the description of behavior. *Journal of General Psychology, 5,* 427–458.

Skinner, B. F. (1935a). The generic nature of the concepts of stimulus and response. *Journal of General Psychology, 12,* 40–65.

Skinner, B. F. (1935b). Two types of conditioned reflex and a pseudo-type. *Journal of General Psychology, 12,* 66–77.

Skinner, B. F. (1938). *The behavior of organisms.* New York: Appleton—Century—Crofts.

Skinner, B. F. (1945). The operational analysis of psychological terms. *Psychological Review, 52,* 270–277.

Skinner, B. F. (1948). *Verbal behavior: The William James Lectures.* www.behavior.org/resources/595.pdf. Accessed 4 Feb 2016.

Skinner, B. F. (1950). Are theories of learning necessary? *Psychological Review, 57,* 193–216.

Skinner, B. F. (1957). *Verbal behavior.* New York: Century.

Skinner, B. F. (1963). Behaviorism at fifty. *Science, 140,* 951–958.

Skinner, B. F. (1969a). *Contingencies of reinforcement: A theoretical analysis.* Englewood Cliffs: Prentice-Hall.

Skinner, B. F. (1969b). An operant analysis of problem solving. In B. F. Skinner (Ed.), *Contingencies of reinforcement: A theoretical analysis* (pp. 133–71). Englewood Cliffs: Prentice–Hall. (First published 1966).

Skinner, B. F. (1971). *Beyond freedom and dignity.* New York: Knopf.

Skinner, B. F. (1974). *About behaviorism.* New York: Knopf.

Skinner, B. F. (1981, July 31). Selection by consequences, *Science*, 213, 501–4.

Skinner, B. F. (1984). *The shaping of a behaviorist.* New York: New York University Press.

Skinner, B. F. (1988). Reply to Stalker and Ziff. In A. C. Catania & S. Harnad (Eds.), *The selection of behavior. The operant behaviorism of B. F. Skinner: Comments and consequences* (pp. 207–208). New York: Cambridge University Press.

Skinner, B. F. (1989a). The origins of cognitive thought. *American Psychologist, 44*, 13–18.

Skinner, B. F. (1989b). The behavior of the listener. In S. C. Hayes (Ed.), *Rule-governed behavior: Cognition, contingencies, and instructional control* (pp. 85–96). New York: Plenum.

Smith, L. D. (1986). *Behaviorism and logical positivism: A reassessment of the alliance.* Stanford: Stanford University Press.

Smith, T. L. (1994). *Behavior and its causes: Philosophical foundations of operant psychology.* Dordrecht: Kluwer.

Staddon, J. E. R., & Cerutti, D. T. (2003). Operant conditioning. *Annual Review of Psychology, 54*, 115–144.

Tolman, E. C. (1932). *Purposive behavior in animals and men.* New York: Century.

Zettle, R. D., & Hayes, S. C. (1982). Rule-governed behavior: A potential framework for cognitive-behavioral therapy. In P. C. Kendall (Ed.), *Advances in cognitive-behavioral research and therapy* (pp. 73–117). New York: Academic.

Zuriff, G. E. (1980). Radical behaviorist epistemology. *Psychological Bulletin, 87*, 337–350.

3

Consumer Choice as Behavior

Introduction

The behaviorist model of consumer choice that must be tested to the point of exhaustion in order to ascertain the necessary position and expository scope of an Intentional Interpretation is derived and described. The contribution of this extensional model of consumer choice, the Behavioral Perspective Model (BPM), based on an empirical research program, is then summarized in three ways. The first is by reference to the operant behavioral economics research program that has tested the fundamental economic and social relationships posited by the model. The second is in terms of further empirical research which has investigated consumers' emotional reactions to situations of purchase and consumption defined by the contingency categories of the BPM. The third is concerned with the interpretation of broader aspects of consumer choice such as saving, the adoption and diffusion of innovations, environmental conservation, and addiction.

© The Editor(s) (if applicable) and The Author(s) 2016
G.R. Foxall, *Perspectives on Consumer Choice*,
DOI 10.1057/978-1-137-50121-9_3

The Behavioral Perspective Model

The Behavioral Perspective Model (BPM; Foxall 1990/2004, 2010a) posits that consumer behavior is influenced by both the economic and technical properties of goods on one hand and the social meaning of acquiring, owning, and using them on the other.[1] People drive cars in order to get around but also in order to be *seen* getting around. They wear clothes not only for protection from the elements but also to show other people how well they are doing at the office; they adorn themselves with jewelry not only to impress their fellows or fit in with social expectations but to raise or confirm their own self-esteem. To the extent that consumption is influenced by these consequences, it is operant; to the extent that it reflects both the functional and the symbolic, it is under the influence of a complex of utilitarian and informational reinforcers. Businesses meet these consumer wants by offering marketing mixes that stress product attributes of both kinds, advertising and distribution channels that complement and enhance them, and price levels that are consonant with both the technical-economic purposes and the social-psychological meanings that the resulting brands address. Both sources of reinforcement belong to a behavior-analytic model of consumer choice. So must the punishing consequences associated with each, for every economic transaction meets with aversive outcomes as well as those that reward. These consequential causes of behavior are depicted on the right-hand side of the BPM (Fig. 3.1).

The Extensional Consumer Situation

On the left of this figure (Fig. 3.1) can be seen the stimuli that set the occasion for these causal consequences should particular acts of purchase

---

[1] This book presents several perspectives on consumer choice: behavioral, action, decision, and agential. I have retained the term Behavioral Perspective Model for the generic or summative model, however, because behavior remains fundamental to the explanatory sequence that becomes apparent as we peruse the various perspectives from which consumer choice may be viewed. Whatever we assume *in addition to* the behavioral perspective as we delve into action and agential characterizations of consumer choice, we never lose the behavioral perspective and its implications for the way in which the additional layers of interpretation are formulated and employed.

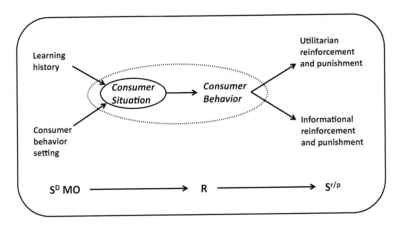

Fig. 3.1 *Summative Behavioral Perspective Model.* The central explanatory device of the model is the relationship between the consumer situation and consumer choice. The model's being essentially an elaboration of the three-term contingency is shown by the correspondence between its main components and discriminative stimuli/motivating operations (S^D, MO), Responses (R), and reinforcing and punishing stimuli ($S^{r/p}$) (Adapted from Foxall (1990/2004), *Consumer Psychology in Behavioral Perspective.* (London and New York: Routledge. Reprinted 2004 by Beard Books, Frederick, MD))

and consumption be enacted. These are the discriminative stimuli (S^D) that set the occasion for reinforcement contingent on the performance of particular acts of purchase and usage, and the motivating operations (MO) that enhance the reinforcing qualities of the products and services obtained and consumed. In a nutshell, S^D are stimuli in the presence of which the individual discriminates behaviorally by performing a response that has previously been reinforced in these or similar circumstances; MO are stimuli that enhance the ability of a reinforcer to strengthen a response. So, while the wording of an advertisement, "*Wizzowash* for whiter clothes!" may be a S^D for buying this product, the accompanying picture of a child wearing pristine, clean clothes might enhance the efficacy of the reinforcer if this symbol has previously been associated with sound parenting and is an MO (Fagerstrøm et al. 2010).

The consumer behavior setting is composed of stimuli that signal the outcomes of behavior—the availability of particular brands, for instance, within a supermarket—and stimuli that motivate the behavior—say a point-of-sale advertisement that emphasizes the unique taste or value-for-money that buying the item will generate. Open settings permit a wider range of behaviors to be enacted than closed settings in which just one or a few behaviors are possible. We can say that the relatively open setting "offers more choices" than the relatively closed if we understand choice to refer simply to opportunities to behave. (For extended discussion of the derivation of the model and its refinement, see Foxall 1990/2004, 2010a, 2015c.)

The scope of consumer behavior settings can, therefore, be described on a continuum from relatively open to relatively closed. This conceptualization is especially relevant to the study of consumer behavior, and particularly, retail research (Yan et al. 2012a, b; Bui Huynh and Foxall 2016). Generally, though not inevitably, in the relatively closed setting, persons other than the consumer arrange the discriminative stimuli that compose the setting in a way that compels conformity to the desired behavior. Such conformity is achieved by making reinforcement contingent on such conformity. The open setting, however, is marked by a relative absence of physical, social, and verbal pressures to conform to a pattern of activity that is determined by others (what ecological psychologists call a behavior program; see Schoggen 1989); it is comparatively free of constraints on the consumer, who, thus, has an increased range of choices. He or she has some ability to determine personal rules for choosing among the products and brands on offer, which stores to visit, and so on. A typical open setting is represented by a departmental store in which the consumer can move from section to section, browsing here, considering there, making a purchase, or leaving altogether to find another store or even giving up on shopping and going home.

In contrast, extremely closed consumer behavior settings are exemplified by the dental surgery or the gymnasium where only one course of action is reinforced and removing oneself from the situation, while not impossible, is fraught with social and, ultimately, health-related costs. Less extreme but still distinctly closed for the consumer behavior context, a bank is usually a physically closed setting, arranged to encourage orderly queuing by customers and to discourage behavior that detracts from the efficient execution of transactions. Social and verbal elements also enter into the closed nature of the setting: the single-file line that leads to the teller window does not encourage conversation, at least not to the point where the business of the bank is likely to be delayed. Social and regulatory aspects of the consumer behavior setting are also apparent in less formal contexts such as having to purchase a birthday gift for a friend, which is closer to the center of the open-closed continuum. The setting is closed insofar as the consumer conforms to social rules that describe moral or material rewards for reciprocity or punishments for ignoring generosity in others, though it has facets of openness stemming from the capacity of friends to depart from social norms or even break the rules on occasion, not only without censure but with a strengthening of the relationship.

Also on the left of the BPM shown in Fig. 3.1 is the consumer's learning history for this and similar products, what he or she has done in the past and the reinforcing and punishing outcomes this has had. The learning history primes the S^D MO that make up the consumer behavior setting and evokes the behavior that will generate or avoid the consequences on offer. It is the consumer situation that results from the interaction of learning history and consumer behavior setting that is the immediate precursor of consumer behavior. The *consumer situation*, which is the interaction of learning history and consumer behavior setting, induces or inhibits particular consumer behaviors depending on whether the consumer behavior analysis is relatively open or relatively closed. In the nonintentional construal of the BPM, the consumer situation thus amounts to the *scope* of the setting, that is, its degree of openness or closeness weighted by the individual's consumption history directly impacts upon the probability that particular consumer behaviors will occur. The consumer situation is the central explanatory device in the BPM, the immediate precursor of operant consumer behavior in this behavioral perspective. Its relationship with operant consumer behavior will remain the essence of the model as we progress to the action, decision, and agential perspectives.

Patterns of Reinforcement

The stimuli that comprise the consumer behavior setting and that enter into the consumer situation prompt the consumer to discriminate his or her behavior by purchasing or consuming certain products and services, marques, and brands rather than others. The behaviors performed are those that have been reinforced in the past and the discriminative stimuli, motivating operations, and learning history that interact to form the consumer situation are associated with utilitarian or functional and informational or symbolic reinforcements that will result from current behaviors. These consequences of behavior, shown on the right-hand side of the model in Fig. 3.1, may be positive or aversive, reinforcing or punishing in their effects on future consumer choice. Utilitarian reinforcers, which are mediated by the products themselves, are associated with the technical and operational qualities of the item bought and consumed. Informational reinforcers are socially mediated, however, and consist of performance feedback on the consumer behavior in question or other behaviors instrumental in making it possible. Almost any car will provide the utilitarian benefits of transporting its owner or driver, that is, "getting from A to B." But a Porsche usually delivers the performance feedback that comes from recognition of the owner's occupational status, social position, and other sources of honor and prestige. Like other socially constructed, symbolic outcomes of behavior, informational reinforcers are relative to the values the community (Foxall 2015c): in a social system conscious of CO_2 emission or fossil fuel consumption, a prestige car might not confer the positive social feedback just assumed, and members of the system may instead approve forms of transportation whose carbon footprint is smaller.

Consumers acquire combinations of utilitarian and informational benefits in the course of buying and using products, represented as a *pattern* of low and high utilitarian reinforcement and low/high informational reinforcement. In the BPM interpretation of consumer choice, the concept of a *pattern of reinforcement* replaces that of schedule of reinforcement, something applicable more to the precision of the closed setting of the laboratory than the construal of complex choices in the open settings of the market place. Defined in terms of pattern of reinforcement, four operant classes of consumer behavior can be discerned from the pattern of high/low utilitarian and informational reinforcement that maintains them: Accomplishment, Hedonism,

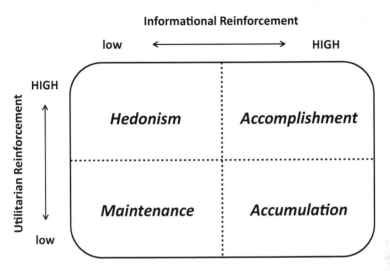

Fig. 3.2 *Patterns of reinforcement and operant classes of consumer behavior.* The patterns of reinforcement that maintain responding define the operant class to which consumer behaviors that have equifinal consequences belong. The labels attached to these operant classes of consumer behavior are arbitrary but have been shown to be accurately descriptive by a large volume of empirical research (Adapted from Foxall (1990/2004), *Consumer Psychology in Behavioral Perspective.* (London and New York: Routledge. Reprinted 2004 by Beard Books, Frederick, MD))

Accumulation, and Maintenance (Fig. 3.2). *Accomplishment* is consumer behavior reflecting social and economic achievement: acquisition and conspicuous consumption of status goods, displaying products and services that signal personal attainment. Both types of reinforcer figure in the maintenance of each of the four classes, though to differing extents. *Hedonism* includes such activities as the consumption of popular entertainment. *Accumulation* includes the consumer behaviors involved in certain kinds of saving, collecting, and installment buying. *Maintenance* consists of activities necessary for the consumer's physical survival and welfare (e.g., food) and the fulfillment of the minimal obligations entailed in membership of a social system (e.g., paying taxes).

The BPM Contingency Matrix

The BPM Contingency Matrix (Fig. 3.3) comprises eight distinct categories of contingencies, the outcome of combining consumer behavior setting scope and reinforcement patterns, each of which encompasses a wide range of consumer situations (Foxall 2010a). The following chapters reveal that the generic BPM shown in Fig. 3.1 can be construed in both extensional and intentional forms and that these offer different levels of explanation of consumer behavior. This theoretical development has inspired not only the empirical research described briefly below but

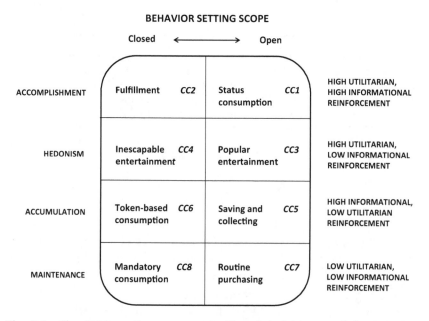

Fig. 3.3 *The BPM contingency matrix*. The eightfold way of the BPM is a functional classification of consumer situations defined in terms of the structural variables of the BPM: the scope of the consumer behavior setting and the pattern of reinforcement. The labels attached to these resulting contingency categories are arbitrary but have been shown to be accurately descriptive by a large volume of empirical research (Adapted from Foxall (1990/2004), *Consumer Psychology in Behavioral Perspective*. (London and New York: Routledge. Reprinted 2004 by Beard Books, Frederick, MD))

a means of interpreting familiar aspects of consumer behavior (Foxall 2010a, 2015c).

Operant Behavioral Economics of Consumer Choice

The contribution of the extensional Behavioral Perspective Model to understanding consumer choice has been reviewed recently in some detail (Foxall 2015a, b, 2016a, c; Foxall et al. 2007) and the following account provides no more than a summary.[2]

An underlying assumption of much of the empirical work inspired by the extensional Behavioral Perspective Model has been that consumers maximize a combination of utilitarian and informational reinforcement subject to their budget constraints. Although there have been tantalizing glimpses of this in the findings of research based on operant behavioral economics, the assumption has only become a conclusion as a result of recent investigations. Early work based on the principles of matching (Foxall 1999a; Herrnstein 1997; see also Baum 1974, 1979, 2015) indicates that consumer behavior is sensitive not only to the price of the brand purchased but to those of its competitors, that consumers maximize their returns in relation to their outgoings, and in ways that reflect

---

[2] Sterling work on the operant behavioral economics of consumer choice has been done by researchers whose first concern has been other than the exploration of the BPM; see, for example, in the context of information foraging, Hantula and Crowell (2015), Hantula et al. (2008), and Kim and Hantula (2016). The special issue of the journal *Managerial and Decision Economics* (2016; published online May 2015) on operant behavioral economics is also of interest in this regard. Recent work that is closely related to the BPM and its testing has also appeared on experimental analysis of consumer choice (Fagerstrøm and Sigurdsson 2016); in-store behavior (Sigurdsson et al. 2016a); online consumer behavior (Sigurdsson et al. 2016b); the role of equivalence classes in consumer choice (Arntzen et al. 2016); consumers' matching behavior (Sigurdsson and Foxall 2016); matching analysis of store choice (Bui Huynh and Foxall 2016); demand elasticity and essential value (Oliveira-Castro and Foxall 2016; Yan and Foxall 2016); triple jeopardy (Rogers et al. 2016); brand market structure (Porto and Oliveira-Castro 2016); consumers' utility functions (Oliveira-Castro et al. 2016); gambling (Dixon and Belisle 2016; Foxall 2016a; Foxall and Sigurdsson 2016); corruption (Luque Carreiro and Oliveira-Castro 2016); motivating operations (Fagerstrøm and Arntzen 2016); decision making (dos Santos and Moutinho 2016); consumer behavior and psychoanalysis (Desmond 2016); ethnography (Hackett 2016); the collective intentionality of car members' clubs (Laparojkit and Foxall 2016); consumer confusion (Anninou et al. 2016), and consumer heterophenomenology (Foxall 2016e).

the predicted patterns of brand and product substitution, independence, and complementarity of economic theory (Foxall et al. 2007; Sigurdsson and Foxall 2016).

These findings generally support the empirical evidence gathered over many years by Ehrenberg and others which has described aggregate patterns of buyer behavior. Most consumers of a product category (say, breakfast cereals) are not brand loyal in the sense that they *always* purchase a particular brand (say, *Shredded Wheat*) *exclusively* on *every* shopping trip. Most people who buy breakfast cereals buy within a subset of the available brands, the ones that through experience they have identified as functionally equivalent, buying one or other brand on each shopping occasion, sometimes buying more than one brand but always within this "consideration set." Their behavior looks random but over time it shows patterns such that some brands are bought more than others but never exclusively. The brands that are bought are similar in that they all provide the same level of utilitarian reinforcement: they are easily substituted one for another, therefore. Some consumers do not practice *multibrand purchasing* in this way. A small percentage of the buyers of a product category are 100 % loyal to a particular brand and each brand has a small proportion of its consumers who exhibit this *sole buying* mode. But most consumers, most of the time, buy a number of brands and show various levels of loyalty to the brands they buy. The relative frequency of buying a brand (the number of times it is bought divided by the number of times the product category is purchased) provides a behavioral measure of loyalty. The important thing is that, generally, consumers buy brands for whose purchase and consumption they have a learning history. Over time they go back to one or other of the brands that they have used in the past and as time goes on brands that have not been bought for a long time are tried again.

However, whereas this descriptive work has simply demonstrated the nature of patterns of consumer choice, the research conducted within the framework provided by the behavioral perspective of the BPM has shown why these patterns take the form they do; it has identified the independent variables of which consumer behavior is a function: prices, as one would expect, but also the utilitarian and informational reinforcement that provides the underlying content of what consumers seek to obtain. Moreover, the analyses we have undertaken indicate, in line with Herrnstein's (1997) theories of matching and melioration, that consumers maximize when making choices on each shopping trip and over a sequence of shopping trips.

The expectation to which this research gives rise—that consumers maximize combinations of utilitarian and informational reinforcement—has been borne out by a series of studies that have employed a variety of methods to estimate the elasticity of demand for consumer goods (Foxall et al. 2004, 2013; Oliveira-Castro and Foxall 2016; Yan and Foxall 2016; Oliveira-Castro et al. 2005, 2008a, b, 2010). Still the evidence that would underpin the assumption on which much of this research was based was elusive until a methodology was devised for the calculation of Cobb-Douglas utility functions indicating that what consumers maximize is indeed a bundle of utilitarian and informational reinforcement (Oliveira-Castro et al. 2015, 2016).

The empirical research program has established the BPM as a viable framework for the investigation of consumer choice. All of the operant classes of consumer behavior based on patterns of reinforcement and all of the contingency categories have received support as means of explaining consumer behavior. The model has proved capable of fostering the behavioral interpretation of such aspects of consumer choice as product, brand, and store selection, the adoption and diffusion of innovations, "green" consumer behavior, and managerial response to consumer demand (Foxall 1996/2016, 1999c, 2016e; Vella and Foxall 2011) and emotional responses to consumer environments of purchase and consumption (Foxall 2011, 2016a; Foxall et al. 2012, 2016c).

Emotion and Patterns of Contingency

Pleasure, Arousal, and Dominance

Another theme of empirical research based on the BPM has investigated the associations between emotional responses to consumer environments of purchase and consumption and the contingencies of reinforcement that govern behavior in such situations (Foxall 1997b, c, 2005, 2011,

2016a, c; Foxall et al. 2012). Three emotions—pleasure, arousal, and dominance—are the subject of a well-researched and validated theory that relates them to the environmental contexts in which they arise (Mehrabian and Russell 1974), from which Mehrabian (1980) argues for their being primary human emotional responses.

Emotion plays a central role in the reinforcement of behavior (for comprehensive accounts, see Foxall 2011, 2016a). Although behavior is often predictable and controllable when we know the pattern of reinforcement that maintains it, that is, the physical or functional benefits of behaving in a particular way (typically provided by product categories) and the social or informational benefits that follow such behavior (typically provided by brands), evolution knew nothing of these commodities when developing our susceptibilities by laying down a genetic basis for reinforcement. All that genes can do is program the particular *goals* that behavior fulfills, the kinds of primary reinforcement that lead to the well-being of the individual and his or her biological fitness (Rolls 2014). The specific products/services and brands that fulfill these requirements in contemporary marketing-oriented economies are the result of an ontogenetic development process that establishes particular secondary reinforcers in the shape of economic and social goods. By obtaining and using these secondary reinforcers, we ensure that the biological needs are met. The consumer, as we have seen, maximizes utilitarian and informational reinforcement but of course he or she has no conception of doing this overtly. Rather we select a bundle of products/services and brands which seem appropriate to us, and our decisions as to which of these goods to include in our shopping baskets are influenced principally by the emotional responses they engender in us. Utilitarian reinforcement derives from those goods that are useful to us in the course of our biological development; they eventuate in *pleasure*. Informational reinforcement derives from environmental feedback on our performance that informs us how well we are doing as members of a social system; it eventuates in *arousal*. The scope of the consumer behavior setting in which we behave eventuates in feelings of *dominance* over our environment. Studies of consumers' responses to the retail and consumption environments in which they operate indicate that these expectations are borne out.

Rolls's (2014; see also Foxall 2016a; Foxall and Yani-de-Soriano 2011) theory of emotion assumes that biologically defined behavioral goals influence what will count as reinforcers: while the overall goals of behavior, the reinforcers that contribute to biological survival and fitness, are therefore genetically regulated, the specific behaviors that achieve these reinforcers are decided by the biological imperatives of the individual (in the case of primary reinforcers) and the social milieux in which he or she operates (in the case of secondary reinforcers). The behaviors whose rate of performance is determined by reinforcers and punishers act can be conceptualized as motivational and emotional: the former resulting from intracranial stimulation, the latter from stimuli originating outside the brain. The identification of reinforcing and punishing stimuli via the sense modalities which inaugurate sensory processing enable the brain to accomplish appropriate decoding and representation of the reward value of reinforcers. Rolls develops a typology of emotions in terms of the contingencies of reinforcement and punishment. However, the BPM Emotional Contingency Matrix (Fig. 3.4) is more relevant to economic behavior in view of its embracing informational as well as utilitarian reinforcement, and is more comprehensive in terms of the functional influence of contingencies.

In summary, utilitarian reinforcement has been consistently shown to evoke a reaction of pleasure; informational reinforcement, one of arousal; and the scope of the consumer behavior setting, feelings of dominance (open settings), and submissiveness (closed settings.) But the interesting finding is that consumers evince a unique pattern of affective responses in terms of pleasure, arousal, and dominance for each of the eight contingency categories composed of varying levels of utilitarian and symbolic reinforcement, and the relative openness or closedness of the consumer behavior setting (Foxall 1995, 1997b, c, 2011; Foxall and Greenley 1998, 1999, 2000; Foxall and Yani-de-Soriano 2005, 2011; Foxall et al. 2012; Yani-de-Soriano and Foxall 2006; Yani-de-Soriano et al. 2013). As noted, the hypothesis that each of the basic emotional responses to environments posited by Mehrabian and Russell (1974) would be uniquely associated with a particular structural element of the consumer situation was borne out. Consumers' verbal references to the experience of pleasure are significantly related to the contingency structure of the situation defined by the BPM. Moreover, approach behavior increases with higher levels of utilitarian reinforcement and informational reinforcement and is highest where high levels of both are combined (Accomplishment) and lowest for combinations of low levels of both (Maintenance). The cross-cultural validity of these results—projects were executed in England, Wales, and Venezuela, the last in Spanish—suggest a robust methodology. Figure 3.4 summarizes the expected and actual results of eight studies. Where an

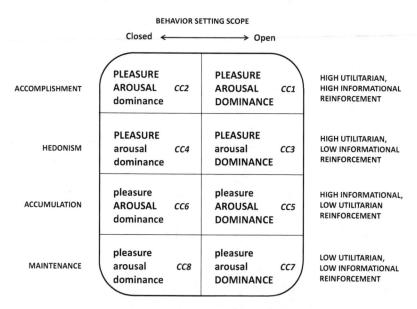

Fig. 3.4 *The BPM emotional contingency matrix.* The figure shows relationships between contingencies of reinforcement defined by the BPM and emotional responses to consumer situations. Studies show that: (a) *pleasure* scores for contingency categories (CCs) 1, 2, 3, and 4 each exceed those of CCs 5, 6, 7, and 8; (b) *arousal* scores for CCs 1, 2, 5, and 6 each exceed those of CCs 3, 4, 7, and 8; (c) *dominance* scores for CCs 1, 3, 5, and 7 each exceed those for CCs 2, 4, 6, and 8. Moreover, (d) *approach-avoidance* (aminusa) scores for CCs 1, 2, 3, and 4 each exceed those for CCs 5, 6, 7, and 8; and (e) *approach-avoidance* (aminusa) scores for CCs 1 and 3 each exceed those for CCs 2, 4, 5, 6, 7, and 8. A further result (f) is that *pleasure* scores for CCs 1, 3, 5, and 7 exceed those of CCs 2, 4, 6, and 8. (For further explication, see Foxall, 2011; Yani-de-Soriano et al. 2013) (Adapted from Foxall (2011), Brain, emotion and contingency in the explanation of consumer behaviour. *International Review of Industrial and Organizational Psychology, 26,* 47–92)

emotional response is in upper case it is relatively higher than when it is in lower case.

Two overarching emotions, pride and shame, identified by Fessler (2001), have been hypothesized as evoked, respectively, by consumer situations marked by high levels of all three of these emotions (CC1 in Fig. 3.3) and low levels thereof (CC8) (see Foxall 2016a). This relationship is shown in Fig. 3.5. This analysis emphasizes that the ultimate rewards that stem from informational reinforcement are the feelings of pride (higher self-esteem) and shame (lower self-esteem) derived from the consumer's self-monitored performance achievements.

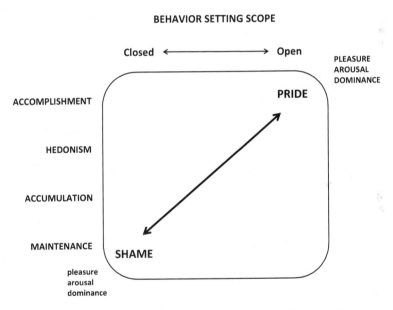

Fig. 3.5 *The BPM pride-shame continuum.* Pride is likely to result from behavior that achieves high levels of utilitarian and informational reinforcement in relatively open settings. Such contingencies evoke high levels of pleasure, arousal, and dominance. Shame is likely to be the result of behavior that leads to low levels of these emotions in relatively closed settings, the result of low levels of utilitarian and informational reinforcement and restricted consumer behavior setting scope (Adapted from Foxall (2016a). *Addiction as Consumer Choice: Exploring the Cognitive Dimension.* (London and New York: Routledge))

Interpreting Consumer Choice

Broad patterns of consumer behavior are amenable to interpretation in terms of the BPM, as the following accounts of consumers' brand and product choice, saving and wealth management, adoption of innovations, and environmental conservation attest. The validity of these behavioral interpretations of consumer choice already exceeds that of most radical behaviorist interpretations of complex behavior (cf., e.g., Skinner 1953a, 1957) in two respects. First, they are based on a wealth of empirical evidence gathered by a large number of nonbehaviorist researchers who have explored these aspects of consumer choice within the conventional marketing framework. Second, they are increasingly validated by the empirical research program of Consumer Behavior Analysis, which has recently been the subject of several reviews, and which has substantiated the underlying model (e.g., Foxall 2015a, 2016a, c).

Brand and Product Choice

Comparatively few consumers seem amenable to the recommendations of marketing textbooks. While many of these tomes exhort managers to ensure the loyalty of their customers and assume that buyers tend to explore the entire array of brands on the market, the consumers themselves staunchly practice multibrand purchasing within a small repertoire of available brands. This repertoire or "consideration set" is composed of tried and tested brands which the consumer knows well through purchase and consumption, a mere subset of the full range of brands within the product category. Each brand of course attracts its quota of "sole purchasers," those who are totally loyal to it, but the majority of consumers select seemingly randomly within their consideration set, sampling several competing versions of the product in the course of a succession of shopping trips.

A customer who purchases a new brand within an established product category is likely to be already a substantial user of the product, someone who is well-versed in the requirements consumers have and the capacity of existing brands to fulfill them. At best, the new brand consumer initially *tries* the new version. A brand that meets the expectations of the consumer, that is, performs at least as well as other members of the product category that are bought, may be included in the consumer's repertoire of acceptable brands. For most consumers, this guarantees nothing other than the possibility of its being chosen again at some future time, and at best selected intermittently. Many new consumer goods fail at this stage, but some go on to be repeat-purchased sufficiently often that they meet their revenue and profit targets and are retained within the firm's portfolio as well as the repertoires or consideration sets of a sufficiently large number of consumers.

Although work in this tradition has described patterns of consumer choice, it has not, except in a few cases, been concerned to establish the determinants of the observed patterns in terms of price and nonprice marketing mix variables. True, some of the research has documented the effects of price promotions on brand purchases, but there has been little systematic analysis of the effects of small differences in price on routine weekly or monthly brand selections. Nor has there been any discussion in this literature of the goals of consumers, their tendencies to maximize or satisfice, for instance, or the underlying motives that propel consumer decision making. Equally importantly, the analysis of aggregate patterns of consumer choice has rested on certain assumptions which, while plausible, have not been supported by systematic empirical evidence. It has been presumed, quite reasonably but without other than face validity, that brands within a product category are functional substitutes for one another. Developments in behavioral psychology and experimental economics have provided the means to overcome these difficulties.

The experimental analysis of behavior has demonstrated that choice and consumption in the confined context of the operant chamber adhere to the laws of neoclassical microeconomics (Kagel 1988; Kagel et al. 1995). Moreover, the extension of behavioral economic methods to the more complex situations of human consumption through applied behavior analyses of more open settings—such as token economies, therapeutic communities, environmental conservation programs, and the purchasing of familiar consumer products in simulated shopping malls—has indicated the robustness of this methodology as a general approach to economic analysis. The recent findings that, even in the relatively open settings of the modern marketing-oriented supermarket, consumer choice also conforms to the patterns established by behavior analysis and behavioral economics has revealed the possibilities of consumer behavior analysis as a means of both extending operant psychology into new areas of human endeavor and enriching that analysis through the absorption of results that are neither apparent nor predictable from prior work in behavioral economics be it with humans or nonhumans.

Saving and Wealth Management

In everyday consumer behavior conflict arises principally between purchasing and saving, something that needs to be phrased carefully. Rather than speaking of immediate or delayed gratification, we must think in terms of immediate or delayed spending, imminent or delayed consumption. "Imminent" permits not only immediate consumption (e.g., of a restaurant meal) and consumption that is slightly delayed to fit into the consumer's usual consumption pattern: buying this breakfast cereal now for consumption in the course of the next seven days. Even this represents a kind of saving insofar as consumption is planned and set out over a period of time. Storing goods for a world catastrophe (as some stocked food for the "Y2K disaster" of fond memory, or as people stock up with basic commodities against a rainy day) involves an extended timeline during which consumption is put off. Saving by definition requires delayed consumption in some form or other which can be classified in terms of how the accumulated funds or wealth are eventually disposed of. Several authors have identified categories of saving behavior and shown their significance in consumer psychology (Wärneryd 1989a). Katona (1975), for instance, defines several kinds of saving: *contractual* (e.g., regular payments of life insurance premiums), *discretionary* (e.g., saving for a planned vacation), and *residual* (e.g., holding money in a current account against irregular expenditures). Lindqvist (1981) goes further by proposing a hierarchy based on four sequential motives for saving: *cash management*, the most frequent motive, arising from the need to synchronize unpredictable payments and cash availability, *buffer saving*, a reserve of funds to meet unforeseen emergencies and their financial consequences, *goal-directed saving*—for a better car or home, etc., and *wealth manage-ment*, the creation and deployment of wealth in order to achieve more with the assets at one's disposal.

A BPM analysis of saving at the extensional level, shown in Fig. 3.6, avoids motives and goals as explanatory constructs and seeks to relate observed patterns of savings behavior to the contingencies likely to main-tain them (Foxall 2015c). At the early stages of the consumer life cycle, saving is related to Maintenance. In open settings, such cash manage-ment consists of residual saving, cash held in current accounts for the purpose of harmonizing receipts and expenditures, saving by default. In closed settings, it takes the form of contractual saving, payments made for credit, insurance, pensions schemes, and so on. In both cases, it is likely to be predominantly contingency-shaped rather than rule-governed. The

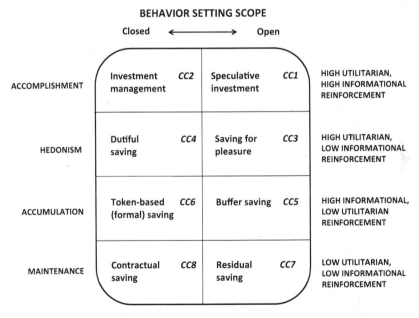

Fig. 3.6 *BPM savings contingency matrix.* This is an evidence-based interpre-tation of the nature of saving and personal asset management based on the economic psychology literature and the reasoning on which the BPM is based (Adapted from Foxall (2015c). *Consumers in Context: The BPM Research Program.* (London and New York: Routledge))

consumer comes directly into contact with the environmental factors that maintain these behaviors and, although some rules may affect specific choices (e.g., regulating the payment of premiums in contractual saving), the behavior is, for the most part, determined by its direct effects.

Additional income is likely to be saved for purposes of Accumulation, that is, with a view to gaining consumer durables, a better home, and so on. In open settings, it takes the form of a basic kind of discretionary saving, saving as a buffer against future misfortune (Katona 1975; Lindqvist 1981; Wärneryd 1989a). This implies formal saving, the regular putting aside of funds into an account which attracts interest. In closed settings, the saving is of a token-economy kind. It consists of accumulating tokens (perhaps through the purchase of products which confer bonuses in the form of additional products—as in frequent customer programs that confer additional air tickets or free gifts—or by a commitment to saving regularly which, when adhered to, provides a higher rate of interest) which give access to other products or prizes which provide mainly utilitarian reinforcement. In both open and closed settings, initially at least, other-rules of a specific nature are likely to influence consumer behavior; such rules specify, for instance, the rate of interest, the number of times a saving act needs to be repeated in order to earn benefits. Tracking is the consumer's likely verbal behavior as he or she follows instructions to: "Do this and that will follow"; to initiate and sustain early saving, however, some plying and augmentals may be necessary. The actual contingencies are likely to assume an important effect as regular saving is maintained by the addition of interest or other benefits.

Further gains in income and/or wealth are likely to lead to saving related to Hedonism which will eventually facilitate higher levels of discretionary spending, perhaps on more luxurious items. In open settings, this could mean saving related to pleasure and fun: saving for vacations, luxuries, home entertainment systems, and so on. In closed settings, it would refer to dutiful saving, as for school fees for one's children, for instance. The benefits of such saving are long deferred and rules are necessary to instigate and sustain this behavior; the contingencies are likely to assume greater control as saving plans mature, enabling spending, which motivates further long-term saving. Both of these are discretionary saving in Katona's terms, though of a more affluent nature than that which was described as Accumulative saving. This is what Lindqvist (1981) refers to as goal-oriented saving (Wahlund and Wärneryd 1987).

The final stage is Accomplishment, which manifests in personal asset management, the use of wealth to create more wealth (Lindqvist 1981; Wärneryd 1989b). In open settings, this wealth management takes the form of speculation for gain and in closed setting as the management of investments. Rules play an important part in both cases: self-rules in speculative investment, and advice from others, such as brokers, in the context of investment management. Tracks and augmentals are likely to be particularly important.

The BPM approach does not simply redescribe the categories developed in other systems but relates patterns of consumer behavior with respect to saving and asset management to the changing patterns of contingencies likely to be operative at different stages in the consumer life cycle. However, it might be objected that, while the interpretation appears plausible, and at least indicates that a behavior analytical account of some specialized aspects of consumer behavior is feasible, it proceeds largely in terms of two components of the model. These are the scope of the behavior setting defined primarily in terms of the nature of the physical and social surroundings in which purchase and consumption occur, and the nature of the pattern of reinforcement apparently maintaining the chosen exemplar behaviors. An interpretative account of a broader sequence of consumer behavior is needed, if we are to adjudge the usefulness of the remaining variables in the model, particularly the role of consumers' verbal behavior. An appropriate sequence is that provided by the adoption and diffusion of innovations. Consideration of the sequence of consumer behaviors that occur over the product-market life cycle permits the extension of the applicability of the model in two ways. First, it allows assessment of the explanatory status of the setting and consequential variables that have not yet been covered, namely effects of consumers' verbal behavior on their nonverbal responses, and the distinction between utilitarian and informational reinforcement. Second, it demonstrates the capacity of the model to account not simply for a sequence of consumer behavior within the context of an individual's economic experience but for an entire sequence of consumption responses involving diverse consumer groups and occurring within a broad social and economic context.

Environmental Conservation

The spoliation of the physical environment is the result of consumer behaviors that are influenced by their consequences, in fact, the pattern of reinforcement that defines the behavior in question as accomplishment, hedonism, accumulation, or maintenance (Fig. 3.7) Each of the major areas of behavior analytical research in this field—the pollution and depletion of fossil fuels caused by private transportation, the similar depletion and pollution caused by domestic energy consumption, the wanton disposal of the products of consumption leading to landfill problems, and the usage of a scarce naturally occurring resource, water—corresponds to one of these classes of operant consumer behavior. The problem of private transportation is one of accumulation: the behavior is maintained by high levels of both utilitarian reinforcement (such as the fun of driving, comfort, flexibility, and the control of one's journey) and informational

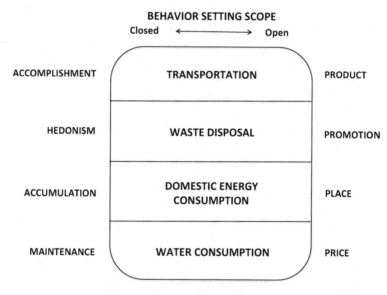

Fig. 3.7 *Environment-impacting consumption: Operant classes and marketing mix elements.* The full reasoning behind the relationships depicted here can be found in Foxall (2015b) (Adapted from Foxall (2015c). *Consumers in Context: The BPM Research Program.* London and New York: Routledge)

reinforcement (speed, low and flexible journey times) and can, therefore, be categorized as accomplishment. A successful demarketing strategy would need to replace this pattern of consequences with one equally motivating (e.g., in the provision of public transportation). Domestic energy usage is based on consequences which include convenience and comfort, and so are generally maintained by high levels of utilitarian reinforcement. Its overconsumption is thus a problem of hedonism. While informational reinforcement (or feedback) is less obvious, it may be important in social situations where visitors are also affected by usage. In recent research, both incentives and feedback have been used alone and in combination to reduce domestic energy consumption with an indication that incentives have the largest effect (cf. Cone and Hayes 1980). Waste disposal is classed as accumulation but the problem is actually manifested in the opposite of accumulation: disposal. Indiscriminate waste disposal has relatively few utilitarian reinforcers other than convenience, but its informational outcomes are extensive if subtle. It confers status through the assumption that someone else will clear up, and it may also imply conspicuous consumption. Intervention may take the form of increasing informational reinforcement by linking the individual's attempts at recycling or saving resources and feeding this information back to them. In the case of domestic water consumption (classed as maintenance) both utilitarian and informational reinforcers are low, compared to the other class of consumer behavior but are not absent. They are related to the consumer's state of deprivation, as domestic water consumption allows us to drink, clean, and wash which are basic human needs. Due to the low levels of both reinforcers it may be the case that the most successful intervention strategy might be punishment. The utilitarian and informational positive consequences are not strongly motivational, and the price elasticity of demand for the commodity is high, so an increase in price would be particularly effective.

The Adoption and Diffusion of New Products

In dealing with everyday consumer choice we have said little about what causes it to change, notably the introduction of new brands, new products, and new practices. Why do established patterns of behavior exhibit dynamic breaks in continuity from time to time? Why do consumers stop buying within their current brand repertoire, if only temporarily, in order to try a new version of the same product? The topic is usually subsumed under the heading of consumer innovation or innovativeness in the marketing literature. But it is also relevant to the understandings of patterns of behavior and their interruption put forward by Ainslie (1992) and Rachlin (1994). Crucially, however, it provides insight into the nature of the quest for evolutionary consistency in the ascription of intentional content on the basis of contingency-shaped molar behavior sequences. In this way, the analysis of consumers' initiating and imitative behaviors becomes a vehicle for discussing the role of evolutionary logic within the framework of exposition for consumer theory worked out in the earlier chapters. The processes should be amenable to analysis in terms of an extensional behavioral science, intentional systems theory, intentional behaviorism, and super-personal cognitive psychology. It should be possible also in this context to explore further the evolutionary basis of complex consumer behavior. This chapter relates consumer innovation to the intentional and behavioral components of explanation found in intentional behaviorism and to super-personal cognitive psychology. Accounting in extensional terms for the diffusion of innovations, from consumer initiation (the earliest trial and adoption of newness) to imitation (later trial and adoption based on the observed experience of initiators), requires a portrayal of the contingencies of reinforcement as they impinge on consumer behaviors over the product and/or brand life cycle.

Rogers (2003) depicts the succession of adopter categories involved in diffusion in terms of a normal distribution of adoption frequencies over time (Fig. 3.8). The rate at which new products diffuse through the social system varies directly with the relative advantage of the innovation, its compatibility with current products and patterns of consumer behavior, its social conspicuousness, and its trialability, and indirectly with the complexity of the innovation and the costs and risks incurred in its trial or adoption. Trial and adoption decisions reflect the consumers' perceptions of these innovation characteristics and the members of the adopter categories shown in Fig. 3.8 show individual differences in their perception in line with the rate at which they try and adopt. Facets of consumers' personalities like flexibility and self-esteem influence their adoption

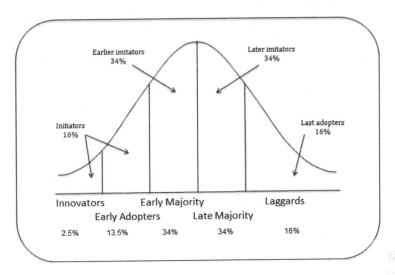

Fig. 3.8 *The BPM diffusion curve.* Adopter categories as defined by Rogers and the BPM. For further exposition, see Foxall (2010a)

decisions, as do their social and behavioral characteristics like socioeconomic status, communications behavior, previous consumer behavior (e.g., being a heavy or a light user of the product category), and pattern of social involvements (Foxall et al. 1998).

The central process in Rogers's (2003) integrative model of the communication of innovations is a cognitive decision strategy which may lead to their trying out a new product and then to their confirming or disconfirming their initial judgment by adopting or discontinuing its use. Diffusion of the innovation through the social system comes about as the various adopter categories respond in turn to the benefits of the product and by their more or less conspicuous consumption of the item communicate it to the next category. The adopter categories are defined by Rogers in terms of standard deviations from the mean time of adoption: the first 2.5 % of adopters being termed "innovators"; the next 13.5 % as "early adopters"; followed by "the earlier majority" (34 %), and a similar proportion who comprise the "later majority." Finally, come the "laggards," the last 16 % of the market. Hence, diffusion is a matter of communication of the benefits of the innovation from one category of adopters to the next (Goldsmith and Foxall 2003).

Figure 3.8 also suggests how the four operant classes of consumer behavior identified by the BPM might account for the diffusion of innovations. Initial adopters (16 % of the eventual market) are consumers whose behavior for the relevant product class/category is described as Accomplishment, that is, the pattern of reinforcement involves high levels of both utilitarian and informational reinforcement. These experienced consumers have considerable product knowledge and expertise and the necessary wealth or income to permit early adoption decisions. By comparison with later adopters, initiators display behavior that is shaped and maintained by the specific pattern of utilitarian and informational reinforcement noted, and a learning history that has seen earlier adoption rewarded. These general interpretations are consistent with the evidence on the adoption of innovations by successive groups of the consumer who compose a social system (Foxall 2010a, b).

Addiction

Addiction defies easy definition but has several characteristics (Foxall 2016a). First, it reflects a tendency to be impulsive, to choose a more immediate reward, even if it is smaller, rather than wait for a greater one. Consumers frequently discount or devalue the future and overvalue immediacy, but this only becomes problematic when their behavior becomes irrational in the sense in which economists use the term. An individual who spends a lot of money trying to lose weight—joining a gym, taking a course, joining a slimming club—but eats fattening foods with abandon is working against himself or herself by investing so much in losing weight only to make sure that this is impossible. When this economic irrationality becomes so marked that it results in the loss of a job because the consumer prefers eating—or it could be drinking, taking drugs, or gambling—to working, then the consumer's life is being disrupted. They may also lose friends and possibly a partner. We can now start to grasp what addiction means. The addict resolves not to eat the fattening food, thoroughly makes up their mind to avoid it, but lapses into binge eating when the opportunity arises; this is followed by further resolve, another lapse, and the cycle continues. It may even get to the point where they actively dislike the substance or behavior but still persist in it.

There are biological dimensions to this too. The addict's brain may change over time so that the impulse to imbibe a particular substance or behave in a particular way (e.g., excessive gambling) becomes easier to give in to. We are more prepared to act in these ways even though the pleasure of doing so has diminished. Scientists used to think that a brain chemical called *dopamine* was responsible for the pleasure of eating, drinking, taking drugs, or gambling but dopamine actually arouses our tendencies to act in particular ways that we have learned, it prepares the way for indulgence. The opioids, another class of chemicals the brain makes, are responsible for the pleasure. The tendency is for dopamine to be released whenever we are in the situations that led to drug taking or whatever in the past and to engender a *craving* for that activity again. The addict *wants* the drug, or food, or to gamble so much that it becomes hard to resist. The paradox is that while the *wanting* increases, *liking* of the substance or the activity diminishes. Situations and the dopamine release for which they are responsible maintain the cycle.

Addiction is a form of consumption. It differs importantly from other kinds of consumer behavior but usually in degree rather than kind. All consumer behavior involves reward, dopamine release, the pleasures evoked by other brain chemicals, and a tendency to repeat the purchasing, owning, storing, and using products and services. And it seems natural to want things sooner rather than later. But most of us avoid consuming so heavily that our behavior becomes economically irrational, losing our friends and possibly our loved ones and our jobs. Impatience may lead consumers to buy on credit or run down their savings, but these are generally temporary effects. If we do go a little too far, we readjust our budgets, get back into the black, and carry on consuming moderately. Fortunately very few consume to the point of addiction as I have described it. There is a spectrum of consumer behaviors from the routine everyday buying of a brand of butter or toothpaste to the compulsion that addiction rests on. In between there are numerous gradations of impulsiveness or impatience that need to become compulsive.

There is, moreover, no need to fear that addiction is irreversible. There were fears when American soldiers who had acquired heroin habits while serving in Viet Nam would continue to use this drug when they returned home. Many did not: on arriving back in the USA the majority became ensconced in the situations that were familiar to them and ceased using the drug. So situations matter. There is also good reason to believe that brain functions can assist in overcoming excessive consumption. While the dopamine system may engender cravings that we act on habitually and without thought, other brain regions, notably the prefrontal cortex, are implicated in inhibiting these impulses, planning for the future, and valuing the larger reward of good health and well-being even though it takes time. It is this cognitive activity with which this book is largely concerned, and understanding its cognitive dimensions elucidates the nature and the possibility of overcoming addiction as problems of consumption (see, for instance, Grant and Potenza 2012; Lewis 2016).

The BPM interprets addiction within a spectrum of consumer choice that ranges from routine purchasing, where consumers discount the future little if at all to extreme consumption which entails compulsion or addiction (Fig. 3.9; for further exposition, see Foxall 2010b, 2016a; Foxall and Sigurdsson 2011). By showing that consumer behavior is generally influenced by similar factors which differ in their magnitude and combined sway over behavior we understand more clearly the nature of addiction. The second is its drawing attention to the cognitive influences on addictive behaviors. Of the three major influences on choice—neurophysiological, situational, and cognitive—the cognitive has been somewhat underdeveloped. The book seeks to redress this imbalance by emphasizing that for some behaviors there are no convincing situational influences—the pattern of rewards available to gamblers for instance often runs entirely contrary to what psychology would predict. This is well-illustrated by the so-called near-miss effect in slot machine gambling: two identical icons along with a third different one are often interpreted as close to the winning combination of three identical icons, a sign that the player is gaining skill in the gambling task. As a result of this cognitive distortion, the near-miss actually motivates further play. Only a cognitive explanation, supported by the neurophysiological evidence, can account for this irrational pattern of play. The treatment of cognition

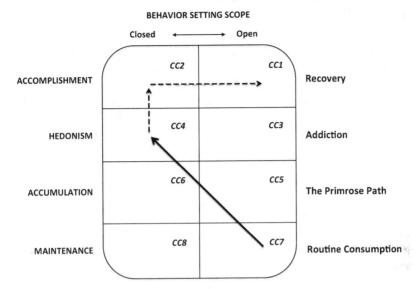

BEHAVIOR SETTING SCOPE

Fig. 3.9 *The BPM course of addiction matrix.* A full exposition of addiction as consumer choice can be found in Foxall (2016a) (Adapted from Foxall (2010b). Accounting for consumer choice: Inter-temporal decision-making in behavioural perspective, *Marketing Theory*, 10, 315–345)

is also unique in that it is pursued according to a strict procedure for cognitive explanation.

Conclusion

In summary, in the behavioral perspective of the BPM, the variables are extensionally defined. The *consumer situation* is simply the interaction of the consumer behavior setting and the learning history. It amounts to the scope of the setting. The consumer behavior setting consists of *motivating operations* (MO), *discriminative stimuli* (S^D), and *rules*. The *pattern of reinforcement* comprises a combination of *utilitarian reinforcement* and *informational reinforcement* (UR and IR). Consumer *behavior* is a response to stimuli and is defined in terms of patterns of reinforcement: accomplishment, hedonism, accumulation, and maintenance.

Bibliography

Ainslie, G. (1992). *Picoeconomics: The strategic interaction of successive motivational states within the person.* Cambridge: Cambridge University Press.

Anninou, I., Foxall, G. R., & Pallister, J. G. (2016). Consumer confusion: A BPM perspective. In G. R. Foxall (Ed.), *The Routledge companion to consumer behavior analysis* (pp. 400–416). London/New York: Routledge.

Arntzen, E., Fagerstrøm, A., & Foxall, G. R. (2016). Equivalence classes and preferences in consumer choice. In G. R. Foxall (Ed.), *The Routledge companion to consumer behavior analysis* (pp. 65–77). London/New York: Routledge.

Baum, W. M. (1974). On two types of deviation from the matching law: Bias and undermatching. *Journal of the Experimental Analysis of Behavior, 22,* 231–242.

Baum, W. M. (1979). Matching, undermatching, and overmatching in studies of choice. *Journal of the Experimental Analysis of Behavior, 23,* 45–53.

Baum, W. M. (2015). Driven by consequences: The multiscale view of choice. *Managerial and Decision Economics,* (Published online May 2015).

Bui Huynh, N., & Foxall, G. R. (2016). Consumer store choice: A matching analysis. In G. R. Foxall (Ed.), *The Routledge companion to cosumer behavior analysis* (pp. 96–120). London/New York: Routledge.

Cone, J. D., & Hayes, S. C. (1980). *Environmental problems/behavioral solutions.* Belmont: Wadsworth.

Desmond, J. (2016). Consumer behavior analysis: A view of psychoanalysis. In G. R. Foxall (Ed.), *The Routledge companion to consumer behavior analysis* (pp. 350–365). London/New York: Routledge.

Dixon, M. R., & Belisle, J. (2016). Gambling behavior. In G. R. Foxall (Ed.), *The Routledge companion to consumer behavior analysis* (pp. 231–241). London/New York: Routledge.

Fagerstrøm, A., & Arntzen, E. (2016). Motivating operations and consumer choice. In G. R. Foxall (Ed.), *The Routledge companion to consumer behavior analysis* (pp. 296–305). London/New York: Routledge.

Fagerstrøm, A., & Sigurdsson, V. (2016). Experimental analysis of consumer choices. In G. R. Foxall (Ed.), *The Routledge companion to consumer behavior analysis* (pp. 25–39). London/New York: Routledge.

Fagerstrøm, A., Foxall, G. R., & Arntzen, E. (2010). Implications of motivating operations for the functional analysis of consumer behavior. *Journal of Organizational Behavior Management, 30*(2), 110–126.

Fessler, D. M. T. (2001). Emotion and cost-benefit assessment: The role of shame and self-esteem in risk taking. In G. Gigerenza & R. Selten (Eds.), *Bounded rationality: The adaptive toolbox* (pp. 191–214). Cambridge, MA: MIT Press.

Foxall, G. R. (1990/2004). *Consumer psychology in behavioral perspective.* New York: Routledge. Reprinted 2004 by Beard Books, Fredericks, MD.

Foxall, G. R. (1996/2016). *Consumers in context: The BPM research program.* London/New York: Routledge. (Library edition 2016).

Foxall, G. R. (1997b). The emotional texture of consumer environments: A systematic approach to atmospherics. *Journal of Economic Psychology, 18,* 505–523.

Foxall, G. R. (1997c). Affective responses to consumer situations. *International Review of Retail, Distribution and Consumer Research, 7,* 191–225.

Foxall, G. R., & Greenley, G. E. (1998). The affective structure of consumer situations. *Environment and Behavior, 30,* 781–798.

Foxall, G. R. (1999a). The substitutability of brands. *Managerial and Decision Economics, 20,* 241–257.

Foxall, G. R. (1999c). The marketing firm. *Journal of Economic Psychology, 20,* 207–234.

Foxall, G. R. (2005). *Understanding consumer choice.* London/New York: Palgrave Macmillan.

Foxall, G. R. (2010a). *Interpreting consumer choice: The behavioral perspective model.* New York: Routledge.

Foxall, G. R. (2010b). Accounting for consumer choice: Inter-temporal decision-making in behavioral perspective. *Marketing Theory, 10,* 315–345.

Foxall, G. R. (2011). Brain, emotion and contingency in the explanation of consumer behavior. *International Review of Industrial and Organizational Psychology, 26,* 47–92.

Foxall, G. R. (2015a). Operant behavioral economics. *Managerial and Decision Economics* (Published online May 2015).

Foxall, G. R. (2015b). Consumer behavior analysis and the marketing firm: Bilateral contingency in the context of environmental concern. *Journal of Organizational Behavior Management, 35,* 44–69

Foxall, G. R. (2015c). Consumers in context: The BPM research program. London/New York: Routledge

Foxall, G. R. (2016a). *Addiction as consumer choice: Exploring the cognitive dimension.* London/New York: Routledge.

Foxall, G. R. (Ed.). (2016c). *The Routledge companion to consumer behavior analysis.* London/New York: Routledge.

Foxall, G. R. (2016e). Consumer heterophenomenology. In G. R. Foxall (Ed.), *The Routledge companion to consumer behavior analysis* (pp. 417–430). London/New York: Routledge.

Foxall, G. R., & Sigurdsson, V. (2011). Drug use as consumer behavior. *Behavioral and Brain Sciences, 34*, 313–314.

Foxall, G. R., & Sigurdsson, S. (2016). When loss rewards: The near-miss effect in slot machine gambling. In G. R. Foxall (Ed.), *The Routledge companion to consumer behavior analysis* (pp. 242–257). London/New York: Routledge.

Foxall, G. R., Goldsmith, R. E., & Brown, S. (1998). *Consumer psychology for marketing* (2nd ed.). London/New York: International Thompson Business Press.

Foxall, G. R., & Yani-de-Soriano, M. Y. (2005). Situational influences on consumers' attitudes and behaviour. *Journal of Business Research, 58*, 518–525.

Foxall, G. R., & Greenley, G. E. (1999). Consumers' emotional responses to service environments. *Journal of Business Research, 46*, 149–158.

Foxall, G. R., & Greenley, G. E. (2000). Predicting and explaining responses to consumer environments: An empirical test and theoretical extension of the behavioural perspective model. *The Service Industries Journal, 20*, 39–63.

Foxall, G. R., Oliveira-Castro, J. M., & Schrezenmaier, T. C. (2004). The behavioral economics of consumer brand choice: Patterns of reinforcement and utility maximization. *Behavioural Processes, 65*, 235–260.

Foxall, G. R., Oliveira-Castro, J. M., James, V. K., & Schrezenmaier, T. C. (2007). *Brand choice in behavioral perspective*. London/New York: Palgrave Macmillan.

Foxall, G. R., & Yani-de-Soriano, M. (2011). Influence of reinforcement contingencies and cognitive styles on affective responses: An examination of Rolls's theory of emotion in the context of consumer choice. *Journal of Applied Social Psychology, 41*, 2506–2535.

Foxall, G. R., Yani-de-Soriano, M., Yousafzai, S., & Javed, U. (2012). The role of neurophysiology, emotion and contingency in the explanation of consumer choice. In V. K. Wells & G. R. Foxall (Eds.), *Handbook of developments in consumer behaviour* (pp. 461–522). Cheltenham/Northampton: Edward Elgar.

Foxall, G. R., Yan, J., Oliveira-Castro, J. M., & Wells, V. K. (2013). Brand-related and situational influences on demand elasticity. *Journal of Business Research, 66*, 73–81.

Goldsmith, R. E., & Foxall, G. R. (2003). The measurement of innovativeness. In L. Shavinina (Ed.), *The international handbook of innovation* (pp. 321–330). Oxford: Pergamon.

Grant, J. E., & Potenza, M. N. (Eds.). (2012). *The Oxford handbook of impulse control disorders*. New York: Oxford University Press.

Hackett, P. M. W. (2016). Ethnographical interpretation of consumer behavior: Employing the behavioral perspective model. In G. R. Foxall (Ed.), *The Routledge companion to consumer behavior analysis* (pp. 366–378). London/ New York: Routledge.

Hantula, D. A., & Crowell, C. R. (2015). Matching and behavioral contrast in a two-option repeated investment simulation. *Managerial and Decision Economics* published online 14 September, 2015.

Hantula, D. A., Brockman, D. D., & Smith, C. L. (2008). Online shopping as foraging: The effects of increasing delays on purchasing and patch residence. *IEEE Transactions on Professional Communication, 51*, 147–154.

Herrnstein, R. J. (1997). *The matching law: Papers in psychology and economics*. In H. Rachlin & D. I. Laibson(Eds.). Cambridge, MA/New York: Harvard University Press/Russell Sage Foundation.

Kagel, J. H. (1988). Economics according to the rats (and pigeons too): What have we learned and what can we hope to learn? In A. E. Roth (Ed.), *Laboratory experimentation in economics: Six points of view* (pp. 155–192). Cambridge: Cambridge University Press.

Kagel, J. H., Battalio, R. C., & Green, L. (1995). *Economic choice theory: An experimental analysis of animal behavior*. Cambridge: Cambridge University Press.

Katona, G. (1975). *Psychological economics*. New York: Elsevier.

Kim, W., & Hantula, D. A. (2016). Consumers as inforagers. In G. R. Foxall (Ed.), *The Routledge companion to consumer behavior analysis* (pp. 306–327). London/New York: Routledge.

Laparojkit, S., & Foxall, G. R. (2016). Collective intentionality and symbolic reinforcement: The case of Thai car-consumer clubs. In G. R. Foxall (Ed.), *The Routledge companion to consumer behavior analysis* (pp. 379–399). London/New York: Routledge.

Lewis, M. (2016). *The biology of desire: Why addiction is not a disease*. Philadelphia: Perseus.

Lindqvist, A. (1981). *Household saving – Behavioral measurement of household saving behavior*. Doctoral thesis. Stockholm School of Economics.

Luque Carreiro, P., & Oliveira-Castro, J. M. (2016). A functional analysis of corruption from a behavioral-economic perspective. In G. R. Foxall (Ed.), *The Routledge companion to consumer behavior analysis* (pp. 258–271). London/New York: Routledge.

Mehrabian, A. (1980). *Basic dimensions for a general psychological theory*. Cambridge, MA: Oelgeschlager, Gunn & Hain.

Mehrabian, A., & Russell, J. A. (1974). *An approach to environmental psychology.* Cambridge, MA: MIT Press.

Oliveira-Castro, J. M., Cavalcanti, P., & Foxall, G. R. (2015). What consumers maximize: Brand choice as a function of utilitarian and informational reinforcement. *Managerial and Decision Economics.* DOI: 10.1002/mde.2722. (Published online May 2015).

Oliveira-Castro, J. M., & Foxall, G. R. (2016). Dimensions of demand elasticity. In G. R. Foxall (Ed.), *The Routledge companion to consumer behavior analysis* (pp. 121–137). London/New York: Routledge.

Oliveira-Castro, J. M., Foxall, G. R., & Schrezenmaier, T. C. (2005). Patterns of consumer response to retail price differentials. *Service Industries Journal, 25,* 309–327.

Oliveira-Castro, J. M., Foxall, G. R., & James, V. K. (2008a). Individual differences in price responsiveness within and across food brands. *Service Industries Journal, 28,* 733–753.

Oliveira-Castro, J. M., Foxall, G. R., James, V. K., Pohl, R. H. B. F., Dias, M. B., & Chang, S. W. (2008b). Consumer-based brand equity and brand performance. *Service Industries Journal, 28,* 445–461.

Oliveira-Castro, J. M., Foxall, G. R., & James, V. K. (2010). Consumer brand choice: Allocation of expenditure as a function of pattern of reinforcement and response cost. *Journal of Organizational Behavior Management, 30*(2), 161–175.

Oliveira-Castro, J. M., Cavalcanti, P., & Foxall, G. R. (2016). What do consumers maximize? The analysis of utility functions in light of the behavioral perspective model. In G. R. Foxall (Ed.), *The Routledge companion to consumer behavior analysis* (pp. 202–212). London/New York: Routledge.

Porto, R. B., & Oliveira-Castro, J. M. (2016). Consumer purchase and brand performance: The basis of brand market structure. In G. R. Foxall (Ed.), *The Routledge companion to consumer behavior analysis* (pp. 175–201). London/ New York: Routledge.

Rachlin, H. (1994). *Behavior and mind: The roots of modern psychology.* Oxford: Oxford University Press.

Rogers, E. M. (2003). *Diffusion of innovations.* New York: Free Press.

Rogers, A., Morgan, P., & Foxall, G. R. (2016). Triple jeopardy in behavioral perspective. In G. R. Foxall (Ed.), *The Routledge companion to consumer behavior analysis* (pp. 150–174). London/New York: Routledge.

Rolls, E. T. (2014). *Emotion and decision-making explained.* Oxford: Oxford University Press.

Schoggen, P. (1989). *Behavior settings.* Stanford: Stanford University Press.

Sigurdsson, V., & Foxall, G. R. (2016). Experimental analyses of choice and matching: From the animal laboratory to the marketplace. In G. R. Foxall (Ed.), *The Routledge companion to consumer behavior analysis* (pp. 78–95). London/New York: Routledge.

Sigurdsson, V., Larsen, N. M., & Fagerstrøm, A. (2016a). Behavior analysis of in-store consumer behavior. In G. R. Foxall (Ed.), *The Routledge companion to consumer behavior analysis* (pp. 40–50). London/New York: Routledge.

Sigurdsson, V., Larsen, N. M., & Menon, R. G. V. (2016b). Behavior analysis of online consumer behavior. In G. R. Foxall (Ed.), *The Routledge companion to consumer behavior analysis* (pp. 51–64). London/New York: Routledge.

Skinner, B. F. (1953a). *Science and human behavior*. New York: Macmillan.

Skinner, B. F. (1957). *Verbal behavior*. New York: Century.

Vella, K. J., & Foxall, G. R. (2011). *The marketing firm: Economic psychology of corporate behaviour*. Cheltenham/Northampton: Edward Elgar.

Wahlund, R., & Wärneryd, K.-E. (1987). Aggregate saving and the saving behavior of saver groups. *Skandinaviska Enskilda Banken Quarterly Review, 3*, 52–64.

Wärneryd, K.-E. (1989a). On the psychology of saving: An essay on economic behavior. *Journal of Economic Psychology, 10*, 515–541.

Wärneryd, K.-E. (1989b). Improving psychological theory through studies of economic behavior: The case of saving. *Applied Psychology: In International Review, 38*, 213–236.

Yan, J., Foxall, G. R., & Doyle, J. R. (2012a). Patterns of reinforcement and the essential value of brands: I. Incorporation of utilitarian and informational reinforcement into the estimation of demand. *The Psychological Record, 62*, 361–376.

Yan, J., Foxall, G. R., & Doyle, J. R. (2012b). Patterns of reinforcement and the essential value of brands: II. Evaluation of a model of consumer choice. *The Psychological Record, 62*, 377–394.

Yan, J., & Foxall, G. R. (2016). The BPM and essential value. In G. R. Foxall (Ed.), *The Routledge companion to consumer behavior analysis* (pp. 138–149). London/New York: Routledge.

Yani-de-Soriano, M., & Foxall, G. R. (2006). The emotional power of place: The fall and rise of dominance in retail research. *Journal of Retailing and Consumer Services, 13*, 403–416.

Yani-de-Soriano, M., Foxall, G. R., & Newman, A. (2013). The impact of the interaction of utilitarian and informational reinforcement and behaviour setting scope on consumer response. *Psychology and Marketing, 30*, 148–159.

4

Beyond Behaviorism

Introduction

Laying the foundations of psychological explanation requires the identification of the limitations or bounds of radical behaviorism. There are three stages in this procedure. First, the essence of an extensional explanation needs to be spelled out so that the pros and cons of this methodology can be appreciated. The purpose of the extensional model of consumer choice is to show where this mode of explanation can no longer give an account of behavior on its own terms. Hence, the second stage requires that the model reveal areas of consumer choice for which the stimulus field on which behaviorist explanation relies cannot be found. This point can only be recognized if we have a clear understanding of the nature of extensional explanation and can diagnose where it runs out. The bounds of behaviorism so distinguished must be classified and the factors that lead to their occurrence singled out. Each of the bounds of behaviorism signals the necessity of an Intentional Interpretation; these "imperatives of intentionality" must correspond to the bounds of behaviorism in which their origins are found. This third stage permits us a first glimpse of the requirements of psychological explanation.

© The Editor(s) (if applicable) and The Author(s) 2016
G.R. Foxall, *Perspectives on Consumer Choice*,
DOI 10.1057/978-1-137-50121-9_4

The Extensional Explanation of Consumer Choice

Extensional Explanation Revisited

We can now return to an examination of the extensional or behavioral perspective of the BPM as summarized in Fig. 4.1. An extensional model incorporates causal influences but does not employ intentional idioms or reasoning to explain its dependent variable, which in this case is rate of responding. Hence, as we saw in Chapter 3, the behavioral perspective of the BPM defines the consumer situation simply as the scope of the current consumer behavior setting, where the experience of consumption meets an opportunity to consume anew. The influence of this consumer situation, the immediate determinant of approach—avoidance responses involved in purchase and consumption, is conceived of entirely in terms of the effect of the external environment on consumer choice. The consumer situation is no more than the range of options available to the consumer as determined by the stimulus antecedents of feasible behaviors, some of which will have been present on earlier consumption occasions; in the presence of the individual's learning history, these initially neutral stimuli are transformed into the S^D and MO that set the occasion for current choice. The consumer's consumption history invests the initially neutral stimuli with a kind of meaning, which consists in no more than the capacity to generate specific kinds of approach and or avoidance

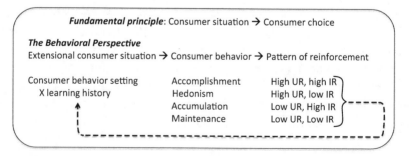

Fig. 4.1 Consumer choice: The behavioral perspective

behaviors; these, in turn, produce the consequences that regulate the rate of recurrence of those behaviors.

An extensional account of behavior, such as that produced by behavior analysis or, as some behaviorists prefer, *behaviorology*, stands in contrast to a *psychological explanation* which posits some form or other of internal representation in order to account for behavior. These ascribed representations, which may take the form of propositional attitudes or perceptual awareness (Bermúdez 2003), are wholly absent from the philosophy of psychology we know as radical behaviorism (Skinner 1974; see also Staddon 2014).

The structure of the extensionally conceived model is such that consumer behavior is portrayed as the outcome of functional relationships between a consumer situation and a response, where the consumer situation is the intersection of a *consumer behavior setting* and a *learning history* of reinforcement and punishment by utilitarian and informational consequences. Consumer behavior setting scope, insofar as it contains the consequences of behavior that have formed the individual's learning history can thus be said to be the "cause" of consumer behavior, in the sense that the behavior is a function of the stimuli that compose consumer behavior setting scope. The consumer situation is thus understood in the extensional model solely in terms of the scope of the consumer behavior setting.

At this theoretical level, both a consumer behavior setting of given scope and the consumer situation simply set the occasion for three types of behavioral consequence: utilitarian reinforcement which consists in the functional outcomes of behavior, informational reinforcement, which stems from the symbolic outcomes, principally performance feedback, and aversive/punishing consequences, the utilitarian and informational costs of purchase and consumption. The components of the model are operationally defined, specified in terms of the functional relationships that stem from their observable impacts upon behavior.

The rationale for building a model of consumer behavior in these terms derives not from the conventional wisdom of hypothetico-deductive scientific methodology but from the need to examine whether a theory of choice can avoid the intentional language of beliefs and desires, that is, statements that do not permit the substitutability of coextensives. The key motivation for this is the finding that both cognitive and behaviorist accounts of consumer choice are equally supported by the empirical evidence on attitudinal—behavioral correspondence (Foxall 1997c, 2005). To favor the former at the cost of the latter suggests the somewhat rigid adherence of an applied field to the prevailing paradigm of the disciplines from which it derives, in this case cognitive psychology. It may also represent an intellectually closed perspective which cannot conceive of explanation in terms not belonging to its chosen framework of conceptualization and analysis. As we have seen, the central fact in the delineation of radical behaviorism is its conceptual avoidance of propositional content. This eschewal of the intentional stance sets it apart not only from cognitivism but from other neo-behaviorisms. Indeed, the defining characteristic of radical behaviorism is not that it avoids mediating processes per se but that it sets out to account for behavior without recourse to propositional attitudes. Based rather on the contextual stance, it provides definitions of contingency-shaped, rule-governed, verbal and private behaviors which are nonintentional. For reasons of disinterested curiosity, therefore, as well as the more pragmatic search for a general explanation of choice, a research program based on the development and evaluation of an extensional model of consumer choice becomes inevitable. This is what the extensional construal of the BPM attempts.

So what have we committed ourselves to in constructing an extensional model of consumer choice? The radical behaviorist explanation that the BPM research program has sought to evaluate is wholly different from an intentional explanation. Indeed, the defining characteristic of radical behaviorism is the dedication of scientific endeavor to the production of a wholly extensional account of behavior. Beginning with radical behaviorism is essential because it is the only means by which we can ascertain how far its linguistic mode will take us in explaining behavior and, therefore, at what point, for what purposes, and in what manner the use of intentional language will be enjoined upon us to complete the task. That is why radical behaviorism is central to the initial stage of the research program described in this book. First, it consists of the identification of the environmental stimuli that control behavior; when these have been identified and described (in nonintentional terms), the behavior has been explained. Second, it resolutely adheres to a form of explanation that strenuously avoids intentional terms such as "believes" and "desires"—it is extensional. The essence of radical behaviorism is the avoidance of intentionality in its scientific discourse (Foxall 2004).

Extensional explanation is the demonstration that a behavior (the dependent variable) is functionally related to particular aspects of the environment and/or neurophysiology (the independent variables). We may refer to these as behavioral explanations and neurophysiological explanations, respectively. This can be achieved most satisfactorily via an experimental analysis since this increases the chances of intersubjective agreement on whether the rules of behavioral syntax have been met. It can also, however, be met where this is appropriate by inferential statistics such as regression analysis. It is least of all possible in the case of behavioral *interpretation* which requires rigorous rules of correspondence to be established. In the case of consumer behavior, and insofar as it falls within the purview of behavioral rather than neurophysiological relationships, an extensional explanation consists in the construction of a consumer situation (defined as the intersection of the consumer's learning history and the stimulus conditions of the social and physical setting in which he or she is located) with the objective of predicting his or her consumption choices. The important matters are, first, that the scientific community can agree verbally that the functional relationship in question has been demonstrated empirically and, second, that they understand consensually the position of this demonstration hierarchy of explanation—interpretation just outlined.

Behavioral Syntax

Behavioral or extensional syntax is a means of encapsulating the basic explanatory system of science in terms of causation. It includes, therefore, the language of explanation adopted by sciences based on the physical, design, and contextual stances (Dennett 1978, 1987; Foxall 1999b). In the case of behavioral science, based on the contextual stance, *behavioral syntax* requires that we identify the three paradigmatic elements S^D, R, and $S^{r/a}$ and the relationships among them such that the rate of R increases when it has been previously followed by S^r, and decreases when it has been previously followed by S^a. In the first case R is said to be reinforced by S^r; in the second, that it has been punished by receipt of an S^a. If these operations have been carried out in the presence of S^D, then in the first instance, R may be enacted in its continued presence even if S^r is not forthcoming; and, in the second, R may be suppressed in the presence of S^D even though S^a no longer ensues. The syntax for attributing operant conditioning may be summarized as the three-term contingency.

The three-term contingency is, however, a syntax for the *interpretation* of results. To say that it is also the syntax involved in designing experiments and formulating hypotheses would render its use circular when it came to post-investigation appraisal of empirical findings. There are no a priori stimuli and responses out there in the world or even in the experimental space: there are only events, some of which reliably precede others such that prediction becomes feasible. But the designation of preceding events as stimuli and those that follow as responses is a theoretical act, an act of interpretation that attempts to make the subject matter intelligible and to suggest the shape of further investigations. The pre-experimental syntax requires the sort of formulation suggested by Dickinson (1980; see also Dickinson 1997) in which E1 is the preceding event after which another event, E2, may or may not occur. The easiest way to use such relationships to study behavior is to present the organism with either an E1 → E2 or E1 → no E2 association and look for behavioral change that indicates that learning has taken place. To jump to the conclusion that "the organism has learned something about the relationship" would entail theorization of a quite different kind from that I am drawing attention to here. If E2 reliably occurs following the presentation of E1, but fails to occur when E1 is absent, we may designate E1 the cause and E2 its effect. To interpret the findings of experiments based on this logic in terms of discriminative stimuli, responses, and reinforcing or punishing stimuli requires multiple findings showing how the rate at which a E2 follows E1 is carefully monitored, the effect of the absence of E1 on the occurrence of E2, and the influence of additional events. E1 may for instance be an event present when E2 was consistently followed by a further event, E3. At the same time we may notice that E2 is performed more frequently when E3 is made subsequently available. We may now argue that E3 is a "reinforcer" in that it "strengthens" E2, and we may observe that even when E3 is not always forthcoming after E2, E2 is now performed more frequently in the presence of E1.[1]

The experimental results showing all these observed relationships among E1, E2, and E3 form a sort of *text*, expressed in the data language of our budding science. To describe E1 as a discriminative stimulus, E2 as a response, and E3 as a reinforcer is to interpret the text, and to understand that this three-term description can be generalized to other situations on the basis of the relationships we infer among the observed events, is a further act of interpreting the text. It is a theoretical procedure, and "discriminative stimulus," "reinforcer," and "response" are theoretical terms, even though they are still defined in the extensional terms suggested by Smith (1994). If we notice that several typographically distinct responses (E2s) are followed by the same E3, we might say that these responses form a single "operant class." This too is a highly theoretical act. Even though we are defining learning in the simple observation-level terms of "an increase in the rate at which a response is emitted," we are making theoretical assumptions about the similarities between the E2s and their relationships with E3. We have moved away from the data language in which our original text was couched and are speaking now in terms of reinforcement, operant classification, and stimulus control. These terms are theoretical, even though they do not entail intentionality. Drawing the conclusion that the "organism has learned something" would be theorization that did involve intentional reasoning, but that is not the sort of theorizing being spoken of here. The reinforcement of one event by another, the inclusion in a single class of events that have similar ramifications, and the transfer of controlling function from one event to another are all inferences rather than straightforward influences. These processes all are described by using language that goes beyond the data language, and the language in which they are described is a language of theory (Zuriff 1985).

---

[1] Something like this sequence of reasoning can be inferred from Skinner's early experimental work and his generalizations therefrom: see Skinner 1931, 1935a, b, 1937, 1938. The development of such a theory is slow and continual: it was not until 1953 that Skinner finally unraveled *negative reinforcement* from *punishment*, for instance: see Skinner (1953a, b).

A similar progression is apparent in the delineation of respondent and operant behaviors, the first *elicited* by a preceding response, the second *emitted*, perhaps spontaneously, by the organism. Neither of the definitional descriptions of these terms is couched in the language of data or observation; they are inferences cast in theoretical terms, which have the effect of determining an ontology of explanation as well as a methodology for experimental research. The idea of a learning history similarly is an inference. A learning history can be mapped out in purely observational terms as a record of an organism's observed responses and their consequences as they occur in experimental situations; this is simply a log of E2s and E3s, perhaps elaborated by the inclusion of E1s, expressed in the language of data. If it is used only to predict and possibly control further behavior of that organism, then this enterprise remains one based on the extensional language of empirical science. However, learning histories are often employed by radical behaviorists as the causal and explanatory element in their science in ways that go beyond simple observation: for example, when the behavior of other organisms is explained in terms of a learning history that is not empirically available or when complex human choice (e.g., of consumers in supermarkets or other large stores) is interpreted as the result of learning histories that can never be observed or reconstructed.

The resultant methodology can, therefore, be depicted as, first, designing experiments or other means of exploring putative functional relationships among events, using the appropriate data language of events; second, describing the experimental results, again in the data language of Es, to compile a *text*; and, third, interpreting the text in the course of intersubjective appraisal to decide how far it supports the syntax of the three-term contingency or any other theoretical system. Insisting that experiments be designed and that, where appropriate, hypotheses be formulated in term of events, while seeking the interpretation of the text resulting from the compilation of data in the theory-laden terminology of the three-term contingency, reduces the likelihood of circular reasoning which would occur if the three-term contingency were also employed in the formulation of hypotheses.

In the closed setting of the operant experiment, it is comparatively easy to adhere to the syntax of behavioral exploration and explanation outlined above. Most of the consumer choice with which we are concerned, however, occurs in the very open settings of the real-world market place. There are, moreover, considerations that apply to the operant model of consumer choice that do not arise in most operant experiments: human economic behavior is shaped and maintained by informational as well as utilitarian reinforcers, for example, requiring that the consequences of behavior be contemplated as a *field* composed of interactive sources of benefit. The antecedent stimuli that set the occasion for consumer behavior also constitute a *field* of discriminative stimuli and motivating operations that interact with one another and with the consumer's learning history to determine the probability of particular behaviors being enacted. The *stimulus fields* represented by the pattern of reinforcement and the consumer situation render explanation and interpretation far more complex than is the experimental case where a closely defined response can be shown with a high degree of reliability to be a function of antecedent and consequential stimuli each of which can be individuated.

Even the field experiments that have been employed in applied behavior analysis and organizational behavior management contexts permit a high degree of conformity in their respective investigations to the stipulations of the three-term contingency. The behavior analysis of consumer choice raises other issues however, which do not normally arise in these contexts. One is the diversity of each consumer's learning history, a variable or set of variables not entirely empirically available and which in any case renders the individual behavior patterns of single consumers somewhat idiosyncratic in terms of testing either psychological and economic theories of decision making or even consonance with the three-term contingency. No one consumer's learning history is going to be typical. This makes the use of aggregated data inevitable and, here, we have shown that careful delineation of the terms of the BPM can lead to results that are generally in line with operant and microeconomic theories, while identifying anomalies that arise from the particularities of human consumer behavior in general and specific culturally defined instances of it. Some of this work has been experimental, some field-experimental, which has allowed the establishment of functional ("causal") relationships between the explanatory variables of the BPM and patterns of the consumer choices of individuals and small groups. Much of the work has involved the regression-based analysis of aggregate consumer behavior which again has tested functional relationships, though they are probably best described as "quasi-causal" in this case. And some of the work has been interpretive. The important matter is that intersubjective agreement is available on the meaning of the results in each case.

The Bounds of Behaviorism

Extensional explanation, then, requires the establishment by one means or another of a *pattern* of operant behavior for which we can establish selection by consequences through identifying the antecedent stimuli that compose the consumer situation and the pursuant stimuli that compose the pattern of reinforcement and punishment. The word "pattern" indicates molar behavior: sequences of responding that can be reliably related to sequences of reinforcement. This requires that the observed behavior conform to the syntax of behavioral explanation just outlined. By "imperatives of intentionality" I mean the circumstances that arise in the extensional explanation of behavior in which the elements of the behavioral syntax cannot be identified empirically and an intentional explanation becomes necessary; these circumstances, by revealing the bounds of behaviorism, make an intentional account imperative. They do not mean that an extensional account has to be abandoned in its entirety; indeed, as the preceding survey of empirical evidence for the BPM showed, the extensional analysis of consumer choice has proved very useful in demonstrating precisely what it is that consumers maximize and how their behavior, understood in terms of the behavioral perspective, adheres to the requirements of microeconomics as well as operant theory. The explanation of behavior in purely extensional terms (i.e., in language which avoids intentionality, displaying referential transparency via the substitutability of coextensive terms) is invaluable for the prediction and control of certain behaviors whose stimulus environments are observable and manipulable.

But this is not always the case. Intentional language is required to account for human behavior for three reasons (Foxall 2004). These three imperatives of intentionality derive from the inadequacies of extensional language to sustain a comprehensive analysis of behavior. First, extensional language is insufficient to account for the continuity of behavior when controlling stimuli cannot be ascertained; second, it is equally unable to deal with the personal level of explanation, that of the whole person rather than its components; nor yet is it able to delimit interpretations of behavior by demarcating the behavioral consequences of which behavior can be said to be a function (Foxall 2004).

Behavioral Continuity and Discontinuity

Why Continuity Matters The plausibility of an extensional radical behaviorist interpretation depends vitally upon its capacity to account for the continuity of behavior. Why should behavior that has been followed by a particular reinforcing stimulus in the presence of a setting stimulus be re-enacted when a similar setting is encountered? Why should a rule that describes certain physical or social contingencies be followed at some future date when those contingencies are encountered? Why can I tell you now what I ate for lunch yesterday? The whole explanatory significance of learning history is concerned with the continuity of behavior between settings and this implies some change in the organism, some means of recording the experience of previous behavior in such a way that it will be available next time similar settings are encountered. There is no other way in which the individual can recognize the potential offered by the current behavior setting in terms of the reinforcement and punishment signaled by the discriminative stimuli that compose it.

The radical behaviorist account of behavioral continuity requires that a common stimulus or some component thereof is present on each occasion that a response is emitted. The stimulus must be either a learned discriminative stimulus and/or a reinforcer. The difficulty with this is that it is not always possible to detect each element of the three-term contingency when behavior is learned or performed. The tendency is, then, to suppose that something occurs within the individual, presumably at a physiological level, that will one day be identified as sufficient to account for the continuity of behavior. But the problem is less one of ontology than of methodology, of the theoretical imperatives involved in explaining the continuity of behavior and therefore the language employed to account for it.

The Continuity of Consumer Situations Although an extensional account facilitates prediction and control by reference to the stimuli that determine the rate of recurrence of behavior, it cannot explain the *continuity of behavior over settings and situations*. As the consumer moves from setting to setting, he or she may be faced with stimuli that differ from those previously encountered; yet they act in a manner consistent with the behaviors displayed in those rather different settings. In contrast, there are other occasions when the pattern of behavior displayed by the consumer in familiar settings deviates markedly from what might be expected, as for example, when a lazy glutton starts to eat less fattening foods and to take up exercise. What accounts for such deviations from patterns of behavior that have hitherto remained constant over time? It is beyond the capacity of a purely extensional model to explain the continuity of behavior across settings or the discontinuity of behavior that occurs when the consumer switches to a new pattern of choice that has not previously been reinforced. The recurrence of the same or similar stimuli in a succession of settings is not generally sufficient for such explanation: only in the most closed experimental setting could it be taken as such. In complex situations of purchase and consumption, it is usually impossible to isolate the stimuli that are responsible for consumer responses with the precision available in the laboratory and without interpretation based on the ascription of intentionality. Moreover, most stimuli differ somewhat from setting to setting. Physiological changes resulting from behaving once in one setting cannot be shown to explain the continuity of behavior even across settings that exhibit stimulus similarities let alone among divergent stimulus contexts. Rules cannot account for behavioral continuity or pattern shifts unless some mechanism of perception, encoding, and interpreting can be identified. (Rules, particularly augmentals, may be motivating operations in an extensional account, but while they may predict or control behavior they cannot *explain* behavioral continuity or deviations from established behavior patterns.) Only by employing intentional language can we provide an explanatory account.

Foxall (2007b) presented the argument for incorporating intentionality into theories of choice on the grounds that an extensional theory could not of itself account for the continuity/discontinuity of behavior (see also Foxall 2004, 2007c, 2008b). Some examples may make this argument more concrete. First, take a person whom we have observed drink alcohol heavily on a daily basis but who, we note, now drinks only on Friday evenings and confines himself to two drinks. As Rachlin (1995) says, we might explain this behavior by saying that the individual concerned has "decided" on this change. The use of intentional language appears inevitable if we are to account for this behavioral discontinuity. At the time when the behavior changed there was no pattern of molar behavior to explain the new pattern of choice. Only the language of decision making suffices to account for the change, and, since it is intentional language, its user is employing intentional explanation. Second, consider a heavy user of the four brands, A, B, C, and D, that comprise this individual's consideration set for a particular consumer nondurable, who now includes a new brand, E, in their repertoire. As is the case for many consumers in affluent societies, we cannot assume anything about the individual's learning history except that they are a heavy user of the product category. It seems impossible to account for their inclusion of the new brand without referring to the individual's beliefs and desires. Finally, let us consider the case of a participant in an operant experiment who maintains their behavior pattern even though the contingencies governing reinforcement of that behavior have changed. Again, there is little we can say about the individual's learning history. It seems reasonable to assume some control of their overt behavior by their private verbal behavior especially since we have no evidence of prior control of overt behavior via instructions. It does not seem that behavior such as this can be explained other than by ascribing certain beliefs and desires to the experimental participant.

These examples of behavioral continuity/discontinuity define a continuum of behavioral change which relates the sequence of observed behavior to changes in the attendant sequence of reinforcement. The behavior of the heavy user of alcohol which reflects some early signs of addiction (such as bingeing followed by remorse which is not sufficient to allay further bouts of heavy drinking) but whose behavior changes to a more restrained pattern of moderated drinking cannot be explained in terms of the contingencies alone. The initial phase leads to aversive consequences which do not reduce the level of alcohol consumption; the subsequent behavior pattern is adopted before the novel consequences of restrained consumption have had time to exert an effect on choice. The abrupt change in the first molar pattern of behavior can be explained only in terms of the individual having made a decision to try a different style of behavior. Such change is described as *major* or *discontinuous*.

The consumer who adopts a new brand also exhibits a change in their sequence of behavior, not by abandoning the existing pattern of choice but by supplementing and extending it. There is a change in behavior but it amounts to no more than trying a new brand in a product category of which the consumer has much experience, that is, a novel version of a familiar pattern of reinforcement. Most consumers of a product category purchase within a small consideration set of tried and tested brands; many, especially the heavier users of the product, try new brands that appear to contain the characteristics of the product class; some of those who try it incorporate the new brand into their future consideration set (Ehrenberg 1988). Most consumers who select a new brand in this way or change to another in their existing consideration set choose one that contains a similar combination of functional and symbolic benefits (the pattern of reinforcement) as existing members of the set (Foxall et al. 2004). The prediction of such behavior follows easily enough from consideration of the contingencies alone (at least for aggregates, not necessarily for individuals) but an explanation of the change itself requires consideration of the processes of comparison and recognition that must precede the change. How are the verbal stimuli (e.g., advertisements) translated into the new pattern of consumer behavior via comparison with the characteristics of the brands already in the consumer's repertoire? Selective perception, beliefs, and desires must be used as part of the explanation of such behavior. It is not sufficient, therefore, to say that more continuous change of this sort, even though it may be readily related to the contingencies, is "explained" by its embodiment of stimulus or reinforcer discrimination and generalization. Use of such terminology merely redescribes the observed choices.

Another example is provided by the behavior of the experimental participant who exhibits rigidity in the face of changing contingencies: the schedule insensitivity that was discussed in Chapter 2. This is an example of behavioral continuity that cannot be explained in terms of the contingencies themselves (Lowe 1983). The situation is exemplified by the consumer who continues to purchase and use a particular brand of razor blades even though the quality of the shave obtained from them has markedly diminished. Why is human behavior so insensitive to changes in contingencies when this is not true of nonhumans? The person presumably has not perceived the change in contingencies and is operating according to a self-generated rule reached in decision making prior to the contingency change. The behavior of persons in this situation often comes to conform to the contingencies after a time. How does this change in perception occur? Is there further decision making?

Another example of the inability to account for the continuity or discontinuity of behavior without recourse to cognitive variables is the self-management which Skinner and other behavior analysts advocate frequently. In self-management, the individual arranges the contingencies of reinforcement in such a way as to change his or her own subsequent behavior. A consumer who overeats, for instance, might take a different route home from work in order to avoid confectionary stores. A student might set the alarm clock in order to rise an hour earlier in order to study. How is self-management possible without a construal of the future consequences of behaviors that have not previously been performed and that are not, therefore, within the current repertoire of the individual? The self-manager has to envision new behaviors and their consequences as mental objects and to weigh the consequences with those of continuing to behave as in the past. Where does this representational activity take place? More importantly, how can the procedures be described other than in intentional language?

Finally, the phenomenon of stimulus equivalence (Sidman 1994) suggests the necessity of turning to cognitive explanation in order to account for the transfer of function when an untrained relationship among stimuli is selected. If an individual is trained to identify stimulus B when presented with stimulus A, and then to identify C when A is presented, a new relationship emerges that has been untrained. Presented with stimulus B, the individual identifies C, even though producing C in the presence of B has never been reinforced. Simply to designate the whole relational frame that links the stimuli in question and the behavioral responses observed as a composite operant (Hayes et al. 2001) seems more like an attempt to save the operant theory than to work out what is actually happening.

The Personal Level of Exposition

Why the Personal Level Matters The personal level of exposition is that of "people and their sensations and activities" rather than that of "brains and events in the nervous system" (Dennett 1969, p. 93). The latter belong to the sub-personal level, that at which an extensional science such as physiology (neuroscience) operates, its mechanistic explanations inappropriate to the explanation of so-called mental entities such as pain and can be understood only at the personal level. The personal level is that at which the organism as a whole can be said to act. And as Dennett notes, both Ryle (1949) and Wittgenstein (1953) point out that it is a stage of explanation that is quickly exhausted because so little can be said at this level. Of his pain, the bearer can say little more than that it hurts, for instance. In Dennett's system, as we shall see, it is the level at which beliefs, desires, and other intentional idioms are ascribed, but for now we are concerned only with the personal level as an analytical tool in extensional behavioral science and its implications for the explanation of behavior.

The personal level has two aspects, a first-personal perspective (that from which one actually feels pain as an inner-body experience) and a third-personal viewpoint (that in which pain is attributed to another person who is sobbing and holding her head as well as referring to "my migraine"). The acceptance of these "subjective" and "objective" understandings of the personal level does not divide cleanly along behaviorist/nonbehaviorist lines. Skinner's analysis of private events can be read as embracing both at one time or another. Dennett's cognitive approach concentrates on the objective, third-personal level which he associates unremittingly with a scientific standpoint, while Schnaitter's (1999) behaviorist view seems ready to endorse the first-personal. Others, such as Searle, fully accept the necessity of speaking in terms of both the first- and the third-personal, and that is the approach taken here.

Whether one assumes that learning takes place as a result of initial exposure to a reinforcing stimulus and that behavioral control is transferred contingently to a paired setting stimulus that acquires discriminatory significance—the standard radical behaviorism view—or that learning usually occurs as a result of observing a conspecific's behavior and its consequences, the only way in which such learning can be described requires the use of intentional idioms. A purely descriptive account can, where this is possible, relate responses to the stimuli with which they correlate, and by which they are therefore predictable and open to influence. This is the essential program of an extensional behavioral science and it is important to the pursuit of Intentional Behaviorism. However, it is not always feasible to make the required connections between environment and behavior, and that this acts as a stimulus to the discovery of an explanation rather than a mere description of behavior and its contextual determinants. The quest for explanation will always be there, should behaviorists choose to adopt it, but the failure of the extensional approach is a catalyst to its implementation. The behaviorist account is both incomplete (Foxall 2004) and fails to come to terms with what is learned in the process of learning. Moreover, as the following section reveals, the attempt by radical behaviorists to formulate a personal level of exposition represents the *reductio ad absurdum* of their mode of explanation.

Radical Behaviorism of the Personal Level of Exposition The difficulty for radical—or any other brand of extensional—behaviorism is that it deals inadequately with neither aspect of the personal level, largely because it confuses them. First note that in the case of the first-personal or subjective level of personhood, radical behaviorism simply has no means of accounting for some behaviors without resorting to intentional language. This stems from the irreducibility of intentional language to extensional and is illustrated by the following examples of people acting contrary to their desires, beliefs, and expectations in ways that cannot be entirely captured in a purely extensional description. Take, for instance, the couple who found themselves married because they went through the motions of a Jewish wedding ceremony, they with all the other participants thinking that they were engaged in an elaborate joke, only to discover that they were in fact married. No-one intended this outcome; one member of the couple fully intended to marry someone else. Another example concerns the Muslim acting with his real-life wife in a television production who, having followed the script to the letter, found himself divorced from both his screen wife and his actual spouse, unable to live with her on pain of being found guilty of adultery. This, again, was contrary to the expectations the entire cast and production team held about the situation. (Both examples are taken from Juarrero 2002.) The point is not that a radical behaviorist interpretation of these behaviors is impossible, or even whether they are actual or anecdotal, but that it can never capture the entire behavior in question without resorting to intentional idioms, that is, without deviating from its commitment to extensional behavioral science.

But the clincher comes from Skinner's statement that a man who is looking intently at his desk, moving papers to look underneath them, knows that he is "looking for his glasses" only because the last time he behaved in this way he came across them. *His* knowledge of what he is doing is gained from the same source as *our* knowledge of what he is doing as we watch him:

> When we see a man moving about in a room opening drawers, looking under magazines, and so on, we may describe his behavior in fully objective terms: "Now he is in a certain part of the room; he has grasped a book between the thumb and forefinger of his right hand; he is lifting the book and bending his head so that any object under the book can be seen." We may "interpret" his behavior or "read a meaning into it" by saying that "he is looking for something," or, more specifically, that "he is looking for his glasses." What we have added is not a further description of his behavior but an inference about some of the variables responsible for it. There is no *current* goal, incentive, purpose or meaning to be taken into account. This is so even if we ask him what he is doing and he says, "I am looking for my glasses." This is not a further description of his behavior but of the variables of which his behavior is a function; it is equivalent to "I have lost my glasses," "I shall stop what I am doing when I find my glasses," or "When I have done this in the past, I have found my glasses." These translations may

seem unnecessarily roundabout, but only because expressions involving goals and purposes are abbreviations. (Skinner 1953a, pp. 89–90)

But, in everyday life, it is only very rarely that we base our statements about our feelings or behaviors on self-observation.[2] A person does not come to understand that he is nervous because he sees his hands shaking and hears his voice quavering. He does not come to *conclude* that he is nervous on the basis of evidence of this kind any more than his saying he has a headache depends on his prior observation of his flushed features, his holding his temples, and his having taken aspirin. As Malcolm (1977) says, "If someone were to say, *on that basis,* that he has a headache, either he would be joking or else he would not understand how the words are used." He argues further that behaviorists have erred by assuming that a psychological sentence expressed in first-personal terms is identical in content and method of verification to the corresponding third-personal sentence. "We verify that another person is angry by the way the veins stand out on his neck, by the redness of his face, and by his shouting. But we do not verify our own anger in this way."

In fact, we rarely attempt to verify it at all. Verification is simply not a concept or operation that applies to many first-person psychological reports, those which are not founded on observation. An individual's statement of purpose or intention belongs to a different class from one made by someone else on the basis of observing that individual. If we see someone turning out his pockets and recall that on previous occasions he has done this before producing his car keys from one of them we can reasonably conclude that he is looking for his car keys this time too. But it would be odd indeed if he himself were to work out what he was doing

---

[2] Daryl Bem, who describes himself as an "unreconstructed radical behaviorist," argues that internal stimuli seldom control a person's behavior. Therefore, "to the extent that internal stimuli are not controlling, an individual's attitude statements may be viewed as inferences from observations of his own overt behavior and its accompanying stimulus variables" (Bem 1967, p. 200). Asked whether he likes brown bread, an individual has access only to the information his wife draws upon to answer the question whether he likes brown bread. He says, "I guess I do, I'm always eating it"; she says, "I guess he does, he's always eating it." He has no privileged source of information that is not available to his wife. "Only to the extent that 'brown bread' elicits strongly conditioned internal responses might he have additional evidence, not currently available to his wife, on which to base his self-descriptive attitude statement" (ibid.). The strongly conditioned internal responses to which Bem resorts are of course intentional representations.

by observing that he was emptying his pockets as he had done in the past when looking for his car keys. If he announced that he must be looking for his car keys at present because he was doing what he had done in the past when finding them had eventuated, we should think him most odd, crazy, to be treated in future with circumspection. The avoidance of such convoluted locutions, which seem to fulfill no function other than to avoid the intentionality of "looking for," "knowing that," and "remembering" involves not only a different kind of verbal description but a different form of explanation.

What Is Learned? For the radical behaviorist, learning is simply a change in the rate of responding that can be traced to changes in the contingencies of reinforcement. Such change might be a switch to a different schedule of reinforcement or it could well be a qualitative change in the nature of reinforcement.

This focus on how the contingencies of reinforcement determine learning is useful in the prediction and possibly the control of behavior but it fails to address some intellectual questions about behavior and learning. It fails to clarify, for instance, *what* it is that is learned when one's behavior is reinforced. Dennett (1969, pp. 33–4) supplies the standard cognitivist answer: what an animal in an operant experiment

> learns, of course, is *where the food is*, but how is this to be characterized non-Intentionally? There is no room for "know" or "believe" or "hunt for" in the officially circumscribed language of behaviorism; so the behaviorist cannot say that the rat knows or believes that the food is at x, or that the rat is hunting for a route to x.

Considerations such as these led some behaviorists to theorize about the nature of learning. This process of coming to terms with intentionality has meant that even mediational theories like those of Hull (Amsel and Rashotte 1984) and Tolman (1932) have given way to an explicit use of intentionality to explain behavior: not on the basis of positing intervening variables but as an inevitable linguistic turn (Foxall 2004). Berridge (2000) makes the progression from mediationism to intentionalism clear in his description of the history of behavioral psychology in the work of

Bolles, Bindra, and Toates. Bolles's (1972) account of behavior in terms of the expectation of utilitarian consequences follows the S–S theory of Tolman rather than the S–R theory of Hull but suggests that what is learned are S–S associations of a particular kind and function: an association is leaned between a conditioned stimulus (CS) and a subsequent utilitarian stimulus (S*) that elicits pleasure. The first S does not elicit a response but an expectation of the second S (S*). Bolles (1972) developed a "psychological syllogism" in which, as Dickinson (1997, p. 346) puts it, "Exposure to stimulus–outcome (S–S*) and response–outcome (R–S*) contingencies leads to the acquisition of S–S* and R–S* expectancies, respectively, that represent these relations. The two expectancies are 'synthesized' or combined in a 'psychological syllogism' so that in the presence of the cue, S, the animal is likely to perform response R." The response becomes more probable as the strengths of the expectancies increase and as the value of S*, which is influenced by the animal's motivational state, increases. Bolles employs this theory to explain why animals sometimes act as though they have received a reward when they have not: for example, the raccoon that washes a coin as though it were food, "misbehavior," or autoshaping, or schedule-induced polydipsia, all empirical instances that research in the 1960s had shown to be contra-indicative of the reinforcement model.

Berridge (2000) argues that, useful as this is, it fails to explain why the animal still approaches the reinforcer (say food) rather than waiting for it to appear and enjoying the S* in the interim. He discusses the approach of Bindra (1978) who proposes the utilitarian transfer of incentive properties to the CS. Bindra accepts the S–S* theory but argues that the S does not simply cause the animal to expect the S*: it also elicits a central motivational state that causes the animal to perceive the S as an S*. The S assumes the motivational properties that normally belong to the S*. These motivational properties are incentive properties which attract the animal and elicit goal-directed behavior and possibly consumption. Through association with the S*, the S acquires the same functions as the S*. An animal approaches the CS for a reward, finds the signal (S) attractive; if the CS is food, the animal wants to eat it. If it is an S for a tasty food S*, the animal may take pleasure in its attempt to eat the CS (Berridge 2000, p. 236; see also Bouton and Franselow 1997). But if

CSs were incentives one would always respond to them whether or not one were hungry. The question is to explain how CSs interact with drive states. Toates (1986), therefore, builds on the Bolles-Bindra theory by positing that both cognitive expectancy and more basic reward processes might occur simultaneously in the individual. All of these theories are necessarily intentionalistic since they deal in expectancies.

Delimitation of Behavioral Interpretation

Why Delimitation of Interpretation Matters The ubiquity of apparent three-term contingencies as we survey life beyond the lab raises difficulties for an interpretative account which is meant to be more than "plausible." As radical behaviorism stands, its program of interpretative research based solely on the criterion of plausibility, there is no way of successfully delimiting the scope of its interpretations so that they meet the standards of validity and reliability that are decisive in qualitative as well as quantitative research.

Rachlin's (1994, 1999) formulation of teleological behaviorism is an ingenious attempt to enhance behaviorist explanation. Its discussion in the present context is not intended to undermine this evaluation but to illustrate the difficulties that radical behaviorism encounters in its interpretations of behavior that is beyond the scope of an experimental analysis.

Teleological behaviorism follows Aristotle in distinguishing efficient from final causes. Efficient causes precede their effects and consist in the set of internal nervous discharges giving rise to particular movements; they would include internal physiological and cognitive precedents of activity. The analysis of efficient causes yields a mechanism that answers the question "*How* does this or that movement occur?" Final causes are consequences of behavior. Moreover, they may fit into one another as the causal web extends outward from the individual who behaves: "eating an appetizer fits into eating a meal, which fits into a good diet, which fits into a healthy life, which in turn fits into a generally good life. The wider the category, the more embracing, the 'more final' the cause" (Rachlin 1994, p. 21). The analysis of final causes is an attempt to answer the question "*Why* does this or that movement occur – for what reason?" (p. 22). The process of finding the causes of behavior is one of fitting the behavior into an ever-increasing molar pattern of response and consequences. The dependent variable in this scheme is not a single response, however, but a temporally extended pattern of behavior. Similarly, the causes of behavior are extended, a series of consequences each nested within others from the closest to the most remote. From these extended patterns of behavior and consequence can be discerned emotional and cognitive behaviors: indeed, the emotion or thinking or believing or knowing *is* the pattern of extended behavior. Rachlin's work in behavioral economics is highly relevant here because an important cause of behavior is the utility function that describes the entire sequence of extended behavior of the individual (e.g., Rachlin 1989).

The causes of behavior are, therefore, to be found in the network of contingencies that control the pattern of behavior of which an observed response (say, drinking or abstaining from alcohol) is but a part. Taking a molar view of environment–behavior relationships (Baum 1973, 2002, 2004), such patterns, rather than single responses, become the unit of analysis. These patterns over time are what give rise to the ascription of mental language to behavior. On this view, patterning is the key to both understanding and modifying behavior. The capacity to embed a desired behavior in a pattern of ongoing behavior is the key to its success. The more long-term a pattern of behavior is, the more costly it is to the individual to interrupt it. The problem presented by the shorter-term (molecular) option's providing greater immediate reward is, he claims, capable of being overcome or ameliorated by embedding that response in a pattern of responses that are extended through time.

A mental event cannot be identified with a single act: it is a pattern of behavior. It is that very pattern of behavior that constitutes the mental event. Moreover, the pattern must be publicly available before it denotes mentality. If nobody sees you holding your head, grimacing, nobody hears you say such things as "Oh, the pain!" then the teleological behaviorist view is that you do not have a headache. If there is no public evidence, then there is no emotion, no mentation. The mental event, the pain in this case, is the very pattern of sustained pain-related behaviors.

But, teleological behaviorism, albeit one of the most meticulous approaches to behaviorist interpretation, still raises the problem of delimiting the range of consequences that can be held to be causes of behavior. What should be included in the utility function of the person whose behavior is being behaviorally interpreted given that numerous consequences can be observed to follow from any behavior that is observed outside the laboratory? This problem is that of equifinality which Lee (1988) identified as an inescapable component of radical behaviorist interpretation.

Decisions, Decisions! Teleological behaviorism is not of itself an extensional behavioral science since it incorporates intentionality in three ways: to designate patterns of behavior, in its exposition of its characteristic mode of explanation, and to account for changes in the pattern of behavior.[3]

Emotionality and cognition consist according to teleological behaviorism in patterns of behavior that are observable by third parties. The emotion/cognition inheres in, is coterminous with the sequence of behavior. Teleological behaviorism provides a means of linking environment–behavior relationships that occur at the super-personal level of analysis, to the ascription of intentionality at the personal level. It thus has much in common with intentional behaviorism, though it does not treat intentionality either a-ontologically or causally.

---

[3] There remains the problem of how the personal level of exposition is to enter this analysis. It is essential in the interpretation of complex behavior to reconstruct at the third-personal level the personal level that the person had (e.g., via heterophenomenology: Dennett 1991a, b). The terms in which we do this rely ultimately on our first-personal knowledge of our intentionality (as I shall argue in Chapter 5, knowledge by acquaintance must precede knowledge by description). It could be argued that teleological behaviorism does not need this level of analysis: in constructing its interpretations, it would be sufficient to deduce the relevant desires, beliefs, emotions, and perceptions from the molar pattern of behavior of the individual. But in this case, why take the trouble of using intentional language at all? The first-personal level is essential to the interpretation of a person's behavior as reflecting his or her having a headache. Only because when I have done those things have I also felt a private sensation of pain in my head can I interpret your behavior as a headache rather than the pre-match ritual of a New Zealand rugby player or antisocial behavior that requires the intervention of trained professionals. Moreover, since I know that on occasion I have had the private sensation of head pain without doing any of those things.

The exposition of teleological behaviorism refers to information in the form of CSs and discriminative stimuli that signal respondent or operant contingencies (Rachlin 1994). Rachlin (1994, p. 33) notes that "Behavioral inferences and models are inferences and models about respondent and operant contingencies that may not be present at the moment but serve as the *context* for current actions." He clarifies this by speaking of the apparently generous behavior of a shopkeeper whose actions might be explicable not in terms of his generosity but by there being a sales promotion in force at the time of his act. The grocer's personal motives cannot be ascertained from his single act but only from the pattern of behavior into which it fits, its context. Surely, to make inferences and build models about behavior and its mental meanings, is to enter nonbehaviorist territory. It goes beyond redescribing behavior in mentalistic terms, for an inference or model involves something over and above the observation of behavior. Why is it necessary to infer the motive of the grocer at all, to even speak in terms of a motive, if this cannot be achieved without knowledge of his behavior which, after all, *is* the motive? Why use this mentalistic term at all?

Teleological behaviorism's accounting for behavioral change emerges from its treatment of the breaking of patterns in the process of self-control. Such an explanation of behavior cannot proceed without the ascription to the individual of intentionality or even cognitive processing. Hence, on the first occasion of one's ceasing the pattern of overeating—say, at one's next meal—there is, by definition, not yet a pattern of reduced or healthy or responsible eating. The initial lone act must be accompanied by the intentionally construed procedure of changing one's attitude or intention, or the attribution of cognitive processing with respect to one's future, novel behavior.

The point is put by Kane in his response to Rachlin's (1995) exposition of self-control. Kane (1995, pp. 131–2) argues that the word "pattern" is ambiguous, referring to either a customary form of behavior, or an internal plan or intention to act in a customary way; while Rachlin attempts to confine the discussion exclusively to the first sense (not an internal state but an overt sequence of acts), Kane believes any theory of self-control must incorporate both senses. A person who has habitually drunk six beers every night may, on sight of his midriff, determine to reduce this to two. After two he is tempted to a third but goes home instead. The drinker's exercise of self-control on the first day after the resolution must involve a pattern-as-internal-cognitive-plan for at that point there is no actual pattern-as-overt-behavior to sustain the exercise of self-control. The only overt pattern in force on that day-after-resolution is the six-beer-a-day pattern and it is this that must be interrupted by the exercise of self-control rather than persisted in. Kane's (1995, p. 113) view is that teleological behaviorism "must make a concession to cognitive theorists on this point or else find some behavioral substitutes for internal plans newly formed by resolutions or choices." Teleological behaviorism claims that choosing is a mental act that is coterminous with a pattern of overt behavior, but at this point the person has committed only one act, an act of thought, that cannot be called a pattern at all, still less a pattern of overt behavior.

The Import of Verbal Behavior

The analysis of verbal behavior is clearly an attempt to deal in extensional behaviorist terms with some of the phenomena that cognitive psychologists deal with in intentional terms. Before assuming that the problems identified as limitations of a behaviorist approach necessitate an intentional account, it is useful to consider whether these problems can be overcome by treating consumer behavior as rule-governed. However, the interpretation of behavior as verbal requires the invention of fictitious causes and, in any case, it entails the "aboutness" which is the defining characteristic of intentional explanation.

In the case of behavioral continuity, especially in the face of changing contingencies, the construction of rules that the individual might be following, even if it is based on their post-experimental verbal debriefing, cannot produce data that can enter into an experimental analysis to demonstrate that rules had been formulated by the participant and were being followed during the second stage of the original experiment (when the reinforcement schedule changed). The assertion that the individual was following certain rules is impossible to verify in the normal course of behavior analytic research and amounts to an explanatory fiction that has the function of saving the behaviorist theory. In any case, the rules would take the form of covert verbal behavior that would be *about* something other than themselves; hence, the explanation in these terms is an intentional one.

This conclusion is also apparent from any attempt to frame the inflexible behavior of the experimental participant in terms of private events, an individual's covert thoughts and feelings that belong to the personal level of exposition. Any attempt to argue that the individual engaged in problem-solving behavior, the conclusions of which persisted beyond the change in the contingencies of reinforcement cannot be other than an invention designed to support the theory when there is no evidence of the kind normally enjoined upon behavior analysts namely experimental (Skinner 1956). Private events are by their very nature both insusceptible to experiment and intentional: thoughts are always *about* something, that is, representational, and most feelings also fall into this category. To employ such constructions in the explanation of behavior is to employ intensional language and thus intentional explanation. The intellectually honest alternative is to acknowledge that no behaviorist (extensional) account that can be subjected to the usual canons of judgment entailed by experimental science is possible, to provide an account that is explicitly intentional, referring to this as an interpretation rather than an explanation.

This, the strategy of intentional behaviorism, is also a means of delimiting behavioral interpretations since, rather than allowing the investigator to multiply possible contingencies ad lib in order to account for observed behavior which is not amenable to an experimental analysis, the analysis of the behavior in terms of what the individual could be expected to desire and believe maintains the intellectual honesty of the enterprise. Naturally, the grounds for such expectations must be made explicit and must conform to a rationale that is constrained by the extensional analyses made available by neuroscience and behavioral science.

The principal reason why the analysis of verbal behavior, including rule-governed behavior, is unable to overcome the bounds of behaviorism is that rule-governed behavior is itself, by its very nature, intentional. Both rules and verbal behavior generally, and the private events which Skinner (1974) defines as thinking and feeling, are inescapably about something other than themselves. The only alternative would be to treat spoken or written verbal rules as extensional constructs, that is, as physical (auditory or visual) stimuli that can be included in the three-term contingency.

Such stimuli would be learned through pairing with other reinforcers but would not have any significance over and above their being material inputs to behavior. This understanding of verbal behavior suffices for the prediction and possibly the control of behavior which are the stated goals of radical behaviorism. Observation of the names of symphonies played at orchestral concerts would enable one to predict a concert goer's attendance, the duration of their wait in the line for tickets, and how much they might pay for them. It is even possible that an analysis of the physical notes comprising the performance would help one refine such predictions. But such understanding of the stimuli under whose control the concert goer's behavior has come to rest scarcely account, in other than the most perfunctory manner, for their attendance at expensive concerts. While this is the only way in which rule-governed behavior can be included in an extensional account of behavior, I shall argue that it is not necessarily the only way in which we can accommodate it.

Toward Psychological Explanation: Representation and Misrepresentation

The heart of radical behaviorism lies in its program of describing behavior in extensional language. And the fact is that the central explanatory device of radical behaviorism, comprising the learning history and the stimulus field required to account for the influence of the current consumer behavior setting, is indeed sometimes empirically unavailable. The use of this linguistic mode and the system of explanation that inheres within it is an essential component of a science of behavior (Foxall 2004). Radical behaviorists invite us simply to invent a learning history when it is not empirically available:

> When the history is unavailable, the behaviorist speculates in the light of what is already known, exactly as in other sciences... In the absence of information, one guesses at the appropriate history... The great advantage of speculating about history, in contrast to fictional present causes, is that it holds out the possibility of replacing guesswork with observation. (Baum and Heath 1992, p. 1316)

But to use extensional language when it is not justified by the interpretations to which experimental and other empirical findings lead cannot be part of this scientific enterprise.

In these circumstances, guesses expressed in extensional language as though they were explanatory can be downright misleading, bringing inquiry to a premature end, and they have no place in science. The use of intentional language is enjoined upon us at this stage, not only because it is the only alternative available once extensional language has been exhausted, but also because, when it is used in an appropriately disciplined manner, its emphasis on the interpretive nature of the account we are giving keeps us honest and spurs further investigation. This is the rationale of psychological explanation.

Psychological explanations are those which employ the idea of internal representations conceptualized as propositional attitudes or perceptual awareness (Bermúdez 2003; see also Foxall 2016a, especially pp. 104–7). Such language demarcates psychology from extensional behavioral science. Employing psychological explanation does not obviate the need for an extensional account. Extensional behavioral science remains an imperative first stage for the explanation of behavior and it is particularly useful insofar as it (i) extends understanding of specific facets of behavior and (ii) guides the timing and content of psychological explanation.

The teleological character of psychological explanations means that they comprehend behavior as goal-directed, something that is not the case for behavior that is mechanistically determined by environmental stimuli. These explanations proceed by the attribution of desires and beliefs on the assumption that the behavior in question is intended to satisfy or embody. Such behavior (that to which psychological explanations are addressed) cannot be accounted for as invariant responses to fixed stimuli (innate releasing mechanisms) which are "innate, unlearned, and involuntary, and that it will occur even when it serves no function" (Dretsky 1988, p. 4). We are referring here to unlearned behavior, derived in the course of the phylogenetic development of the organism, and its form remains largely if not entirely unaltered by the ontogenetic development of the organism.

In line with the principle of "explanatory minimalism" which underpins the initial stage of Intentional Behaviorism, psychological explanations are needed when stimuli of this kind cannot be detected.

Explanatory minimalism, however, is concerned also with more complex patterns of stimulation and behavior than innate releasing mechanisms embody. Behavior may be accounted for also by classical and operant conditioning which by no means entail invariant relationships between stimulus and response, as is evinced by the phenomena of stimulus and response generalization which involve the transfer of function from the stimulus or response contained in a conditioning procedure. Hence, the crux of what we mean by psychological explanation is its comprehension of a creature's behavior not in terms of the stimuli that impinge upon it but an understanding of how the creature must represent its environment (Bermúdez 2003). That such capacities are within the realm of evolutionary development is suggested by Shapiro (1999, p. 97):

> In essence, we should expect an organism to have evolved a psychological solution to some problem when the problem requires the organism to have more information about a feature of its environment than cues in its environment provide. When the information an organism can mindlessly detect falls short of the information the organism actually possesses, it is because psychological processes are present to span the gap.

As long as the operant paradigm is successful in the prediction and control of behavior, we may learn much about that behavior by viewing it as mechanistic. However, when an Intentional Interpretation is required to render some aspects of the behavior intelligible, our adoption of the intentional perspective makes possible a psychological explanation. It is of course impossible to ascertain the actual representations employed by a creature to guide its behavior: psychological explanation deals only in the representations that an investigator ascribes to the creature in the course of making its behavior intelligible.

The Imperatives of Intentionality

Each of the bounds (or limitations) of behaviorism we have identified has associated with it an imperative of intentionality which is necessary for the alternative explanation of behavior. Table 4.1 summarizes the

Table 4.1 *The bounds of behaviorism, the imperatives of intentionality.* The table relates each of the bounds of behaviorism to its corresponding imperative of intentionality

Bounds of behaviorism	Imperatives of intentionality
1. *Accounting for behavioral continuity and discontinuity.* The limitation of a behavioral analysis is established when the antecedent and consequent stimuli required to explain the behavior in terms of the *n*-term contingency cannot be reliably identified via third-personal observation	1. *Establishment of the intentional grounds of behavioral continuity and discontinuity.* To supply alternative account in intentional terms, especially desires and beliefs. (i) Determine, first, what intentionality can be inferred to account for behavior for which behavioral syntax is available. (ii) Apply this intentionality account to behavior for which no such behavioral explanation is possible. This ascription of intentionality is third-personal, exactly as Dennett proposes for IST
2. *Rendering the personal level of exposition meaningful.* The behaviorist's notion of private events is an attempt to account for behavior in terms of a subjective phenomenology. This is inherently intentional. A more scientifically acceptable account is required	2. *Provision of an account of first-personal experience.* Supply a heterophenomenology of personal experience, especially in terms of emotion and perception. The result is still third-personal but is as close as possible to the individual's phenomenology. The methodology and results are unashamedly intentional
3. *Delineating behavioral interpretation.* Behavioral interpretation lacks a means of establishing limits of stimulus proximity/ remoteness. How distant in time and/or space can a stimulus be and still provide a plausible account of behavior? The limit can only be established by considering what the individual can reasonably have known when he or she acted	3. *Establishment of stimulus proximity.* There are two aspects to this. The first is (3a) *the contextual delimitation of the behavioral interpretation.* We delimit the extensional behavioral interpretation by (i) establishing the limits of remoteness to be reached before a functional interpretation must be deemed implausible (which entails identifying the range of stimuli that can be invoked to interpret behavior as operant); (ii) providing an alternative account of the behavior in terms of desires, beliefs, emotions, and perceptions. The second is (3b) *scoping out the Intentional Interpretation:* by establishing the boundaries of the required Intentional Interpretation, we avoid the fanciful extension of what we are saying in terms of intentionality. But by determining what needs to be explained at the intentional level of exposition, we necessarily restrict both the extensional interpretation and the Intentional Interpretation. This second stage ensures that our response to the need to delimit the behavioral interpretation is matched by a corresponding delineation of the intentional alternative

intentional strategy that is appropriately required to meet each of the bounds of behaviorism.

Intentional Continuity and Discontinuity

The first limitation of behaviorist explanation arises from an inability to provide an account of behavior that conforms to the rules of behavioral syntax, that is, that cannot identify the stimulus conditions that would account for observed behavior in extensional terms. The aim of the intentional strategy in this context is to reconstruct the framework of desires and beliefs that would account for observed behavior for which an extensional syntax is unavailable. The first imperative of intentionality is therefore to present an account of the behavior in terms of appropriate desires and beliefs. The principles of Intentional Interpretation necessitated by these considerations form the following methodology: *first*, the rigorous demonstration of the inability of extensional syntax to account for the behavior (or its aspects); if this is accomplished, the behavior in question is referred to as "intentional behavior"; *second*, construction of an intentional account of similar behavior where the behavioral syntax requirements are fulfilled; this is then transferred to the situation in which these requirements cannot be met to provide a basis for evaluating the following operations in terms of their producing a credible interpretation; *third*, explication of the intentional behavior in terms of the intentional consumer situation where references to the content of desires, beliefs, emotions, and perceptions are supported by molar operant behavioral accounts of this or similar behavior and species-general neurophysiological correlates of behavior; the intentional consumer situation will include reference to the consumer's learning history and the nature of the pattern of reinforcement prefigured by this intentional situation.

The beliefs, desires, emotions, and perceptions that should be ascribed are those that, in Dennett's words, the consumer *ought* to have by virtue of his or her history and situation, that is, the learning history and consumer setting in which it is located. This explication of intentional behavior consists therefore in the reconstruction of the consumer situation along intentional lines. *Fourth*, further explication of the intentional behavior in terms of the cognitive consumer situation where references to the content of decision making are supported by molar operant behavioral accounts of this or similar behavior and species-general neurophysiological correlates of behavior; the cognitive consumer situation will include reference to the consumer's learning history and the nature of the pattern of reinforcement prefigured by this cognitive situation. The decision-making processes that should be ascribed are those that the consumer ought to have by virtue of its history and situation, that is, the learning history and consumer setting in which it is located. This explication of cognitive behavior consists, therefore, in the reconstruction of the consumer situation along cognitive lines.

First-Personal Experience

The intentional strategy in this case involves consumer heterophenomenology (Dennett 1991a; Foxall 2016e), a special instance of Intentional Interpretation in which the verbal reports of individual consumers provide data. The interpretation made of these reports can be corroborated/extended by the use of the general elements of Intentional Interpretation listed above.

Stimulus Proximity

Contextual Delimitation We cannot assume that any and every ramification of a response counts as a controlling consequence of the emission of similar responses in the future. To make this assumption is to presume too much about the generalization of responses, the situations in which they occur, and their outcomes. There must come a limit to the range of behavioral aftermaths that can enter into an interpretation of observed activities, even when a whole sequence of similar responses is accompanied by a series of similar sequels. Similarly, the antecedent stimuli that set the occasion for reinforcement of a response must be determined by careful experimental analysis and cannot be assumed to have this effect simply on the basis of their propinquity to the response. To think otherwise is to invite a *post hoc, ergo propter hoc* fallacy in the form of what purports to be a scientifically causal statement: my train does not move off each morning because I take a seat in it; my failing an examination is neither a consequential cause of my taking it nor necessarily an outcome that punishes my further involvement in examinations. We need to be able to establish relationships between bits of behavior that occur in non-experimental contexts, which we are pleased to call "responses," and the preceding and subsequent elements of the environment that we choose to call "stimuli," that are based on more than casual observation or even high levels of correlative association. Failure to work out a logic of behavioral interpretation that avoids these simple miscalculations precludes the establishment of operant behavioral Intentional Interpretation as a plausible extension of the experimental analysis of behavior. However, it is difficult to achieve such a logic without resort to Intentional Interpretation.

Unless the outcomes of a behavioral response or patterns of behavioral response can be directly or through analogue incorporated into a functional analysis based on either an experimental or quasi-experimental (regression-based) analysis, the causal relationships between behavior and its reinforcing and punishing consequences cannot be reliably established. The alternative is to restrict the interpretation to the desires, beliefs, emotions, and perceptions the individuals involved could reasonably be expected to have held at the time of their performing the observed behaviors. We cannot include the exploding of nuclear weapons on civilian populations among the causal consequences attributed to the prosecution of basic physics research into the behavior of fundamental particles constituting matter, even though one led to the other. We can, however, delimit our interpretation by referring to the goals (desires) and information (beliefs) available to the scientists at the time of their basic discoveries. The resulting Intentional Interpretation helps delineate the operant behavioral interpretation. However, the Intentional Interpretation must itself be delimited so that it does not reproduce the very errors of unwarranted generality of which we have accused operant interpretation.

Scoping Out It is important to establish limits for the Intentional Interpretation that becomes necessary as a result of our inability to account for behavior according to the extensional syntax outlined above. Otherwise the temptation to extend the intentional account may lead to unwarranted speculation about the mental processing involved. Like the operant behavioral interpretations that ensconce any and all outcomes of a behavior pattern as causal consequences, Intentional Interpretation may ramify endlessly unless it is kept in check.

The scoping out of an Intentional Interpretation involves specifying the cognitive operations necessary to reach the decision that would explain the observed behavior. Its aim is to reach an understanding of the procedures necessary to reconstruct the logical progression from problem specification and goal determination through examination of the options available to achieve or at least approximate this objective function to the selection of a particular course of action as optimal or satisficing and the implementation of the plan that ensues.

Bibliography

Amsel, A., & Rashotte, M. E. (Eds.). (1984). *Mechanisms of adaptive behavior: Clark L. Hull's theoretical papers with commentary.* New York: Columbia University Press.

Baum, W. M. (1973). The correlation-based law of effect. *Journal of the Experimental Analysis of Behavior, 20,* 137–153.

Baum, W. M. (2002). Molar versus molecular as a paradigm clash. *Journal of the Experimental Analysis of Behavior, 75,* 338–341.

Baum, W. M. (2004). Molar and molecular views of choice. *Behavioral Processes, 66,* 349–359.

Baum, W. M., & Heath, J. L. (1992). Behavioral explanations and intentional explanations in psychology. *American Psychologist, 47,* 1312–1317.

Bem, D. J. (1967). Self-perception: An alternative interpretation of cognitive dissonance phenomena. *Psychological Review, 74,* 188–200.

Bermúdez, J. L. (2003). *Thinking without words.* Oxford: Oxford University Press.

Berridge, K. C. (2000). Reward learning: Reinforcement, incentives, and expectations. In D. L. Medin (Ed.), *The psychology of learning and motivation, 49* (pp. 223–278). San Diego: Academic Press.

Bindra, D. (1978). How adaptive behavior is produced: A perceptual—motivation alternative to response reinforcement. *Psychological Review, 81,* 199–213.

Bolles, R. C. (1972). Reinforcement, expectancy, and learning. *Psychological Review, 79,* 394–409.

Bouton, M. E., & Franselow, M. S. (Eds.). (1997). *Learning, motivation, and cognition: The functional behaviorism of Robert C. Bolles.* Washington, DC: American Psychological Association.

Dennett, D. C. (1969). *Content and consciousness.* London: Routledge and Kegan Paul.

Dennett, D. C. (1978). *Brainstorms.* Montgomery: Bradford.

Dennett, D. C. (1987). *The intentional stance.* Cambridge, MA: MIT Press.

Dennett, D. C. (1991a). *Consciousness explained.* London: Penguin Books.

Dennett, D. C. (1991b). Real patterns. *Journal of Philosophy, 88,* 27–51.

Dickinson, A. (1980). *Contemporary animal learning theory.* Cambridge: Cambridge University Press.

Dickinson, A. (1997). Bolles's psychological syllogism. In M. E. Bouton & M. S. Franselow (Eds.), *Learning, motivation, and cognition: The functional behaviorism of Robert C. Bolles* (pp. 345–268). Washington, DC: American Psychological Association.

Dretsky, F. (1988). *Explaining behavior: Reasons in a world of causes.* Cambridge, MA: MIT Press.

Ehrenberg, A. S. C. (1988). *Repeat buying* (2nd ed.). London: Griffin.

Foxall, G. R. (1997c). Affective responses to consumer situations. *International Review of Retail, Distribution and Consumer Research, 7,* 191–225.

Foxall, G. R. (1999b). The contextual stance. *Philosophical Psychology, 12,* 25–46.

Foxall, G. R. (2004). *Context and cognition: Interpreting complex behavior.* Reno: Context Press.

Foxall, G. R. (2005). *Understanding consumer choice.* London/New York: Palgrave Macmillan.

Foxall, G. R. (2007b). Explaining consumer choice: Coming to terms with intentionality. *Behavioral Processes, 75,* 129–145.

Foxall, G. R. (2007c). Intentional behaviorism. *Behavior and Philosophy, 35,* 1–56.

Foxall, G. R. (2008b). Intentional behaviorism revisited. *Behavior and Philosophy, 37,* 113–156.

Foxall, G. R. (2016a). *Addiction as consumer choice: Exploring the cognitive dimension.* London/New York: Routledge.

Foxall, G. R. (2016e). Consumer heterophenomenology. In G. R. Foxall (Ed.), *The Routledge companion to consumer behavior analysis* (pp. 417–430). London/New York: Routledge.

Foxall, G. R., Oliveira-Castro, J. M., & Schrezenmaier, T. C. (2004). The behavioral economics of consumer brand choice: Patterns of reinforcement and utility maximization. *Behavioural Processes, 65,* 235–260.

Hayes, S. C., Barnes-Holmes, D., & Roche, B. (Eds.) (2001). *Relational frame theory: A post-Skinnerian account of human language and cognition.* New York: Kluwer.

Juarrero, A. (2002). *Dynamics in action: Intentional behavior as a complex system.* Cambridge, MA: MIT Press.

Kane, R. (1995). Patterns, acts and self-control: Rachlin's theory. *Behavioral and Brain Sciences, 18,* 131–132.

Lee, V. L. (1988). *Beyond behaviorism.* London: Erlbaum.

Lowe, C. F. (1983). Radical behaviorism and human psychology. In G. C. L. Davey (Ed.), *Animal models of human behavior* (pp. 71–93). Chichester: Wiley.

Malcolm, N. (1977). Behaviorism as a philosophy of psychology. In N. Malcolm (Eds.), *Thought and knowledge* (pp. 85–103). Ithaca: Cornell University Press.

Rachlin, H. (1989). *Judgment, decision, and choice: A cognitive/behavioral synthesis.* New York: Freeman.

Rachlin, H. (1994). *Behavior and mind: The roots of modern psychology.* Oxford: Oxford University Press.

Rachlin, H. (1995). Self-control: Beyond commitment. *Behavioral and Brain Sciences, 18,* 109–159.

Rachlin, H. (1999). Teleological behaviorism. In W. O'Donohue & R. Kitchener (Eds.), *Handbook of behaviorism* (pp. 195–215). New York: Academic Press.

Ryle, G. (1949). *The concept of mind.* London: Hutchinson.

Schnaitter, R. (1999). Some criticisms of behaviorism. In B. A. Thyer (Ed.), *The philosophical legacy of behaviorism* (pp. 209–249). Dordrecht: Kluwer.

Shapiro, L. A. (1999). Presence of mind. In V. G. Hardcastle (Ed.), *Where biology meets psychology: Philosophical essays* (pp. 83–98). Cambridge, MA: MIT Press.

Sidman, M. (1994). *Equivalence relations and behavior: A research story.* Boston: Authors Cooperative.

Skinner, B. F. (1931). The concept of the reflex in the description of behavior. *Journal of General Psychology, 5,* 427–458.

Skinner, B. F. (1935a). The generic nature of the concepts of stimulus and response. *Journal of General Psychology, 12,* 40–65.

Skinner, B. F. (1935b). Two types of conditioned reflex and a pseudo-type. *Journal of General Psychology, 12,* 66–77.

Skinner, B. F. (1937). Two types of conditioned reflex: A reply to Konorski and Miller. *Journal of General Psychology, 16,* 272–279.

Skinner, B. F. (1938). *The behavior of organisms*. New York: Appleton—Century—Crofts.

Skinner, B. F. (1953a). *Science and human behavior*. New York: Macmillan.

Skinner, B. F. (1953b). Some contributions of an experimental analysis of behavior to psychology as a whole. *American Psychologist, 8,* 69–78.

Skinner, B. F. (1956). A case history in scientific method. *American Psychologist, 11*(5), 221–233.

Skinner, B. F. (1974). *About behaviorism*. New York: Knopf.

Smith, T. L. (1994). *Behavior and its causes: Philosophical foundations of operant psychology*. Dordrecht: Kluwer.

Staddon, J. E. R. (2014). *The new behaviorism*. Hove/New York: Psychology Press.

Toates, F. (1986). *Motivational systems*. Cambridge: Cambridge University Press.

Tolman, E. C. (1932). *Purposive behavior in animals and men*. New York: Century.

Wittgenstein, L. (1953). *Philosophical investigations*. (G. E. M. Anscombe. & R. Rhees (Eds.), trans: Anscombe, G. E. M.). Oxford: Blackwell.

Zuriff, G. E. (1985). *Behaviorism: A conceptual reconstruction*. New York: Columbia University Press.

5

The Ascription of Intentionality

Introduction

Since this chapter proposes the use of intentional idioms to explain consumer behavior, it is important to establish the bases of such terminology in human experience and then to show how we can apply this knowledge in the third-personal interpretation of choice. This chapter is concerned, therefore, with the origins of subjectively held intentionality in the knowledge by acquaintance that is the stuff of conscious experience. This proceeds to a discussion of how we can ascribe intentionality to explain the behavior of ourselves and others in a manner that is not speculative and whimsical but part of a genuine scientific endeavor to *explain* consumer activity.

Conceptual Dualism

Minds and Bodies

The philosophical conundrum known as the "mind-body problem" asks how material beings living in a wholly physical universe can have subjective mental experiences that do not appear to follow physical laws yet either

© The Editor(s) (if applicable) and The Author(s) 2016
G.R. Foxall, *Perspectives on Consumer Choice*,
DOI 10.1057/978-1-137-50121-9_5

influence our behavior or must be taken into consideration in explaining it. How can desires and beliefs determine choice? Are the reasons we give for acting in a particular way in any sense the causes of that behavior? There is no easy answer to this problem and most attempts at its philosophical resolution seem to rest on no more than monistic assertions that all is matter or all is mind, or on sleight-of-hand reasoning that allows the same entity to count here as matter, there as mind. In one way or another, authors who seek to maintain a materialist ontology struggle to reconcile the very traits that make us human, the "life of the mind," with our evolution as animals in an all-too-effable world. The mind-body problem is not identical with that of using intentional versus extensional language and explanations but it is an important complicating factor. I shall suggest that it is, for now at least, also a linguistic or conceptual rather than an ontological problem. That is, the world, including ourselves, is indeed material but we have more than one way of experiencing it, talking about it, and using its contents to explain behavior.

McGinn (2004) draws upon Russell's (1912) distinction between *knowledge by acquaintance* and *knowledge by description* to ground his conception of the relationship between the mind (consciousness) and the body (brain), and to argue for the irreducibility of the former to the latter. Knowledge by acquaintance arises through direct experience, as in my knowing that the sky is darkening as I watch the clouds move across the sun. Knowledge by description relies on the reports of others: if I have never left England, my knowledge that even on a perfect summer's afternoon, day can turn rapidly to night without the intervention of a period of dusk, can come only from the descriptions of people who have witnessed other climes for themselves. In the first case, my knowledge is nonpropositional: I just know how things are. In the latter case where a visitor to say Australia has described to me that dusk is there short-lived, it is propositional: I now know that p. Even knowledge I have gained personally by acquaintance can be subsequently related to myself and others propositionally.

There is, then, a sense in which I can claim to know my own thoughts and feelings directly, that is by being personally acquainted with their contents. The skeptic, of course, would deny that anyone other than he or she has thoughts and feelings: the privacy of firsthand phenomenal experience renders consciousness by definition inaccessible to other. Such consideration might be taken as justifying a solipsistic stance but it would render discourse on consciousness sterile. Like most people, I infer that other humans, who are after all physiologically similar to me and whom I can assume to have evolved by means of the same biological and social processes, have a private consciousness on the basis that their behavior, especially their verbal behavior, is consistent with this assumption. To take the solipsistic stance is therefore surely to assert that one is a special creation. To expand Descartes's axiom, "I think; therefore, I am. You are; therefore, you think."

Bear in mind that this reasoning might not convince the determined skeptic and that our granting reality to the private consciousness of each and every human being does not mean that subjective experience can enter directly into a scientific, experimental analysis of behavior. At best, we may claim that measures of behavior, especially verbal behavior, and neurophysiology constitute proxy variables for consciousness. Note also that even radical behaviorism embraces the existence of such private events as thinking and feeling (Skinner 1945, 1974), though it casts them as responses and thus denies them causal efficacy.

Our knowing our consciousness by acquaintance rather than by description is sufficient, McGinn argues, to establish that there is a mind-body problem. Moreover, for all that knowledge by acquaintance is nonpropositional, it is genuine knowledge: it is through knowing by acquaintance that we understand at all what consciousness is. Knowledge by acquaintance is prerequisite to knowledge by description and propositional knowledge would be impossible without it. It is knowledge by acquaintance which, by providing implicit understanding of the phenomena of consciousness, legitimizes our using mental language to make our own and others' behavior intelligible, to the extent that the limitations of our introspection permit. Knowledge by acquaintance is, therefore, prior to knowledge by description. Even if I am a research biologist, my knowledge of photosynthesis is by description; but, whoever, I am, my knowledge of my elation is by acquaintance. As McGinn (2004, p. 8) puts it, "No propositional knowledge would be possible unless we know some things in a non-propositional way."

Intersubjective Agreement

This fundamental distinction between two kinds of knowledge, and the manner in which they are related, requires elaboration. To reiterate, my phenomenological intentionality, in common with everyone's desires, beliefs, emotions, and perceptions, for that matter, is not publicly observable and, therefore, not accessible of itself to a scientific analysis, something that Dennett (e.g., 1991a) is rightly at pains to point out. I claim that what I take to be my desires, beliefs, emotions, and perceptions helps me to make sense of my behavior. Moreover, the intentionality I ascribe to others on the basis of what I observe them to do and the circumstances of their behavior helps me make sense of them. But my subjective intentionality cannot directly form part of an approach to understanding that demands third-personal agreement, that is, the scientific enterprise. Of course, statements, perhaps verbal, which purportedly describe this private intentionality can, to the extent that they receive intersubjective agreement from my fellow-investigators, with respect to their nature and significance, provide the justification of a more sophisticated Intentional Interpretation of behavior. But this is a different point from any insistence that my assertion of what I know by acquaintance suffices to establish its reality and efficacy.

   The foundations of the concepts we employ in Intentional Interpretation of behavior, whether understood as *abstracta* or *illata* (which are defined below), or simply as *mental constructs*, are located, therefore, ultimately in what we take to be first-personal knowledge by acquaintance. But it does not follow that the assertion of my knowing these phenomena by acquaintance suffices to establish their reality or that it grounds them sufficiently that they can form the basis of scientific enquiry. Radical behaviorists such as Skinner claim that private events can enter into a science of behavior on the basis of their being observed, albeit solely by the person whose thoughts and feelings they are. To Skinner, for whom the objective and the subjective are, therefore, identical, observation by one person is no different from observation by many. This is not my claim. Intersubjective agreement forms the basis of scientific inquiry and is at the root of concepts like desires and beliefs in which Intentional Interpretation consists. But the experience to which the commonly asserted statements about intentionality purportedly refer have, in themselves, no place in science. To the degree to which they receive intersubjective corroboration they lie at the heart of the philosophical grounding of scientific conceptualization and analysis. Of course, I have or think I have knowledge so ineffable that I cannot formulate it propositionally but by its very nature it is in itself not empirically available for scientific scrutiny.

McGinn's (2004, p. 8) statement which we have noted that "No propositional knowledge would by possible unless we knew some things by acquaintance," could, therefore, be restated—admittedly less pithily—as "Propositional knowledge would not be possible unless our statement 'We know that p' were accepted by the scientific community as consonant with its knowing by acquaintance at the first-personal level, and which they could only express publicly in terms of propositional statements identical to our own." Hence, this common knowledge is the basis of scientific propositional knowledge in the context of any theory of behavior that relies on the ascription of intentionality and cognition to predict and explain behavior. Knowledge by description is grounded in knowledge by acquaintance; extrinsic knowledge, in intrinsic.

This is the essential point of Dennett's (1991a) heterophenomenology which is an attempt to translate knowledge by acquaintance into knowledge by description.[1] It is not a link to consciousness; it is simply the best method we have of getting at the consciousness of the person whose behavior we wish to interpret. Dennett's starting point for heterophenomenology, the subjective experience of individual, private consciousness, does not seem to differ from Strawson's or McGinn's: everyday self-experience. What Dennett is saying is that this is not sufficient for a scientific analysis (this is much what I mean when I say that the objects of intentionality cannot be subjected to an experimental analysis). The closest one can get to this first-person consciousness is to translate it into third-person propositions which are then taken as a text for scientific investigation. So, we are not dealing with the consciousness firsthand when we analyze these verbal propositions: we are dealing with verbal behavior: for example, *I believe that p*. Moreover, since we cannot translate these propositional data into extensional language without altering

---

[1] For an exposition in the context of consumer psychology, see Foxall (2016e).

(adding to) their meaning, our interpretations must themselves take the form of intentional idioms: *she believes that p*, and so on.

The knowledge that grounds an Intentional Interpretation of behavior is the propositional knowledge held in common by the members of the scientific community that they agree forms a veracious account of their first-person knowledge by acquaintance of their consciousness. That is, the grounds are not the knowledge by acquaintance itself but the commonly held third-person accounts of it. The grounds of third-person Intentional Interpretation also include the beliefs that the interpretations we observe through knowledge by acquaintance are reasons for how we behave or should behave.

A Conceptual Distinction

Whereas concepts like my experience of euphoria are introspectively ascribed, those like photosynthesis are perceptual concepts. The problem of mind-brain relationships stems from the impossibility of making appropriate connections between the two kinds of concept. What is required is a novel kind of concept that falls into neither camp but mediates between them, thereby melting away the conceptual dualism that lies at the heart of the difficulty. Without such bridging concepts, we have knowledge by acquaintance of consciousness which is captured only in introspective concepts, and knowledge by description of the way in which the brain works which are caught only by perceptual concepts. The solution to the mind-body problem lies in discovering a concept that spans the two domains, the *biconditionality*. McGinn argues that this is impossible.

Referring to the required concept which will solve the problem of finding the a priori entailments, spanning the explanatory chasm, as "P," he notes that given our present cognitive capacities P will either be an introspective concept or a perceptual concept. Thus the conceptual dualism that is the essence of the problem will not have been overcome. There appears no means of bridging the gap: "Our concepts of consciousness are acquaintance-based, but any objective description of conscious states are not – so the latter can never adequately capture the former" (McGinn

2004, p. 22). Heterophenomenology does not meet this need, but then Dennett never expected it would. Neither an objective phenomenology nor a subjective physiology can be had. "What would a concept of consciousness be like that was not acquaintance-based, that did not require being conscious in order to possess it?" (p. 22). The inescapable conceptual dualism with which McGinn presents us constantly suggests an ontological dualism where there is none.

The subjective experience we call consciousness can never constitute the stuff of scientific examination because it can never be publicly experienced or intersubjectively evaluated. So the task of science becomes that of examining the third-personal texts that arise from individuals' statements (knowledge by description) of what they experience (knowledge by acquaintance), that is, what they desire, believe, feel, and perceive. This is the methodology of Dennett's heterophenomenology, but it can be put to a special purpose in the service of science. In this case, it is not confined to the linguistic analysis of whatever statements an individual happens to make in response to a request to express his or her personal consciousness. It becomes, rather, the critical examination of numerous individuals' statements of this kind that seeks to establish their commonalities. In other words, it probes the degree of interindividual accord there is to be found among these statements severally given. This is, of course, precisely what psychometric tests of cognition and emotion elicit from a sample whose responses are typically averaged and compared in terms of central tendency. But these data can also form the basis of Intentional Interpretation, the justification and refinement of the constructs of folk psychology as the basis of psychological explanation.

By framing the problem as conceptual, we avoid both the dualism involved in accepting that there are two ontologies and the intricacies of identity theories that seek to marry them together. Nor does the kind of functionalism proposed by Dennett suffice to solve our problem. Dennett argues that to have beliefs and desires is simply to be predictable by the intentional stance. But to adopt this stance is to ascribe *third-personal* consciousness, albeit as a conceptual exercise, to the system that is to be predicted. Our problem is to deal with the *first*-personal experience which we know by acquaintance. It follows that all attempts to solve the mind-body problem entail a miraculous jump from one side to the conceptual divide to the other without the aid of the essential bridging concept. This can be achieved only by arguing that one kind of concept in the biconditionality actually belongs to the other category. This is precisely Dennett's strategy when he decides that the intentional stance can be applied at the sub-personal level (Dennett 1978, 1987, 1991a). The same applies in the case of panpsychism, the doctrine that "everything having a physical aspect also has a mental or conscious aspect" (Freeman 2006, p. 1; see also Strawson 2006, and the essays following). By adopting one or other of these mechanisms of transformation, the authors give themselves permission to cross the line of biconditional separation at will.

These comments are not meant to suggest that Consumer Behavior Analysis be preoccupied with the knowledge by acquaintance we have at our subjective conscious experience. Rather, the aims at this stage are (a) to acknowledge the existence of such experience, whatever its precise form and import; and (b) to argue that this knowledge by acquaintance is the basis of the knowledge by description we draw on when we use intentional language (or the idealized language of desires and beliefs that we use to make our own and others' behavior intelligible in a scientific context).

Most philosophers of mind and cognitive scientists wish to avoid substance dualism in accounting for the differences between the apparently physical and the apparently mental. That difference is a deep and possibly unbridgeable conceptual chasm that could only be crossed by the invention of suitable bridging concepts. Since a bridging concept, as far as we can imagine it with our present cognitive capacities would have to be either a physical or a mental concept, it would not be able to do the job. Conceptual dualism boils down to verbal dualism: we have two languages to describe the behavioral realm but they carry with them distinctly different criteria for the truth value of their statements and therefore incommensurable explanations of behavior. Both are required in order to present as comprehensive an account of behavior as we are capable of. The task of a theory of behavior is to show how, despite the conceptual chasm, they may work together to provide that account.

Of course, there is nothing other than materiality to work with. We have only neurons and behavior, both of which are physical elements: no claim is being made that there are entities other than the physical. The important point is that we have to speak of the physical universe using more than one linguistic mode. This is the source of our conceptual dualism, which is of course ultimately a verbal dualism.

Summing-Up

While knowledge by acquaintance may genuinely be a part of the individual's phenomenology, it is necessarily first-personal: any record of it is therefore a third-personal account, knowledge by description. The only way in which conscious experience can enter into a scientific analysis is through its transformation into a text that is generally available, a third-personal artifact. While knowledge by acquaintance, conscious experience, can be accepted as real on this basis, it is of limited scientific value in its own right. We can ascribe to people the intentionality they "ought" to have given their history and present position, partly as suggested by their verbal accounts of their private thoughts and feelings, and this may be useful in rendering their behavior intelligible or predictable. Can we improve on this state of affairs?

The Ascription of Intentionality

Afferent-Efferent Linkages

It is common for philosophers of mind to assume without offering justification that the grounds for intentional explanation are self-evident and to propose a scheme for its achievement without further ado. A notable exception is Daniel Dennett whose earliest work dealt painstakingly with the validation of intentional reasoning and a detailed scheme for the ascription of intentionality (e.g., Dennett 1969). This chapter discusses Dennett's logic for the ascription of intentionality and for a two-stage approach to cognitive psychology and offers an alternative two-stage methodology for the present purpose of deriving and justifying a cognitive explanation of consumer choice. Although recognizing and adapting the invaluable positive contribution of Dennett's thinking on these matters, I am critical, notably of the way in which he attributes intentionality at the sub-personal level of exposition and propose an alternative methodology for psychological explanation.

Since we cannot avoid intentionality even if, with the radical behaviorists, we confine the aims of intellectual inquiry to the prediction and control of behavior, we must address the question of how intentionality can be responsibly ascribed. Dennett (1969) proposes that we can do so on the basis of the evolutionary consistency of the afferent–efferent[2] linkages identified in (extensional) neuroscience. The result is an a-ontological basis for intentional explanation as an additional interpretation of physiological mechanisms, a "heuristic overlay" of Intentional Interpretation placed upon neuroscience but not part of its extensional program.

Dennett (1969) argues that a purely intentional psychology is impossible because its explicative terms are tautologically derived from its observations of that behavior. A more appropriate basis for psychology would be to add a layer of Intentional Interpretation to the theories and findings of physiology. Those extensional theories cannot of themselves account for the personal level of analysis, that of "people and their sensations and activities" rather than that of "brains and events in the nervous system" (Dennett 1969, p. 93). The personal level is that at which the person knows what it is to feel pain but cannot express this in a way that is further analyzable. Similarly, the abstractions of intentional analysis (beliefs, desires, and so on) are attributed at this level. Dennett is careful to point

---

[2] *Afferent* refers to moving or carrying inward or toward a central part and may refer to blood vessels or nerves, and so on. Veins which carry blood toward the heart, or nerves conducting signals to the central nervous system (CNS) are, therefore, referred to as *afferent*. Blood vessels or nerves carrying blood or signals away from the heart or CNS are, by contrast, known as *efferent*. Closer to the present context, the terms denote functions of neurons which are cells in the nervous system that transmit impulses to other neurons. The important components from the point of view of the current discussion are the cell body itself which is broadly similar to other types of cell, containing for instance a nucleus (though differing in other respects that do not concern us here), and the fibers that project from it, dendrites and axons. Dendrites, of which there are a number to each cell, receive signals from other neurons which are accordingly *afferent*. Axons, of which each cell has only one, transmit signals to other neurons which are, therefore, *efferent*. Closer still is the sense in which these terms are used to denote the functions of neurons by reference to the direction in which they transmit impulses: *toward* the CNS in the case of afferent or sensory neurons, *away from* the CNS in the case of efferent or motor neurons. Connecting the two types of neuron, within the CNS, is a third kind of nerve cell, the interneuron. Although both afferent and efferent neurons are found primarily in the peripheral nervous system (PNS), they are defined functionally and in relation to the CNS.

out that the resulting heuristic overlay adds nothing to the neurophysiological account but provides a means of prediction. The mechanistic explanations provided by sub-personal neuroscience are not appropriate to the explanation of so-called mental entities such as pain. While there is a good understanding of the neurological basis of pain, Dennett asks whether the presumed evolutionarily appropriate afferent-efferent networks underlying this understanding are sufficient (they are certainly necessary) to account for the "phenomena of pain." So, he asks, does pain exist over and above the physical events that constitute the neurophysiological network? (Dennett 1969, p. 91).

Now, there are no events or processes in the brain that "exhibit the characteristics of the putative 'mental phenomena' of pain" that are apparent when we speak in everyday terms about our experiencing pain. Such verbalizations are nonmechanical, while brain events and processes are mechanical. The only distinguishing feature of pain sensations is "painfulness" which is an unanalyzable quality that allows of only circular definition. (It is unclear for instance how an individual distinguishes a sensation of pain from a nonpainful sensation.) It is at the personal level that pain is discriminated, not the sub-personal: neurons and brains have no sensation of pain and do not discriminate them. Moreover, pains, like other mental phenomena, do not refer: our speaking of them does not pick out *any thing*. Pain is simply a personal-level phenomenon that has, nevertheless, some corresponding states, events, or processes at the sub-personal, physiological level. This is not an identity theory: Dennett does not identify the experience of pain with some physical happening; he maintains two separate levels of explanation: one in which the experience of pain, while felt, does not refer, and one in which the descriptions of neural occurrences refer to actual neural structures, events, and states in which the extensionally characterized science deals.

The task now becomes that of ascribing content to the internal states and events. The first stage is straightforward: since intentional theory assumes that the structures and events they seek to explain are appropriate to their purpose, an important link in this ascription is provided by hypotheses drawn from the natural selection of both species and of brains and the nervous system. A system which through evolution has the capacity to produce appropriate efferent responses to the afferent stimulation it encounters, clearly has the ability to discriminate among the repertoire of efferent responses it might conceivably make. Its ability so to discriminate, to respond appropriately to the stimulus characteristics of its complex environment, implies that it is "capable of interpreting its peripheral stimulation," of engendering inner states or events that cooccur with the phenomena that arise in its perceptual field. If we are to call this process intelligent, something must be added to this analysis, namely the capacity to *associate* the outcomes of the afferent analysis with structures on the efferent portion of the brain.

The import of Dennett's argument is that the linkages between afferent and efferent neurons evolved in the course of natural selection to solve the problem, as it were, of how the organism "knows" the appropriate response to produce in the face of a particular stimulus. If sensory neurons signal the availability of food to a hungry animal, for instance, it produces the appropriate response of approaching the stimulus and devouring it. Dennett argues that in this instance, we are justified in saying that the animal *desires* the food and *believes* that acting in this manner will procure it. The purpose of his inquiry is to determine how intentional terms, inescapable because of their general usage and carrying important implications for explanation in view of the meanings assumed by sentences that carry them, can be legitimately employed in psychology.

For instance, in order to detect the presence of a substance *as food*, an organism must have the capacity not only to detect the substance but thereafter to stop seeking and start eating; without this capacity to associate afferent stimulation and efferent response, the organism could not be said to have detected the presence of the substance *as* that of food. Dennett uses this point to criticize behaviorists for having no answer to the question how the organism selects the appropriate response. There is a need to invest the animal which has discriminated a stimulus with the capacity to "know" what its appropriate response should be. (In fact, behaviorists have ducked this problem by designating it a part of the physiologist's assignment and drawing the conclusion that the behavioral scientists need be concerned with it no longer (Foxall 2004). The conventional behaviorist wisdom over the kind of cognitive ascription to which Dennett refers is that it amounts to no more than "premature physiology.")

The content of a neural state, event, or structure relies on its stimulation *and* the appropriate efferent effects to which it gives rise, and in order to delineate these it is necessary to transcend the extensional description of stimulus and response. It is necessary to relate the content to the environmental conditions as perceived by the organism's sense organs in order that it can be given reference to the real-world phenomena that produced the stimulation. And it is equally important to specify what the organism "does with" the event or state so produced in order to determine what that event or state "means to" the organism. An aversive stimulus has not only to be identified along with the neural changes it engenders to signify that it means danger to the animal; in addition, the animal has to respond appropriately to the stimulus, for example, by moving away. Failure on its part to do so would mean that we were not justified in ascribing such content to the physiological processes occurring as a result of the stimulation. If we are to designate the animal's activities as "intelligent decision making" then this behavioral link must be apparent. Only events in the brain that appear appropriately linked in this way can be ascribed content, described in intentional idioms.

Level of Exposition

How are the intentional ascription and the extensional descriptions provided by neuroscience to be related? The ascribed content is not an additional characteristic of the event, state, or structure to which it is allocated, some intrinsic part of it discovered within it, as its extensionally characterized features are discovered by the physiologist. It is, Dennett explains, a matter of additional *interpretation*. The features of neural systems, extensionally characterized in terms of physiology or physics, are describable and predictable in those terms without intentional ascription which makes reference to meaning or content. Such a scientific story, consisting in an account of behavior confined to talk of the structure and functions of neural cells and so on, is entirely extensional in character. But such an extensional story could not, according to Dennett, provide us with an understanding of *what the organism is doing*. Only an intentional account can accomplish this, "but it is not a story about features of the world *in addition to* features of the extensional story; it just describes what happens in a different way." Such an extensional theory would be confined to the description/explanation of the *motions* of the organism rather than of its *actions*.

The legitimate ascription of content relies emphatically upon the clear understanding of the nature of the personal level of analysis, a matter on which Dennett has proved extraordinarily flexible over the years. The logic of intentional ascription derives from the evolutionary imperative that a creature must, in order to survive and reproduce, generate environmentally appropriate behavior—its responses must be appropriate to the stimuli that impinge upon it. Only an intelligent creature can produce the right behavior in the circumstances it faces, that is, a creature whose nervous system can generate the efferent behavior that matches the afferent stimulus in order to increase its biological fitness. There is a need to invest the animal which has discriminated a stimulus with the capacity to "know" what its appropriate response should be, and such an intelligent capacity can be specified only in intentional terms. We have not identified some additional characteristic of the physiology of the creature by ascribing content to it in order to account for the intelligence it exhibits: we have simply provided *additional interpretation*.

Such ascription is unnecessary to the research program of the physiologist who characterizes the features of neural systems via extensional physics or biology, and who for the purposes of neuroscience has no need of intentional ascriptions that refer to meaning or content. A simple example of the kind of afferent-efferent linkage Dennett is talking about is: sight of a particular foodstuff (afferent sensory input) leading to approach behavior mediated by motor neuron activity in requisite muscles: the intentional inference is that the organism *wants, needs, has a positive attitude toward, intends to get* the food. But the ascription of wanting, intending, and so on, is not part of the physiology: it is not part of extensional neuroscience which deals with the sub-personal level: it belongs only at the level of the person since only a whole organism can be said to do these things.

Dennett provides the example of a hungry dog which, on being presented with meat, lays it on a pile of straw and sits on it rather than eat it. Our knowledge of the afferent events in the dog's brain confirms that they are the usual olfactory, visual, and tactile responses to food that the dog has always shown in the past. However, the operation of its efferent system leads on this occasion to curious responses that fit in with neither the phylogenetic history of its species nor its peculiar ontogenetic development. Because the dog's behavior is inappropriate we cannot understand it on the basis that the meat was interpreted as food but nor do we have grounds for any other interpretation: perhaps the dog mistook it for a brick or is fantasizing that it is an egg he must sit on to hatch. There is no clue to this from his afferent state. If the behavior is unintelligible in biological terms, no particular Intentional Interpretation follows.

The conclusion he draws from this is that "one can only ascribe content to a neural event, state, or structure when it is a link in a demonstrably appropriate chain between the afferent and the efferent" (Dennett 1969, p. 78). He goes on to reiterate that the content one ascribes to such events, states, or structures is not something additional to the extensional characterization of how neural systems are constituted and work, based as they are on firing rates, exchanges of neurotransmitters as a result of the operation of action potentials, and so on; it is entirely a matter of extra *interpretation* of those events. And he points out that even the most thorough extensional account of those events would always have one deficit in that it could not inform us "*what the animal was doing*" (ibid., emphasis in original). Crucially, "a solely biological, non-Intentional story of behaviour should be possible in principle, but it would be mute on the topic of the actions (as opposed to motions), intentions, beliefs and desires of its subjects" (Dennett 1969, p. 79).

Dennett attributes the behavior of the animal to the efferent system. He makes the claim that a neural state's content depends not only on the source of stimulation that leads to an afferent reaction but also to its corresponding efferent activity which leads to an appropriate behavioral response. Ascription of such content depends, first, on the stimulus conditions that bring about an afferent response. It is this process that provides the reference of the events within the nervous system to happenings in the world. An afferent event is thus a response to or, as Dennett puts it, a report on the environmental events that brought it into being. Optic nerve fibers of frogs respond to small dark objects because the appropriate neural firings occur only if reports of such stimuli are received by the retina. But the meaning of such an event to the individual animal relies also on what it does with that event. A link between an environmental event and a withdrawal reaction may be established evolutionarily when the event signals danger or pain. However, this Intentional Interpretation would be inappropriate on an occasion when the animal failed to respond with withdrawal. The stimulus clearly did not mean danger or pain *to this animal*. As Dennett comments (1969, p. 85) "propitiousness or adaptiveness of behavior is at least a necessary condition of intelligence." The problem with Dennett's account comes up in his next sentence: "This immediately establishes a limit on the events and states within the brain to which the investigator can ascribe content" (Dennett 1969, pp. 85–6). The difficulty is not that Dennett has failed to make good points about the necessity of ascribing content in order to explain the animal's behavior; nor that his assumption that neurophysiology must be one source of constraint on the ascription of intentionality is other than sound. It is the positioning of the ascribed content in his scheme of exposition that is troublesome. The assumption is that content is to be ascribed at the sub-personal level.

There is no reason to attribute intentionality to any level other than the personal in order to overcome the problem that Dennett has identified of explicating what the animal is doing. The view that an Intentional Interpretation is required is unobjectionable; the necessity of ascribing intentionality in these circumstances is not in dispute. But at what level of exposition can this ascription be legitimately made? The ascription of intentionality is not properly to the efferent system but to the person, and therefore belongs at the personal level of exposition. The purpose of this ascription of intentionality is to explicate behavior, a personal level phenomenon in terms of desires and beliefs, which are personal-level phenomena. The content ascription is not actually to the efferent level of neuronal functioning—it is an ascription made at the personal level to explain a response (in terms of its appropriateness), given that the afferent response to the stimulus cannot do this. That there has to be a post-afferent judgment about what is appropriate ("I believe that this is food") does not of itself locate this intentional ascription at the level of efferent neural events. It is exactly as Dennett says another level of interpretation but part of the interpretation is the view that this intentionality is attributable only at the personal level.

The Intentional Stance

Dennett's (1987) idea of the intentional stance represents a prominent innovation in the philosophy of mind. While remaining a-ontological about the nature of intentionality, the intentional stance proposes that the behavior of humans, many animals, and some mechanical devices such as computer programs can be predicted and partially explained by the ascription to them of the desires and beliefs that they "ought" to have, given their history and current circumstances. Moreover, being predictable in this way is all that is required for the intentional system so identified to be described as having desires and beliefs and other aspects of intentionality; that is the only qualification necessary to be a believer or one who desires.

The intentional stance is one of several stances relevant to the explanation of the behavior of living entities and physical systems. Dennett speaks of the *physical stance* and the *design stance*, for instance, and we have already encountered the contextual stance (Foxall 1999b) in which an entity is understood insofar as we attribute to it a susceptibility to operant conditioning: human behavior, for instance, is predictable in terms of its contingent reinforcers and punishers.

Dennett's system of stances, with the addition of the contextual stance, is valuable, though I disagree with his positions on the range of entities to which the stances, notably the intentional stance, can be applied, and on the question of the levels of exposition to which each stance is relevant.

Range of Applicability

In Dennett's approach, whatever is predictable by means of the application of the intentional stance is an intentional system. If this stance works, it is permissible to apply it; moreover, as I have mentioned, the predictive attribution of intentional idioms is all there is to having desires and beliefs. However, I do not agree that the intentional stance is applicable everywhere it predicts successfully—it is only applicable where the other stances are not relevant. The adoption of the intentional stance is necessary only when other stances do not suffice to explain the behavior in question. For physical entities the physical and design stances suffice; for animals, the contextual stance; only for humans the intentional stance and even then only for the whole person. The contextual, physical, and design stances are fully capable of explicating the behavior of physical systems and many animal systems and it is not therefore necessary to call upon the intentional stance to do so. Insofar as intentionality is a linguistic phenomenon, the intentional stance is similarly relevant to the use of intentionality in verbal behavior. That is, it can only explain the behavior of creatures that can employ intentional language to understand their own and others' behavior.

Dennett claims, as we have seen, that it is both possible and useful to construe systems as intentional, and thus to use the intentional stance in the explanation of their behavior, even though other stances can be applied to them. Steward (2012) argues that there are systems, such as thermostats, toward which it is simply not necessary to take the intentional stance to understand why they behave as they do. Single-celled creatures such as paramecia also come into this category. This is consistent with my argument that the contextual stance suffices to account for much animal behavior, and the physical stance in instances such as the thermometer and chess-playing computer programs. We can, she says, account for the behavior of a computer or a program without attributing to it the status of an agent. This alone disqualifies the system from being an agent: "Folk psychology is not a metaphysical necessity for the explanation of the changes that occur within any artificial system of this sort that has so far been invented" (Steward 2012, p. 105). Moreover, and this is crucial, she further asserts that the capacity of agents to settle matters renders them insusceptible to the physical stance: if there are such things as agents they are not explicable by the physical stance. The import of this reasoning is that the range of applicability of the stances is demarcated not by the pragmatic benefits of using the intentional stance wherever its assumption of agency and even its demonstrable contribution to predictability of the system are evident. It is ruled out on epistemological grounds.

Relevance to Levels of Exposition

Stances are on this view specific to particular levels of exposition. Extensional stances such as the physical and contextual apply to the sub-personal and super-personal levels, respectively, while the intentional and design stances apply to the personal level of exposition. (The design stance is simply an application of the intentional stance with a particular goal in mind. It is an attribution of intentionality to another person or persons, not to a physical system that is being unraveled.) It is inappropriate and unnecessary to apply the intentional and stances to the sub-personal or super-personal levels of exposition.

There is always a sense in which it is possible to predict the behavior of an entity by describing what it does in terms of what it wants to do. My car moves me about and I could predict its behavior by saying that this is what it wants to do. Especially when it fails to move I might demand "Why doesn't my car want to go today?!" But this is an example of everyday parlance, not a scientific explanation. Dennett (e.g., 1996) argues that using the intentional stance in situations like this is permissible because it makes the prediction of the system easier than using the physical or design stance. It is easier to use intentional language of the computer program that I am playing at chess, ascribing to it the desire to get my king into check and deducing that it therefore wants to get my knight out of the way. This is clearly easier than going through details of how the computer program was written and trying to work out what instructions it will next give rise to. Everyday talk is, of course, superior in this situation but it is not behavioral science. Dennett does not, moreover, specify when the use of the physical stance becomes sufficiently ineffective to justify employing the intentional stance. Just because using the nonintentional stances would be cumbersome and time-consuming does not mean that they are not the correct means by which the behavior of the system ought to be scientifically explained or predicted. An intentional system would then become any system that can *only* be explained and predicted by use of the intentional stance. A human being thus becomes an intentional system when the behavior can no longer be explained by the contextual stance, and intentional idioms must be used to interpret and possibly predict it. The criterion that the intentional stance is necessary only when the stances that proceed in terms of extensional language are exhausted is far more precise a guide to scientific practice. More precisely, we say that *the intentional language required by the intentional stance is to be used only when extensional language has failed or no longer suffices.* This is clearly not the case for entities that are explicable in terms of the physical stance of the design stance; even though to do so may be painstakingly arduous, it is the appropriate scientific procedure.

For which entities can the intentional stance then be employed? There are two answers to this. First, the intentional stance might be applicable only to living entities whose gross behavior can be explained only by that stance rather than by the contextual or physical stance. Any animal, therefore, the behavior of which cannot be explained by physical or contextual means is thus amenable to analysis by means of this stance. Second, the intentional stance might be applicable only to living entities that can act intensionally when intensionality is defined as a linguistic convention. This would confine it to creatures which can discriminate their behavior and the reasons why they engaged in it. It applies therefore only to post-infantile humans. However, animals that can be shown to act intentionally, for example, in deceiving conspecifics or predators, could also be considered.

Summing-Up

Before proceeding to Dennett's classification of intentional psychologies, this is a fitting point at which to summarize his argument thus far and to note where I deviate from it. Content, he says, can be ascribed to a neural event when it is a link in an *appropriate chain* between afferent and efferent which has been selected in the course of the phylogeny of the organism in question. The content is not something to be discovered *within* this neural event but is an extra interpretation, the rationale of which is not to understand better the operation of the subsystem per se but to provide a local justification for the ascription of appropriate content at the personal level. The ultimate justification for such ascription is provided by evolutionary thinking—the intelligent brain must be able to select the appropriate response to a specific stimulus. Why should this be less the case for the link between extensional operant analysis and the personal level of analysis than for that between physiology and that level? A totally biological theory of behavior would still not be able, Dennett claims, to account for *what the animal is doing* in the sense that what it is doing is looking for the food. Intentional ascription simply describes what a purely extensional theory would describe, nothing more, but in a different way. This different way may be useful to the physiologist, however. Neuroscience that does not view neural events as signals, reports, or messages can scarcely function at all. No purely biological logic can tell us why the rat knows which way to go for his food. Nor can any purely contextualistic (e.g., operant) logic reveal this in the absence of some sort of "Dennettian overlay." In neither case does the proposed intentional ascription detract from the extensional version of events but adds an interpretation that provides greater intuitive understanding of the system. Hence, the sub-personal level is coterminous with that of an extensional science such as physiology, which is mechanistic in the explanations it provides.

However, I have argued that intentional explanation simply *does not belong at this level* and that we cannot add content to this level without violating its integrity as a conventionally scientific (i.e., extensional) approach to theory. We may need to make ascriptions of content, i.e., the attribution of intentional idioms that make certain behaviors of the organism intelligible—pain, for instance, or other emotional activity. And we are entitled to do this when extensional modes of explanation no longer suffice. But such addition of content is at the personal level of explanation. This is the sole level at which the experience of pain, the holding of desires and beliefs, and perceiving can be comprehended. There is a sharp epistemological dichotomy here between the personal and sub-personal levels of explanation: at one of which it is appropriate to include intentional explanation, the other serving as a basis for legitimately doing so but remaining intact as an extensional level of understanding. The guiding principle by which content is added is evolutionary logic: the process of natural selection that produced the findings identified at the level of physiology (or other science that treats sub-personal events and processes) must provide the logic by which activities that are proposed in order to explain or predict the behavior of the whole organism. But being constrained by extensional science is not the same as adding content at its level of operation and relevance.

Bibliography

Dennett, D. C. (1969). *Content and consciousness*. London: Routledge and Kegan Paul.

Dennett, D. C. (1978). *Brainstorms*. Montgomery: Bradford.

Dennett, D. C. (1987). *The intentional stance*. Cambridge, MA: MIT Press.

Dennett, D. C. (1991a). *Consciousness explained*. London: Penguin Books.

Dennett, D. C. (1996). *Kinds of minds: Towards an understanding of consciousness*. London: Weidenfeld and Nicholson.

Foxall, G. R. (1999b). The contextual stance. *Philosophical Psychology, 12*, 25–46.

Foxall, G. R. (2004). *Context and cognition: Interpreting complex behavior*. Reno: Context Press.

Foxall, G. R. (2015c). Consumers in context: The BPM research program. London/New York: Routledge

Freeman, A. (Ed.). (2006). *Consciousness and its place in nature*. Exeter: Imprint Academic.

McGinn, C. (2004). *Consciousness and its objects*. Oxford: Oxford University Press.

Russell, B. (1912). *The problems of philosophy*. London: Home University Library.

Skinner, B. F. (1945). The operational analysis of psychological terms. *Psychological Review, 52*, 270–277.

Skinner, B. F. (1974). *About behaviorism*. New York: Knopf.

Steward, H. (2012). *A metaphysics for freedom*. Oxford: Oxford University Press.

Strawson, G. (2006). Realistic monism. In R. Freeman (Ed.), *Consciousness and its place in nature* (pp. 3–31). Exeter: Imprint Academic.

6

Intentional Psychologies

Introduction

The discussion of ascribing intentionality leads to consideration of Dennett's (1987) intentional stance as a means of generating a first approximation of the behavior of an intentional system by treating it in an idealized manner as a utility maximizer that has the intentionality apt to it given its circumstances. This somewhat rough and ready initial analysis needs to be borne out, if it is to count as a useful explanatory approximation, by an empirically substantiated cognitive account of how humans make decisions. In Dennett's formulation this entails the devising of a sub-personal cognitive psychology: in the Intentional Behaviorist formulation it is a matter of devising both micro- and macro-cognitive psychologies that show how the intentionality assumed in the Intentional Interpretation could have been generated. We thus arrive at a theoretical framework that can be used to interpret and explain consumer choice.

© The Editor(s) (if applicable) and The Author(s) 2016
G.R. Foxall, *Perspectives on Consumer Choice*,
DOI 10.1057/978-1-137-50121-9_6

Three Intentional Psychologies

Dennett's (1981) distinction among three *kinds* of intentional psychology, is based on the argument that folk psychology (the first kind of intentional psychology) provides a source of the other two—*intentional systems theory* (IST) and *sub-personal cognitive psychology* (SubPCP) which play important roles in psychological explanation. Folk psychology provides a nonspecific and unhelpful causal theory of behavior. Folk psychology, moreover, is abstract: the desires and beliefs it employs are not necessarily components of the "internal behavior-causing system" to which they are attributed. Beliefs are concepts like that of center of gravity; the calculations to which the concept leads are akin to those involving a parallelogram of forces rather than cogs and levers. Folk psychology is therefore instrumentalist rather than realistic in the sense that most realists would require. For Dennett, "people really do have beliefs and desires, on my version of folk psychology, just the way they really have centers of gravity and the earth has an Equator" (Dennett 1987, p. 52). Following Reichenbach he employs the ideas of *abstracta* which are "calculation-bound entities or logical constructs" and *illata* which are "posited theoretical entities" (p. 53). Folk psychology uses but does not clearly distinguish the logical constructs that are *abstracta* and the causally interacting *illata*, but Dennett proposes refining it by devising two theories: "one strictly abstract, idealizing, holistic, instrumentalistic – pure intentional systems theory – and the other a concrete, microtheoretic science of the actual realization of those intentional systems – what I will call sub-personal cognitive psychology" (p. 57).

Each of the two additional intentional psychologies Dennett proposes rests integrally on one or other of these types of concept. IST draws upon the notions of belief and desire but provides them with a more technical meaning than they receive in folk psychology. It is a whole-person psychology, dealing with "...the prediction and explanation from belief—desire profiles of the actions of whole systems... The *subject* of all the intentional attributions is the whole system (the person, the animal, or even the corporation or nation rather than any of its parts...)" (Dennett 1987, p. 58). Intentional systems theory is a competence theory in that it specifies the functional requirements of the system without going on to speculate as to what form they might take. The necessity of this general level theory is that of providing an account of intelligence, meaning, reference, or representation. Intentional systems theory is blind to the internal structure of the system. Akin to decision theory and game theory, it is "similarly abstract, normative, and couched in intentional language" (p. 58) and, while it uses the common terms beliefs and desires, it endues them with technical meaning. IST deals with the system as a whole, instrumentally, and is not concerned with how the system is structured to implement the mechanisms that realize the system's behavior. But "there must be some way in which the internal processes of the system mirror the complexities of the Intentional Interpretation, or its success would be a miracle" (p. 60). This is the task of SubPCP, a performance theory, charged with explaining how the brain can be both a semantic engine, concerned with determining what stimulus inputs mean, and a syntactic engine, a neurophysiological mechanism which does no more than distinguish inputs according to their physical character. So, how *does* the brain get semantic meaning from syntax? Before examining this question, it is useful to look a little more closely at the *abstracta-illata distinction*.

"Intentionally Characterized"

Abstracta are calculation-bound: they are the concepts necessary in order to make the calculation work, the theory account for the observation. This does not mean that they are not real in some sense (Dennett 1991b). *Illata*, by contrast, are concrete: electrons, neurons, satellites, for example. Centers of gravity and the Equator are *abstracta*-type constructs for which we can work out necessary properties like where they are or what they do by reference to what we know about *illata*. Intentional states are *abstracta* but not *illata*: they do not literally inhabit people's heads. But *illata* as Dennett conceives the concept are a little more than electrons, neurons, and satellites: in SubPCP, *illata* are "intentionally characterized" elements (especially when they are parts of neurophysiological systems). And, while electrons are *illata*, a piece of magnetized iron contains no magnetic state existing within itself. When we talk about the iron's "magnetic condition," this is an *abstractum*. All that exist in the piece of metal are atoms of iron. Having a belief is like this. Being an "intentionally characterized" neuron is said by Dennett to be more concrete, to constitute a variable that can play a part in psychological theory and experiment.

The capacity of *abstracta* to interrelate, predict, and partly explain behavior itself suggests some underlying mechanism to which intentional systems theory does not on principle address itself. Any intentional system of interest would surely have a complex internal structure and chances are this will be found to resemble closely the instrumental Intentional Interpretation. Hence, SubPCP is tasked with explaining the brain as a syntactic engine (as opposed to the task of IST which is to explain it as a semantic engine). A person who has only been a passenger in a car might pursue such an approach to a theory how the engine works by conjecturing that it must have a means of generating motive power or, even, that it must be capable of transforming linear movement into rotary. "Motive power" and "transformation" are, at this stage, no more than highly abstract notions that point to the more specific parts out of which the engine and other apparatus within the car must be constituted, *abstracta*. This theory, highly abstract as it is, could still lead to predictions such as that a car without such means of power and transformation would not move.

Mixing, Merging, and Flipping

Let us return to the question of how the brain derives semantic meaning from syntactical mechanics. Syntax is not a determinant of semantics; so the brain cannot accomplish this task. But Dennett claims it can *approximate* this impossible task by *mimicking* the behavior of the impossible object (the semantic engine). It capitalizes on similarities between "structural regularities – of the environment and of its own internal states and operations – and semantic types" (Dennett 1987, p. 61). An animal needs to *know* when it has finished feeding but it has to settle for a sensation in its throat and a stretched stomach to signal this since these mechanical operations usually accompany its actual goal. The purpose of sub-personal cognitive psychology is to formulate and evaluate models of how nature assembles these near-enough activities.

There are difficulties, I think, with Dennett's using the word "approximates" which implies *"almost is."* It might be better to emphasize that the syntax of the brain *correlates with* the semantic meaning we ascribe, but this might not go far enough for Dennett. The problem with taking physical entities like neurons and giving them an intentional characterization is that the resulting construct is located at the sub-personal level of exposition. This is just a means of seeming to find the bridging concept of which McGinn (2004) speaks but it could also be interpreted as mental sleight of hand. It is the notion of "almost" or "just" that Dennett uses to smuggle in the idea that things are agents that is disconcerting. The use of intentional language to describe the functions of inanimate objects softens us up for the conclusion that they are intentional systems and then that they are agential. A thermostat, for instance, whose designer augments it with additional functions, "chooses the boiler fuel, purchases it from the cheapest and most reliable dealer, checks the weather stripping, and so forth" (Dennett 1987, p. 30). Dennett's conclusion is that the feature-enhancement of the thermostat enables us to attribute an increasingly sophisticated semantic characterization of the system, at least in practical if not principled terms.

Elton (2003) conducts an examination of Dennett's methodology, in which he characterizes this as the conclusion that "cunningly constructed mechanistic devices just can exhibit the powers of agents, such as sensitivity to reasons" (Elton 2003, p. 83). Although they do this in "a partial and limited way," it is nevertheless "a brute fact that, by close examination of cases, we can come to see." Moreover, we can overcome our bafflement at how this is so by "flipping" between the intentional stance and the design or physical stance. Dennett's strategy, he points out, involves taking the intentional stance toward physical systems and "by switching from the physical or design stance and back to the intentional stance, we come to see how an intentional system, an agent, can be made out of nothing more than correctly arranged mechanistic parts" (pp. 84–5). Elton admits that while many will see this as a deeply suspect methodology based on fancy rhetoric he is not one of them; he admits however that Dennett's approach is highly contestable. Indeed, it is difficult to see it otherwise. It is, of course, a sign of mental agility to be able to view facts normally thought of from the perspective of one stance from the point of view of another, and this might well lead to conceptual block-busting as new ways of looking at old puzzles suggest solutions to problems that would otherwise be intractable. "Intentionally characterized" physical systems are not the bridging concepts that would be required to overcome the mind-body problem. At any one time, we are using either a physical stance or an intentional stance depiction of the mechanical system that is the thermostat. The design stance does not accomplish this either since it is merely the intentional stance applied to the desires and beliefs of the designer of a particular system.

Both thermostats and robots can be described in intentional language so that we think of them as choosing and seeking but using such language does not make the machine an intentional system. It is unlikely that we can even predict such systems from the intentional stance with greater accuracy than knowing the designer's intentions would allow. The designer is, after all, the person who does the choosing and programming.

The situation does not improve when Dennett specifies the function of SubPCP. It is he says to construct and then test models of activities such as pattern recognition or stimulus generalization, concept learning, expectation, learning, goal-directed behavior, problem-solving "that not only produce a simulacrum of genuine content-sensitivity, but that do this in ways demonstrably like the way people's brains do it, exhibiting the same powers and the same vulnerabilities to deception, overload, and confusion. It is here that we will find out good theoretical entities, our useful *illata*…They will be characterized as events with content, bearing information, signaling this and ordering that" (Dennett 1987, p. 63).

Indispensable as a competence theory is, there has to be some underlying internal structure that accounts for the capacity of the various abstracta that are the components of intentional systems theory to predict systemic behavior at the personal level so well. Discovering this structure and its workings is the task of the third kind of intentional psychology: sub-personal cognitive psychology, the task of which consists in "[d]iscovering the constraints on design and implementation variation, and demonstrating how particular species and individuals in fact succeed in realizing intentional systems" (Dennett 1987, p. 60). The task of the brain in IST, then, is semantic: it must decipher what its stimulus inputs mean and then respond with appropriate behavior. But to the physiologist the brain is no more than a *syntactic* engine: it "discriminate[s] its inputs by their structural, temporal, and physical features and let[s] its entirely mechanical activities be governed by these 'syntactic' features of its inputs" (Dennett 1987, p. 61). The necessity of bridging this gap, of explaining how the mechanistic brain extricates meaning from physical stimuli requires that these physical, and especially neurophysiological, entities be intentionally characterized. This is Dennett's means of bridging the divide between mind and body. *Illata* are his bridging concepts.

The process of intentional characterization that forms the essential component of the reversals that permit a naturalistic explanation of the behavior revealed by IST entails more than flipping between the intentional and physical stances. It requires also flipping between levels of exposition, from the personal to the sub-personal and back, and between the system under explanation and the environment in which it is operating.

> In order to give the *illata* these labels, in order to maintain any Intentional Interpretation of their operation at all, the theorist must always keep glancing outside the system, to see what normally produces the configuration he is describing, what effects the system's responses normally have on the environment, and what benefit normally accrues to the whole system from this activity... The alternative of ignoring the external world and its relations to the internal machinery... is not really psychology at all, but just at best abstract neurophysiology – pure internal syntax with no hope of a semantic interpretation. Psychology 'reduced' to neurophysiology in this fashion would not be psychology, for it would not be able to provide an explanation of the regularities it is psychology's particular job to explain: the reliability with which 'intelligent' organisms can cope with their environments and thus prolong their lives. Psychology can, and should, work toward an account of the physiological foundations of psychological processes, not by eliminating psychological or intentional characterizations of those processes, but by exhibiting how the brain implements the intentionally characterized performance specifications of sub-personal theories. (Dennett 1978, p. 64)

Dennett's (1969) apparent establishment of a clear distinction between the personal and sub-personal levels is blurred by the claim that we must be constantly "flipping" between the two so that we can ascribe content to entities that belong emphatically at the sub-personal level. The sheer ingenuity of this move does not exempt it from being a leap too far.

Shifting Emphases

We should now take stock of Dennett's altering conception and attribution of importance to the distinction of personal and sub-personal levels of explanation. Four distinct phases are apparent in his thought. The first is the so-called categorical distinction (held in varying forms by Davidson 1980; Davies 2000; Elton 2000; Gardner 2000; Hornsby 2000) which maintains the analytical difference between these levels of explanation that Dennett set out in 1969. Dennett here holds to a strict personal/ sub-personal distinction, using the latter to ascribe intentionality at the personal level. He also maintains a strict difference between extensional and intentional sciences, claiming that both are necessary. The role of behavior appears important here because it is to its explanation that the ascription of intentionality is ostensibly directed. But it receives no explicit definition or analysis: it is taken as a given, albeit an important one.

In the 1970s, and certainly by the early 1980s, Dennett's criterion for the ascription of content changed from one that was explicitly justifiable on biological grounds to that of the predictability of behavior. This progression, by means of the introduction of the intentional stance, marks the abandonment of the personal level as a seriously entertained analytic category. The distinction between personal and sub-personal, crucial to the originally argued basis for the legitimate ascription of content, is lost as the intentional stance comes to be applied to sub-personal units in order to predict them. We shall shortly see that the mereological fallacy, inherent in Dennett's reasoning, rules out such a move, despite the stand on realism that Dennett takes. Behavior is still important because its predictability is a criterion of the legitimate ascription of the mental. But it still receives no additional analysis nor yet definition.

The third phase comes with Dennett's attempt to include cognitive functioning at the sub-personal level: the so-called sub-personal cognitive psychology that he has made the center of his philosophy of psychology.

The sub-personal that is now the focus of attention is that of an intentional level of analysis that spans the divide between neurology and the personal. The categorical distinction is being further eroded. Behavior now is more sidelined than before. But is the notion of sub-personal cognition sustainable? Or does cognition belong at the personal level?

The final phase (so far) is Dennett's explanation of consciousness. By now any suggestion that the personal is important appears to have been lost—though Elton disagrees—as the quest is for the heterophenomenological interpretation of behavior at the third-personal level. But Elton claims that consciousness can only be entertained at the personal level. Behavior … is presumably important again because it is the basis of heterophenomenological attribution of the content of consciousness. But what are the rules for legitimately ascribing content now? It seems that Dennett has lapsed into the very loose mode of intentional attribution that *Content and Consciousness* was to guard against!

The shift in emphasis is apparent to other commentators, too. Hornsby (2000), for instance, detects a subtle difference between Dennett's (1969) treatment of the personal and sub-personal levels and his later usage which inheres in his (1978, p. 154) argument that the behavior of the person as a whole is the outcome of the interactive behavior of its various subsystems (Hornsby 2000, pp. 16–17). This is a departure from his earlier insistence that to move to the sub-personal level, that is, to the operation of the central and peripheral nervous systems, is to leave behind the personal level of explanation of sensations, intentionality, and behavior. Hornsby argues that this is inconsistent with the proscription on using sub-personal level findings to understand the personal level. Why-questions about the behavior of an actor in an environment can be answered only at the personal level. It is Dennett's later claim that the program of sub-personal cognitive psychology is to show how the physicalist findings of sub-personal extensional science can be used to interpret a fully realized intentional system operating at the personal level that is the problem. She seeks, moreover, to maintain the distinction between personal and sub-personal levels of explanation by arguing that intentional phenomena are real at the levels of persons but merely as-if constructions at the sub-personal level (Hornsby 2000, pp. 20–21). The attraction of this clear distinction is that it maintains the independence of the personal level as a basis of explanation but permits the intentional stance to be operated at the sub-personal level for purposes of predicting the behavior of subsystems.

Elton (2003) also notes the progressive deemphasizing of the personal/sub-personal distinction in Dennett's work. While it is "central" to Dennett writing in 1969, and "recurs more or less intact" in his 1978 book *Brainstorms*, it loses its prominence thereafter. Elton remarks that Dennett speaks of the sub-personal level but neglects the personal and he cites Dennett's "Three Kinds of Intentional Psychology" paper (1981/1987) in support. Even speaking of the sub-personal had dropped by 1991 when Dennett published *Consciousness Explained* (see Elton 2003, p. 110). It is possible, as Elton proposes, that although the terminology has been abandoned, the spirit has not. But I believe there is more than a change of emphasis in Dennett's use of the intentional stance at the sub-personal level.

It is also the case that Dennett's use of intentional language evinces subtle differences at the personal and sub-personal levels. A limit to the extent to which sub-personal entities can be described intentionally is imposed by the capacity to describe the entire system in idealized intentional terms (Dennett 1978). A capacity to believe *that p* which is attributed to a sub-personal component of the system is justified only if the rational, idealized system has already been shown to believe *that p* on the basis of this belief's having been ascribed to it as consistent with its history and present circumstances and to have been found predictively true of the system at this personal level.

The possibility of describing sub-personal elements agentially and intentionally also is justified by the idea of homuncular functionalism. Taking the intentional stance toward the task of designing a computer to solve a particular problem, the designer can characterize the machine intentionally by saying that it "can solve that problem." The design of the computer requires the planning of subsystems that have their own intentionally characterized task, and these have subsystems or homunculi that have their own intentionally characterized tasks to perform. The resulting finite regress continues until the homunculi have such simple jobs to do, like adding and subtracting, that they can be supplanted by mechanical devices. On either of the criteria for the applicability of the intentional stance discussed above, Dennett's idea of homuncular functionalism would fail. It is doubtful that the physical entities that intervene between the personal level and the obviously stupid molecular level can be intentional in Dennett's sense. These entities would certainly fail on the second criterion which confines the use of the intentional stance to intensional beings. But do we want to draw the intentional circle as tightly as that? Would they also fail on the first criterion which proposes that the intentional stance can be applied only to entities whose behavior cannot be explained more appropriately by any other stance? Clearly, these entities are physical and therefore ultimately explicable and predictable in terms of the physical stance. On the argument that anything that can be explained and predicted from the physical stance does not qualify to be explained/predicted by the intentional stance, there is no reason to apply the intentional stance to them. We have no reason to speak of them in terms of their desiring and believing other than as a simple way of speaking. Agreed, this could be a useful *façon de parler* but it is hardly a scientific explanation.

The Mereological Fallacy

It seems preferable to keep the personal, sub-personal, and indeed the super-personal quite distinct in terms of the kinds of language that can be used at each. This conclusion is borne out by what he has written in response to Bennett and Hacker's (2003; Bennett 2007) argument that the intentional stance when assumed in regard to the sub-personal rests on the "mereological fallacy." The mereological fallacy is the attribution to the parts of a system of processes, events, or behaviors that properly belong only at the level of the system as a whole. Dennett's reply indicates both the equivocation and the confusion. On the one hand, he is at pains to point out that, in *Content and Consciousness*, he advocated the personal/sub-personal distinction being made in such a way as to maintain their separateness with respect to the appropriateness of ascribing intentionality. On the other, he makes a plea for the as-if use of intentional language to redescribe what is already covered by the extensional language of neuroscience. If this is the basis of his additional heuristic overlay, then there can be no objection, but it is essential to point out that such reinterpretation belongs to another level of discourse and explanation than the extensional, that it belongs in fact at the personal level.

Summing-Up

Before launching an alternative to Dennett's proposal I should like to summarize the points of agreement and disagreement. Let me say at the outset, however, that none of this should be interpreted as wanton criticism of Dennett's work, which embodies one of the most considered attempts to overcome the problems identified above. I cannot escape the thought, however, that it is essentially a competence—rather than a performance—theory. It specifies the conditions a conceptual analysis of the relationships between the sub-personal and personal levels of exposition would have to meet. But, in its reliance on flipping between stances and its attachment of significance to "almost as if" definitions and associations, I believe it to fall short as yet of a means of testing cognitive theories by means of *illata*.

First, Dennett's framework and that which I shall propose have in common an emphasis on intentionality as linguistic, a means of distinguishing one type of language from another, and consequently one kind of explanation from another, rather than a distinction between the mental and the physical.

Second, there is common recognition that a scientific analysis based on intentionality shows that it is only ascribable. There are ways of getting at the first-personal expedience of desires, beliefs, emotions, and perceptions through heterophenomenology (Dennett 1991a, b; Foxall 2016e) but this provides third-personal texts for analysis by trained investigators. From this scientific purview, it is the case that all there is to an entity's being an intentional system is its amenability to another's understanding, explaining, or predicting its behavior by means of the ascription of desires and beliefs. But this point is not incompatible with the assumption that people actually have desires and beliefs in some sense. We all have knowledge by acquaintance, though this cannot enter into scientific analysis, and may or may not be causal. Without knowledge by acquaintance, knowledge by description would be impossible.

Third, there is agreement on the necessity of a two-part methodological strategy for psychological explanation, and there is no questioning the fact that I am here following Dennett's lead, albeit critically. In Intentional Behaviorism, the first stage of psychological explanation does not take precisely the form of IST, but the initial stage or its psychological treatment of consumer activity, Intentional Interpretation, is broadly similar in intention and procedure. The subsequent stage of psychological explanation, Cognitive Interpretation, is rather distinct from Dennett's SubPCP, however.

As Dennett (1978, 1987) argues, the necessary first stage in building a cognitive theory of behavior is to treat the individual as an agent who acts rationally and whose desires and beliefs can be reconstructed by considering what the idealized system "ought" to do given its temporal, physical, and social circumstances. In Intentional Interpretation the system is treated as though it were economically rational. The idealized account must be testable. In the case of IST, this is through the construction of *illata* which can enter into psychological theories for examination; in the process, the strategy moves from a competence theory to a performance theory that contains hybrid variables. In the case of Intentional Behaviorism, it is by seeking to show that cognitive processing theory gives rise to the beliefs and desires that the idealized account projects. This is another layer of competence-theory testing. Performance theories are the province of the extensional sciences of neurophysiology and behaviorology.

There is full agreement, therefore, that the competence theory of idealized theory of behavior requires grounding. But the second stage of theory development (entailing in Intentional Behaviorism the presentation of micro- and macro-cognitive psychologies, MiCP and MaCP) and Dennett's SubPCP are parallel research programs. They will not converge because there is no place for the idea of *illata* in Intentional Behaviorism, which views the testing of the models that form MiCP and MaCP as the province of neuroscience and extensional behavioral science.

A Methodology for Psychological Explanation

A Two-Stage Approach

The idea of a two-stage procedure proposed by Dennett has much to commend it. It allows, first, a quick assessment of a system in order to test whether it is an intentional system, and this identifies the aspects of the Intentional Interpretation that require justification at a more general level of explanation. However, while sharing this much, the scheme I propose here differs in three important respects from Dennett's. First, the criteria for determining what is an intentional system differ from those Dennett suggests. That is, the range of applicability of the concept differs from his more inclusive conception. Second, the criterion of predictability is not employed to determine whether a system is intentional. Dennett's intentional stance approach states that any system that can be predicted by the attribution to it of desires and beliefs appropriate to its history and current setting is an intentional system. But prediction does not constitute explanation and it is explanation that we require from the intentional level of exposition. And, third, the relationship between the Intentional Interpretation/IST stage and that of Cognitive Interpretation/SubPCP differs between the two proposals.

Range of Applicability

Dennett, as we have seen, defines an intentional system as an entity the behavior of which can be predicted by ascribing to it the desires and beliefs it ought to have given its circumstantial position and goals. Any system that can be so predicted is an intentional system and all there is to having desires and beliefs is to be predictable via their idealized ascription. The viewpoint from which such ascription and prediction occurs is *the intentional stance*. While adopting this general strategy, I would like to confine the range of entities to which the status of intentional system can be attributed.

Intensionality is principally a linguistic phenomenon that consists in sentences in the form of propositional attitudes that embody *aboutness* or content. Such sentences do not permit the substitution of codesignatives without losing their truth value; they display also intensional inexistence in that the objects represented by their content exist within the attitude expressed; and, if the objects to which the content refers do not exist, the truth value of the sentence is not affected. In addition, it is impossible to translate intentional sentences into extensional sentences without changing their meaning, principally through the addition of information. It seems neglectful of these considerations if we fail to take them into account when delineating what can be regarded as an intentional system.

We might therefore wish to confine the capacity to be an intentional system to entities that can display the linguistic ingenuity required to reflect an understanding of these "rules of intentionality." The argument would be that only systems that can display an underlying comprehension of intentionality via their linguistic dexterity could qualify as intentional systems. However, this would be unduly restrictive since it would confine intentionality to humans who were sufficiently mature and intelligent to cope with linguistic usages of this kind. Behaviors that do not in the first instance appear to be linguistic bear at least one of the defining characteristics of intentionality (namely, *aboutness* or content) and perform functions similar or identical to those of intentional language: the waggle dances of honey bees are a conspicuous example. A less confining understanding of intentionality than specialized linguistic capability is therefore justified.

What we are trying to do in setting criteria for the ascription of intentionality is to divine intellectual ability to understand and appreciate the intricacies of intentional usage and the meanings it conveys when incorporated into social intercourse (usually with conspecifics). One criterion of this would be the ability to employ language in such a way as to demonstrate this linguistic ingenuity. A less constrictive criterion is the capacity to behave intentionally, perhaps through gestures and other forms of symbolic behavior: even though these are not linguistic in the narrow sense, they constitute verbal behavior insofar as they are socially mediated communications. This criterion works well in a quite distinct approach to verbal behavior, that of Skinner (1957) in which gestural behaviors are deemed to be verbal because of their function. Adopting this characterization of intentionality, we would include the behaviors of pre-literate infants and some nonhuman animals. *We would be confining the designation "intentional system" to entities that can demonstrably employ the intentional stance for themselves, that can demonstrably function as agents rather than pre-programmed machines.* This would include some animals, in addition to by far the majority of humans. It would, however, exclude machines such as robots and software such as chess-playing computer programs.

Predictability

Any claims that machines or programs might have to being intentional systems stem from the ability to predict their behavior by treating them as such. However, on a pragmatic level, there is seldom anything one can say about the "desires and beliefs" of those systems that Dennett maintains can be predicted in this way that is not obvious already from knowing how they were designed and what they are supposed to do. Translating this information, gained from the design stance, into the simplistic notions of the intentional-stance-so-deployed adds nothing or next to nothing. If intentionality is to be detected in the case of designed artifacts, it is the intentionality of the designer. What was he or she trying to achieve? What information did he or she base the design on? The designer must, therefore, also be an intentional system in the sense in which I have defined it. It is his or her beliefs and desires, embodied in the designing of the artifact, that we must discern in order to predict the machine or its software.

To imagine that we can predict specifics of behavior from the kind of qualitative ascription of desires and beliefs that are open to us as hetero-phenomenologists is an unfounded assumption. Except in the grossest terms we cannot so predict. By gross, I mean coarse-grained and therefore liable to be trivial. Anything more detailed or important is likely to be unpredictable. Brand choice is the essence of what academic marketing is concerned to explain (Foxall et al. 2007). Yet, even so basic an aspect of consumer behavior as a consumer's brand choice on the next shopping occasion is generally unpredictable, though we can predict his or her product choice reasonably well, and we can predict relative brand choice over a longer period. Gross prediction may suffice for folk psychology but it is hardly a suitable criterion for either the attribution of the status of intentional systems to entities, or the explanation of the behavior of an intentional system. An intentional consumer almost by definition has brand attitudes, yet they are poor predictors of their next behavior except in the relatively rare cases of sole purchasers. Prediction is possible in the closed setting of the operant laboratory or other closed setting. But it is notoriously difficult in the case of the immediate circumstances of the open settings represented by supermarkets. This, after all, is our motivation for moving to the intentional level of exposition because we seek something over and above the operant paradigm when the consumer's behavior entails misrepresentation. Moreover, the kinds of prediction of consumer behavior we are likely to be in a position to make are somewhat trivial.

Moreover, we have no means of delineating the intentionality we should ascribe thus appropriately for an individual. We can, using the multiattribute models such as the theory of reasoned action and the theory of planned behavior (Fishbein and Ajzen 2010), along with suitable additional variables, arrive at verbal constructions of the beliefs, attitudes, and intentions that predict behavior of a large aggregate of respondents. But this is not the same as predicting an individual's behavior from his or her intentionality even if it is ascribed on the basis of the rigorous methods provided by Ajzen, Fishbein, and others. The multiattribute models predict aggregate behavior to the extent they do by evening out the effects of unpredictable and indeed unknowable-in-advance situational interventions that occur during the time that elapses between the expression of intentionality and the opportunity to behave in a corresponding manner. This hardly corresponds to the predictive evidence we would require before assigning the status of an intentional system as Dennett proposes.

The function of the Intentional Interpretation is to explain the behavior of the consumer in intentional terms, treating him or her as an idealized system and deducing his or her intentionality from what we know of his or her history and current position. We can do this to some extent on the basis of what we know of him or her from the use of the extensional model. In order to specify the intentionality of the consumer we also need to generate an intentional or action perspective on consumer choice within the BPM which delineates which aspects of intentionality belong where in the model and their likely effects on behavior. In explaining extensionally the behavior of the previously encountered consumer who tries a new brand (E) of a product category, we assume that he or she seeks to maximize utilitarian and informational reinforcement within a budget constraint. The consumer's intentionality can then be outlined as follows. The consumer *desires* to maximize utilitarian and informational reinforcement, *believes* that using a subset of the available brands that compose the product category will achieve this, *perceives* brand E to be similar in function to A, B, C, and D, and *expects* to maximize the emotional outcomes of reinforcing consequences (pleasure, arousal, and dominance) by trialing E, since if this comes up to scratch it may either improve the overall quality of the consideration set (perhaps by dropping a low performing brand) or enhance the efficiency of the set by giving another choice, enabling the consumer, for instance, to buy the by-now familiar E when it is the cheapest available brand.

Now, this is clearly an *explanation* of consumer's behavior. It is not a prediction; predicting these things could be accomplished on the basis of what we know as a commonplace about consumers. This explanation is based on the pattern of behavior that the extensional model has identified as standard—that is, maximization of utilitarian and informational reinforcement, formation of a consideration set, purchase predominantly within this set, evaluation in practice of the brands in the consideration set, readjustment of the consideration set, etc. It has to be consistent with the general intentional or action perspective on consumer choice, which has to be pre-specified. We know from that that consumers add to and subtract from their consideration sets from time to time. We can predict when they are likely to do this from noting when a new brand comes on to the market. The problem for an extensional explanation of trialing E is that the consumer has no learning history with respect to this brand. Even if we note that he or she sees advertisements describing this brand as having the same product attributes that are the functional minimum for all brands in the product category, we have to explain how it is that he or she comes to perceive this brand as potentially equivalent and is willing to try it. This is an explanation rather than a prediction. Predictions are going to be trivial, very coarse-grained, pretty obvious from extensional accounts. Explanation is the better criterion. So… how do we test this? We cannot test an *Intentional Interpretation* directly for its elements are not such that they can enter into an experimental or correlational analysis. We would use the extensional sciences for testing but it is unlikely they would add much in this case that we do not know. So that would be a fatuous prediction. We have to evaluate (perhaps not test) the Intentional Interpretation by showing that it is consistent with cognitive theory. However, the Cognitive Interpretation cannot make assumptions of intentional functioning that are not borne out at the level of the Intentional Interpretation.

That it is extremely difficult, perhaps impossible, to predict something novel on the basis of an Intentional Interpretation that is not already either known to be true from our extensional knowledge of the situation or as easily predictable from that knowledge is illustrated also by the case of schedule insensitivity mentioned earlier. Once the schedule has been changed, we might for instance predict that a player will quickly form new beliefs and desires at this stage that reflect the new contingencies. In fact this is not the case since players' behavior does not come into line with the new contingencies so quickly. We might then predict that the player will change his or her behavior pattern only after the beliefs carried over from the first set of contingencies are manifestly inefficient. That is, we turn to the prediction that he or she will continue to play under the strategy determined by his or her decision processes formed in the earlier phase of the experiment until losing consistently makes him or her realize that this strategy is wrong, pay attention to the new contingencies, and change decision strategy. All this is mental. If this proposed mental activity could be used to formulate a novel prediction of behavior the upshot would be a rigorous test of the Intentional Interpretation. The problem is that each changing "prediction" is simply chosen to conform to a pattern of behavior that has just been observed rather than one that will come into being. At each stage, however, we are very usefully *reexplaining* behavior in intentional terms because there is no reliable input from the stimulus field to allow us to account for the behavior in terms of extensional behavioral science.

The Cognitive Interpretation

If the Intentional Interpretation cannot be substantiated on the basis of predictions that follow from it, nor by a sub-personal cognitive psychology that conveniently straddles the personal and sub-personal levels of exposition, on what basis is it to be critically examined? One possibility is the reconstruction of desires and beliefs that would be consistent with observed behavior. By showing that this intentionality (a) is consistent with the individual's behavior given his or her history and situation, and (b) plausibly underpins the observed behavior pattern in a rational individual, we might argue that we had adduced some "evidence" for the model. Ensuring that the reconstruction is consistent with what we know of the behavior through neuroscience and behaviorology would inspire additional confidence in the Intentional Interpretation. However, while reconstruction of this kind forms part of the necessary method of formulating the Intentional Interpretation, it is for this very reason impermissible as a test of the Intentional Interpretation. Critical comparison of the Intentional Interpretation with what we know through the extensional sciences of the behavior in question amounts in any case to post-diction rather than prediction of the behavior.

Another possibility involves comparison of the *Intentional Interpretation* (Stage One of the psychological explanation) with a *Cognitive Interpretation* (Stage Two). This subsequent stage entails examination of a theory of decision making, not formulated by the author of the Intentional Interpretation but an independent theory, which we can examine in order to determine whether the intentionality ascribed in the course of the Intentional Interpretation could be likely to generate the desires, beliefs, emotions, and perceptions in terms of which the Intentional Interpretation proceeds. Such theories need to be multidisciplinary formulations that have strong empirical support and that convincingly link cognitive functioning with neurophysiological events and the effects of the stimulus field provided by the environment on behavior. In other words they must convincingly relate their explanations of what is occurring at the personal level to considerations that arise at the sub-personal and super-personal levels.

It is desirable, moreover, that the Intentional and Cognitive Interpretations, having been shown to be logically consistent (in the sense that the cognitive structure and functioning posited in the latter is capable of and likely to engender the desires, beliefs, emotions, and perceptions that form the intentionality assumed in the former), should lead to hypotheses that generate further empirical investigation.

Relationship Between the Stages

Dennett proposes the building first of an intentional systems theory (IST) of idealized behavior which is then substantiated by a sub-personal cognitive psychology (SubPCP) which shows how the behavior of the intentional system so described could be instantiated at the SubPCP level of causal influence. The SubPCP account is itself constrained by the intentional ascriptions made in the course of developing the competence-theory level IST: for instance, perception of certain aspects of the environment is not feasible in the course of constructing the sub-personal cognitive-psychological account if such perception has not been shown to be instrumental in predicting the behavior of the idealized intentional system. The SubPCP approach entails the devising of a performance theory based on *illata* which are capable of inclusion in scientific hypotheses. Although I appreciate the ingenuity of this approach, I have noted difficulties with the way in which it is implemented. The role of the Cognitive Interpretation in Intentional Behaviorism is therefore somewhat different.

First, the Cognitive Interpretation is a higher-order competence theory than the Intentional Interpretation. It is capable of explaining a much larger realm of intentionality than the Intentional Interpretation, and several alternative Intentional Interpretations might be justified in terms of a Cognitive Interpretation. Second, the Cognitive Interpretation remains a competence rather than a performance theory. Performance theories are provided by the extensional neurological and behavioral sciences. Third, the variables on which the Cognitive Interpretation is based are *abstracta*, albeit of a higher level than those involved in the Intentional Interpretation. Crucially, however, they do not purport to be *illata*. Fourth, Dennett assumes that only sub-personal cognitive psychology contributes to the substantiation of the idealized and rational system examined by IST. But this overlooks the super-personal cognitive psychology which also determines the validity of the Intentional Interpretation. It is true that operancy acts ultimately through neurophysiology but (a) we cannot know precisely how particular, say, reinforcing stimuli instantiate sub-personal neurophysiology, and (b) our knowledge of operancy is insufficient to allow us to make judgments about the implications of the Intentional Interpretation. Intentional Behaviorism explores the implications of sub-personal and super-personal influences on behavior in its bifurcation of the second stage of its explanatory system into micro-cognitive psychology (MiCP) which relates the Intentional Interpretation to neurophysiological concerns, and macro-cognitive psychology (MaCP) which relates it to operancy. Finally, the Cognitive Interpretation should provide an agenda for further extensional research.

Summing-Up

This approach to the explanation of behavior has several implications. First, it avoids the instrumentalism of which Dennett's adoption of the intentional stance has often been accused. Bechtel (1985) points out that Dennett invites us to see how the design of a system (in terms of SubPCP) might cause it to behave in a fashion consistent with its intentional construal (in IST). Bechtel argues that the power of Dennett's suggestion is reduced by his (Dennett's) taking an instrumentalist rather than a realist approach to mental phenomena. "Sub-personal analyses are to explain how a mechanism could perform *as* something intentional, that is, as something fully rational" (Bechtel 1985, p. 475).

However, the approach I suggest avoids the charge of instrumentalism. The existence of desires and beliefs is assumed on the basis of my personal subjective experience which I generalize to others on the basis of their behavior, especially verbal. I also assume that a rational system will behave consistently with its beliefs and desires. I cannot know the desires and beliefs of another system, but I can infer what they would be if I assume the system to which I attribute them is rational and if I know its history and current circumstances. Thus far, my intentional strategy, if not my ontological assumption, is that of Dennett, though I would confine its applicability as indicated while Dennett would apply it also to nonanimate systems like computer programs. Given my ontological assumption, my use of the strategy avoids instrumentalism.

Second, the proposed understanding of Intentional Interpretation confines the ascription of intentionality to the personal level. The use of the intentional stance is reserved for the prediction of the behavior of those whole beings that can display intentional behavior, be it linguistic or nonlinguistic. The intentional stance cannot be used at the sub-personal or super-personal level, treating the relevant entities as if they were intentional systems. There are other ways of predicting their behavior that are more precise. Neurons are not intentional systems. This has implications for some of Dennett's attributions of choice, freedom, consciousness, and agency to systems at the sub-personal level and, given his thesis of the accumulation of intentionality via the decreasing stupidity he infers of homunculi as they rise in the hierarchy of biological complexity, at the personal level, too.

Third, in instances such as playing a computer at chess or slot machine gambling, the player may take the intentional stance to predict how the machine or program will perform. But the inferred intentionality in question is that of the designer. The player may take the design stance toward the machine as an indication of how it will function and may use the information so gained to infer the motivations of the designer. The player may also treat the machine as though it were a person and speak of its goals (desires) and information (beliefs) as though it were a decision-making entity. But this is just everyday folk psychology; it is not a scientific stance adopted on the assumption that the system is rational and involving determining the system's history and current circumstances. The machine is known to have certain deign features that determine its behavior: its personification reflects a shorthand way of speaking rather than a scientific strategy.

Fourth, this proposed approach also avoids the mereological fallacy since it eliminates the ascription of states that can characterize only the system at the personal level to the sub-personal level (or for that matter the super-personal).

None of this is to automatically rule out the desirability of grounding cognitive theories of behavior in neurophysiological substrates. I am just not convinced that Dennett's proposed means of achieving this is justified since it involves mixing the languages of cognition and neurophysiology in what seems an ad hoc manner. For me, the idea of sub-personal cognitive psychology based on *illata* does not solve the mind-body problem: it just accentuates it. It is necessary, though, to try to overcome the impasse that McGinn (2004) speaks of rather than resting on the conclusions of the new mysterianism. The second stage of psychological explanation, Cognitive Interpretation, is a step in the direction of linking with neurophysiology, more tentative than Dennett's and not one that goes all the way to resolving the conceptual dichotomy.

Bibliography

Bechtel, W. (1985). Realism, instrumentalism, and the intentional stance. *Cognitive Science, 9*, 473–497.

Bennett, M. R. (2007). Neuroscience and philosophy. In M. Bennett, D. Dennett, P. Hacker, & J. Searle (Eds.), *Neuroscience and philosophy: Brain, mind, and language* (pp. 49–69). NY: Columbia University Press.

Bennett, M. R., & Hacker, P. M. S. (2003). *Philosophical foundations of neuroscience*. Oxford: Blackwell.

Davidson, D. (1980). *Essays on actions and events*. Oxford: Clarendon Press.

Davies, M. (2000). Persons and their underpinning. *Philosophical Explorations, 3*, 42–60.

Dennett, D. C. (1969). *Content and consciousness*. London: Routledge and Kegan Paul.

Dennett, D. C. (1978). *Brainstorms*. Montgomery: Bradford.

Dennett, D. C. (1981). Three kinds of intentional psychology. In R. Healy (Ed.), *Reduction, time and reality*. Cambridge: Cambridge University Press.

Dennett, D. C. (1987). *The intentional stance*. Cambridge, MA: MIT Press.

Dennett, D. C. (1991a). *Consciousness explained*. London: Penguin Books.

Dennett, D. C. (1991b). Real patterns. *Journal of Philosophy, 88*, 27–51.

Elton, M. (2000). Consciousness: Only at the personal level. *Philosophical Explorations, 3*, 25–40.

Elton, M. (2003). *Daniel Dennett: Reconciling science and our self-conception*. Cambridge: Polity.

Fishbein, M., & Ajzen, I. (2010). *Predicting and changing behavior*. New York: Psychology Press.

Foxall, G. R. (2016e). Consumer heterophenomenology. In G. R. Foxall (Ed.), *The Routledge companion to consumer behavior analysis* (pp. 417–430). London/New York: Routledge.

Foxall, G. R., Oliveira-Castro, J. M., James, V. K., & Schrezenmaier, T. C. (2007). *Brand choice in behavioral perspective*. London/New York: Palgrave Macmillan.

Gardner, S. (2000). Psychoanalysis and the personal/sub-personal distinction. *Philosophical Explorations, 3,* 96–119.

Hornsby, J. (2000). Personal and sub-personal: A defence of Dennett's early distinction. *Philosophical Explorations, 3,* 6–24.

McGinn, C. (2004). *Consciousness and its objects*. Oxford: Oxford University Press.

Skinner, B. F. (1957). *Verbal behavior*. New York: Century.

7

Consumer Choice as Action

Introduction

This chapter spells out the philosophy of explanation devised in Chapter 6 in the context of the psychological explanation of consumer choice. It works through the operations involved in Intentional Interpretation: the adoption of the intentional stance, treating the consumer as an intentional system, and assuming it to be a rational maximizer of utility. It goes on to describe the Behavioral Perspective Model in terms of an intentional depiction of consumer choice. In this perspective, the consumer situation is defined in intentional terms as comprising the consumer's desires, beliefs, emotions, and perceptions, and patterns of reinforcement and punishment are conceptualized as future payoffs and costs that the consumer mentally envisions.

The conceptualization of intentionally explained behavior as action rather than behavior has far-reaching implications for the nature of the consumer and of consumer choice. There are some commonalities with the agency incompatibilism (Steward 2012) which argues that the dogma of universal determinism that every happening in our lives was determined at the beginning of the universe cannot be true if some events

© The Editor(s) (if applicable) and The Author(s) 2016
G.R. Foxall, *Perspectives on Consumer Choice*,
DOI 10.1057/978-1-137-50121-9_7

remain "up-to-us." While determinism would leave no room for the future to be open, to be unsettled, there are aspects of our activities that are "up-to-us," even if they are only the timing of when they occur or their precise topography. Self-movement can be attributed only to a creature that can make itself move, and of such an entity we can make an owner-body distinction: indeed, the capacity to own one's body is the essence of agency. Since "there are things which can make their bodies move – i.e., agents—the future is open" (Steward 2012, p. 17). Such an entity must also have a mind—have certain mental predicates. It must be "up to" this entity what it does; such an entity must be capable of settling matters. Its capacity for action suggests its agency.

An Intentional Interpretation is proposed on the basis of the Continuum of Consumer Choice, which locates various modes of consumption according to the degree to which they entail discounting future rewards. Many of the modes of consumer behavior described in Chapter 3 in relation to the extensional perspective of the BPM are analyzed here in terms of intentionality. This depiction of consumer choice leads on to the Cognitive Interpretation which is the subject of Chapter 8.

Intentional Interpretation

When extensional language is not possible because the rules of behavioral syntax cannot be met (e.g., the required stimuli cannot be identified to third-person satisfaction), it is necessary to employ intentional language. In order to avoid undisciplined use of this mode of expression, it is necessary to establish guidelines for its deployment. The aim of Intentional Interpretation in the context of consumer behavior is the construction of a consumer situation defined in terms of the beliefs, desires, emotions, and perceptions of the individual *qua* consumer (the "intentional consumer situation") in order to make his or her behavior more intelligible, consistent with what is known of patterns of consumer choice via the extensional model. The procedure is a-ontological: there are no preconceptions as to whether consumers actually have in some sense the intentionality ascribed to them in order to make their behavior more comprehensible. This mirrors Dennett's instrumentalism.

The procedure for Intentional Interpretation follows the methodology that comprises the *principles of Intentional Interpretation* which is based on the following sequence: adopt the intentional stance, treat the consumer as an intentional system, and understand the system as ideally rational. It is then feasible to ascribe to the system the intentionality it should have given its history, current circumstances, and motivation.

Adopt the Intentional Stance

An intentional system is an entity the behavior of which can be explained *only* by the ascription to it of intentionality, principally beliefs, desires, emotions, and perceptions. An entity becomes an intentional system when all or some aspect of its behavior can be accounted for only by the intentional stance.

The intentional stance is the ascription of intentionality to an entity in order to explicate its behavior when the extensional stances have been exhausted in this endeavor. The explication of behavior in these terms ("intentional behavior") is undertaken in terms of the ascription of appropriate beliefs, desires, emotions, and perceptions to the individual. The ascribed intentionality must be consistent with the beliefs, desires, emotions, and perceptions that a rational individual who performed the observed behavior would hold or experience (Box 7.1).

Treat the Consumer as an Intentional System

Dennett's intentional systems theory (IST) portrays the system in an idealized fashion, as an optimally behaving organized structure to which we ascribe the desires and beliefs that such a system ought to have given its history and current circumstances. The intentional system I am proposing is essentially similar to Dennett's but it is possible in the case of Intentional Interpretation to be more specific about the behavior of the system. First, we can employ the findings of the extensional or behavioral perspective of the BPM to characterize the nature of the consumer-as-intentional-system, to refine our assumption about the nature of its

Box 7.1 Summary of the Intentional Stance

Philosophy of explanation:

Philosophy of explanation explains and interprets choice as the result of the interaction of the consumer situation delineated by the consumer's desires, beliefs, emotions, and perceptions as these relate to his or her consumption history and the opportunities for the maximization of subjectively assessed utilitarian and informational reinforcement offered by the current setting.

Method:

Given the history and current circumstances of the consumer, constructs the intentionality he or she ought to have in order to explain his or her choice.

Epistemology:

The relationships between the consumer situation and the actions of the consumer are described intentionally. The action of the consumer is accounted for in terms of the nature of the intentional consumer situation.

Success criterion:

The generation of an intelligible account of consumer choice that is not amenable to an extensional explanation by the reconstruction of the consumer's intentionality. This intentional interpretation must be consistent with theories of cognitive structure and processing and neurophysiologies! research.

Scope:

Human action, and the actions of animals to which intentionality can be properly ascribed.

Agency:

Agency is attributed to the individual consumer.

optimizing behavior, and to outline the general patterns of its behavior. This last is as important in ruling out uncharacteristic behaviors as it is in including those that have actually been observed. Hence, the consumer is treated as a system that is economically rational insofar as he or she maximizes a utility function composed of bundles of utilitarian and informational reinforcement. He or she minimizes the monetary costs involved in obtaining varying quantities of utilitarian and informational reinforcement over time according to the principle of cost matching. His or her behavior is sensitive to price changes in accordance with the basic economic theory of demand. He or she has desires, beliefs, emotions, and perceptions consistent with these behaviors which comprise his or her intentional consumer situation.

Understand the System as Ideally Rational

The principles of Intentional Interpretation form the following methodology. First it is imperative that we demonstrate rigorously the inability of extensional syntax to account for the behavior (or its aspects). Accomplishing this provides confidence that the behavior in question may be regarded as intentional behavior. Second, is the construction of an intentional account of similar behavior where the behavioral syntax requirements are fulfilled; this is then transferred to the situation in which these requirements cannot be met. This intentional account then provides a basis for evaluating the following operations in terms of their producing a credible interpretation.

Third is the explication of the intentional behavior in terms of the intentional consumer situation where references to the content of desires, beliefs, emotions, and perceptions are supported by molar operant behavioral accounts of this or similar behavior and species-general neurophysiological correlates of behavior. The intentional consumer situation will include reference to the consumer's learning history and the nature of the pattern of reinforcement prefigured by this intentional situation. The beliefs, desires, emotions, and perceptions that should be ascribed are those that, as we have seen, the consumer "ought" to have by virtue of its history and situation, that is, the learning history and consumer setting in which it is located. This explication of intentional behavior consists, therefore, in the reconstruction of the consumer situation along intentional lines.

Fourth, it is possible to put forward further explication of the intentional behavior in terms of the cognitive consumer situation. In this case, references to the content of decision making are supported by molar operant behavioral accounts of this or similar behavior and species-general neurophysiological correlates of behavior. The cognitive consumer situation will include reference to the consumer's learning history and the nature of the pattern of reinforcement prefigured by this cognitive situation. The decision-making processes that should be ascribed are those that the consumer again "ought" to have. This explication of cognitive behavior consists, therefore, in the reconstruction of the consumer situation along cognitive lines.[1]

The Action Perspective of the BPM

The Intentional Consumer Situation

The consumer situation and its relationship to consumer behavior remains the essence of the model but the components of the situation are conceived intentionally and behavior is replaced with action. The conception of the consumer situation is no longer simply the scope of the consumer behavior setting; it is now a complex of intentionally specified influences on choice.

The central explanatory component of the BPM, the *consumer situation*, is also redefined in the action perspective. Whereas in the extensional model we could delineate the consumer situation only as the interaction of the consumer behavior setting and the learning history, a construction that avoids intentionality, it is now possible to portray consumer situations in terms of a nexus of beliefs and desires which have become feasible means of expressing the emotional and intellectual outputs of consumption experience (Fig. 7.1).

---

[1] The methodology that Dennett (1991a, b) terms *heterophenomenology* is a special case of Intentional Interpretation in which the verbal reports of individual consumers provide data. The interpretation made of these reports can be corroborated/extended by the use of the general elements of Intentional Interpretation listed above. (For discussion in the context of consumer psychology, see Foxall (2016e).

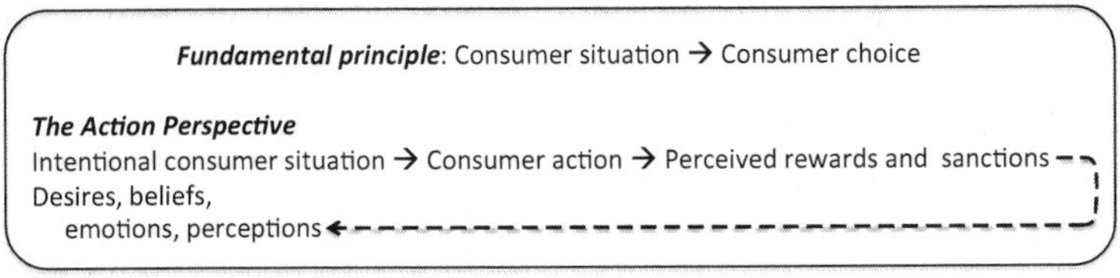

> **Fundamental principle**: Consumer situation → Consumer choice
>
> **The Action Perspective**
> Intentional consumer situation → Consumer action → Perceived rewards and sanctions ⌐ ┐
> Desires, beliefs,   ¦
>   emotions, perceptions ◄ – ┘

Fig. 7.1   Consumer choice: The action perspective

Patterns of Reinforcement

In a sense, the pattern of reinforcement is inherent in the consumer situation even in the behavioral perspective of the BPM since the learning history encompasses what the consumer's prior experience is in behaving in particular ways, the consequences that have followed such behavior, and the effects these have had on the probability of further behavior of the same kind in similar settings. However, we now envision this experience in terms of the consumer's desires, beliefs, emotions, and perceptions. The goals toward which the consumer's behavior is moving him or her are ultimately those established genetically in the course of a phylogenetic history; these lay down what primary reinforcers and punishers influence his or her behavior and toward the acquisition of which he or she is therefore motivated. In addition, the secondary reinforcers whose power to motivate has been acquired in the course of an ontogenetic history can be added to the desires that shape consumer behavior. The consumer's beliefs about his or her prior behavior, the events that followed from it, their effect on behavior, and the ensuing emotional rewards act within this consumer situation to prime the setting stimuli to effect a particular pattern of behavior. For these beliefs, the consumer is dependent on memory, particularly episodic memory.

Consumer Choice as Action

In seeking the explanation of consumer activity that is not under stimulus control, we are reconceptualizing it as action rather than behavior. The essence of this distinction casts behavior as activity (bodily movement) that is caused by elements of the environments that are external to the person. So understood, the environment includes the person's body as well as the immediate situation. Actions, by contrast, are under personal control; they are *intended*[2] by the actor (Taylor 1964). They involve *trying* to achieve an end (Hornsby 1981).

To count as an action, an activity must both achieve its end, and be intended by its enactor. But how can we tell that an activity was intended? Dennett might say that if this assumption helps us predict the behavior then it was intended, for being so predictable is all there is to intending an action. For something to be an action in a stronger sense than this, it must be an intentionally directed activity that brings about an appropriate result: "With action, we might say, the behavior occurs because of the corresponding intention or purpose; where this is not the case, we are not dealing with action" (Taylor 1964, p. 33). It is necessary, then, that the activity occurred *because of* the intention of the actor.

Activity$_I$ and Activity$_T$ Whereas a behavior is construed as happening because of causes to which the individual is involuntarily subjected, action is usually defined, in Dretske's (1988, p. 3) words as "either itself something one does voluntarily or deliberately (e.g., playing the piano) or a direct consequence, whether intended and foreseen or not, of such a voluntary act (e.g., unintentionally disturbing one's neighbors by intentionally playing the piano"). Hornsby (1981) distinguishes these meanings by the subscripts $_I$ for intransitive and $_T$ for transitive: My arm's moving$_I$, as opposed to My moving$_T$ my arm. The two are related insofar as My moving$_T$ my arm is the cause of My arm's moving$_I$.

While behavior involves bodily movements, including mental events as well as physical, actions are bodily movements of a particular kind. As Hornsby (1981) points out, "The melting$_T$ of the chocolate" is something a person or agent does whereas "The melting$_I$ of the chocolate" is something that happens to or within the chocolate. Actions are transitive, not intransitive, movements. Hence, a movement of the body (which is

---

[2] In the everyday sense rather than in terms of intentionality as discussed in Chapter 2.

an intransitive activity) is not necessarily a bodily movement (that is a transitive activity).[3]

While both behavior and action refer to bodily movement, they are, respectively, described by the intransitive and transitive moods of the verb *to move*. Hence, the meaning of "The moving of my arm" depends on whether the gerund *moving* is understood intransitively ("My arm's moving") or transitively ("*My* moving my arm"). The first refers to the physical disturbance of my arm, perhaps by someone else or by the jolting of the car in which I am traveling; the second, to the moving of my arm *by me*. Understanding actions to be bodily movements requires that the moving in question is transitively portrayed. As noted, actions are bodily movements$_T$, which are among the possible causes of bodily movements$_I$.

Hence, to label an activity "action" is akin to alluding to a prior cause for a bodily movement inasmuch as it excludes other antecedent causes such as reflexive stimulation or being acted upon by another person (Taylor 1964, p. 33). If events such as these could be shown to account for the activity, action explanation would be ruled out.[4] A rival account is one in which the behavior would have occurred on the basis of some other antecedent, such as an environmental stimulus, regardless of the existence or nonexistence of the intention. If an activity is to be classified as an action, we must be unable to account for it by some causal antecedent such that the antecedent and the behavior are not related by a law that is itself dependent on a law or rule that governs the intention or purpose.

---

[3] Steward (2012) includes as actions, movements which are not "intentional" in the Anscombe-Davidson sense, that is, things like jiggling one's foot while writing (p. 34). Presumably she means actions of which one is not aware; certainly she says she means those that are not done intentionally. This is similar to the distinction between contingency-shaped and rule-governed behavior. She is making her definition of action broader than others have employed because she wants to delineate her notion of *settling* more finely. She argues that things done absent-mindedly are still movements of one's body by oneself and thus qualify. These are all settlings by the individual of "how things are to be in respect of [their] body at certain times" (ibid.).

[4] "To call something an action... does involve ruling out certain rival accounts, those incompatible with the implied claim that the intention brought about the behaviour" (Taylor 1964, p. 34). This is exactly the principle that the search for the bounds of behaviorism has ruled by. But the consideration of intentional behavior as action allows a more rigorous treatment.

Action and Responsibility There are two kinds of law here and the difference between them is illustrated by the following example. I can account for the activity of someone smiling at me by means of a law that says "She smiles at everyone who enters her store" or "She smiles at all her friends." If she is a shopkeeper, her purposes might include encouraging shoppers to buy more or, if she is outgoing, to maintaining harmonious relationships. Taylor would classify these reasons as the conditions of this person's behavior on the grounds that they are conditions of her intending or purposing to behave in this manner. The behavioral regularities she displays are regularities in her intentions or desires. But it would not make sense to classify her behavior as an action on the grounds that she had been conditioned to smile whenever the bell on the door of her shop rang. We can, moreover, in these cases, alter her behavior by giving her reasons for being less sensitive to shoppers or keeping her friends. By contrast, her smiling whenever the bell rang would be independent of any desires or intentions that arise from the ringing of the bell. Such smiling does not constitute an action.

Taylor relates action to responsibility: categorizing an activity as an action is to account for it in terms of a person's "desires, intentions, and purposes. And this is why we hold [him or her] responsible" (Taylor 1964, p. 35). There may, he admits, be "gradations." An attribution of responsibility is entirely ruled out, however, if it is possible to show that no intention was relevant to it. He summarizes his position:

> Thus the laws by which we explain action must be such that the antecedent is the condition of the agent having a certain intention or purpose, whether because it gives rise to a desire, or is the object of a certain policy, so that the regularity in his behavior is conditional on the regularity of his intentions or purposes. A behaviour law which fulfils this condition can be called a 'law governing action', while one which relates antecedent to behavior unconditionally can be called a 'law governing movement'. The point could then be put this way, that action can only be accounted for by laws governing action; that once we can explain behavior by laws governing movement, we are no longer dealing with action. (Taylor 1964, p. 36)

The redescription of behavior as action provides an explanation by revealing the goal for the sake of which the behavior was enacted. How does this differ from an explanation in terms of operant conditioning? It would be an *interpretation* in Skinner's sense since the actual conditions would not be present to support definitively the conclusion that this was operant behavior: there would be no stimulus conditions from which to establish that a particular element of the environment had, through repeated pairing, become a discriminative stimulus, nor that the outcome picked out by the goal had actually reinforced the behavior, perhaps rather than rewarding the behavior. In the absence of these stimulus conditions being previously related to the behavior, we are not able to offer an explanation in operant terms. We do not have the evidence to support an extensional account based on behavioral syntax.

How is it possible to differentiate an activity that is "directed" (i.e., goal-directed, purposive), such as standing as a candidate in an election, from one which is not, such as an eye blink? In particular, how can the many activities that fall between these easily classifiable examples be categorized (Taylor 1964, p. 29; see also Ryle 1971; Geertz 1973)? One way of resolving this is to look for the stimulus conditions governing each kind of activity. Skinner (1953a, pp. 110–113) distinguishes "involuntary" behavior, that which is predictable and controllable by means of Pavlovian conditioning from that which is "voluntary," that is (not voluntary at all but) under the control of operant contingencies. Though both are equally determined by environmental circumstances, the latter appears to be deliberate or purposive but is actually as much under the control of external variables as that which results from the responses established by classical conditioning. Not all behavior falls easily into one or other of these camps, however. In the closed setting of the experimental chamber, it is possible to identify elements of the environment as discriminative stimuli, reinforcers, and punishers, and to record the pattern of defined responses that occur in the presence of the former to produce the latter. However, in the open settings in which much consumer choice takes place, it is frequently impossible to delineate the three-term contingency so definitively. It is certainly not feasible to assign a history of reinforcement and punishment to consumers with anything approaching the specificity and determinativeness possible in operant experiments with rats and pigeons.

There are two ways in which an inability to locate the stimulus conditions that might constitute the reinforcement contingencies that explain
consumer behavior could arise. First, even if we have good reason to
expect a particular behavior to be the result of operant contingencies
(e.g., this has been demonstrated under experimental conditions), we
may not be able to locate, in the field, the variables of which it would be
a function on the basis of this expectation. Second, they may not actually
exist, as for instance in the case of so-called automatic reinforcement or
the intraverbals necessary to make particular grammatical usages possible
(Smith 1994). In these cases, intellectual integrity compels us to treat
the behaviors in question as under intentional control; this is true even
of a behavior that is topographically identical to behavior that can be
traced to environmental stimulation. Note that this rules out the kind
of behavioral interpretation to which Skinner (1957) laid claim, much
of which was unprincipled speculation. It applies, for instance, to the
attribution of stimulus control to "seeing in the absence of the thing
seen." We may, therefore, be dealing with an activity that can be categorized as *behavior* when it is demonstrably under contingency control or as
an *action* because the sole manner of accounting for it is by the ascription
of intentionality.

Summing-Up: Behavior versus Action We can now categorize activity as
follows, where *B* refers to behavior and *A* to action:

> *B1* is an activity that is the result of Pavlovian (classical or respondent)
> conditioning and is clearly behavior in the sense that can be explained in
> terms of environmental stimulation, at least to the extent that it is predict-
> able and controllable.
>
> *B2* is an activity that results from operant conditioning, that is, that can
> be reliably traced to its stimulus conditions, being either contingency-
> shaped by direct contact with the controlling variables, or rule-governed,
> in the sense that it results from the stimulation provided by verbal behavior
> which is understood as a series of audible productions that have become
> discriminative stimuli and/or motivating operations through pairing with
> primary reinforcers.

A1 is activity for which there is no discernable stimulus field, activity which can, therefore, be accounted for only by the ascription of intentionality. Activity of this kind must be classed as under intentional control even though there exists the possibility of its (or, more accurately, of topographically similar responding) being explained in the less-complex context of the operant chamber by means of discernable stimuli. (There may, indeed, be no apparent topographical distinction between *B2* and *A1* in the absence of detailed empirical scrutiny of the potential stimulus field.)

A2 is activity for which it is unlikely that stimuli could conceivably be found that could enter into an experimental analysis (as in automatic reinforcement, or publicly unvoiced intraverbal control of behavior).

To treat activity as behavior (i.e., to classify it as either *B1* or *B2*) is to view it as determined, not under personal control but under that of the environment. It is to adopt the contextual stance, to work exclusively within a descriptive-behaviorist framework of conceptualization and analysis. Assuming we would wish to use the term in these circumstances, what would "agency" mean (a) if the contingencies were assumed to be naturally occurring, and (b) if the contingencies were manipulated by another person? In the case of *B1* and *B2*, the locus of the utility function is the individual but the elements entering into it are all present in the environment (usually in the product or service that is consumed). The locus of causation is therefore the environment (that is where the reinforcers, of which behavior is demonstrably a function, are located). In the case of *A1* and *A2*, the utility function is still that of the individual (and it still exists, therefore, at the personal level) but it is now conceived in terms of felt emotion, i.e., at an intra-personal level). In the case of *A*, we are interpreting activity as influenced by desires, beliefs, emotions, and perceptions, including the desire for optimal levels of pleasure, arousal, and dominance, and the beliefs that particular activities will deliver this emotional satisfaction via the attainment of the appropriate reinforcers, plus perceptions of how the world works and has worked (i.e., a learning history). This is *action* rather than behavior since the mainsprings of the activity are "mental" rather than physical (or, more precisely, can be described only in intentional language).

Does the understanding of activity as action rather than behavior impose upon us the view that both agency and causation now reside within the individual? Even in operant terms,[5] causation might be said to be within the individual if it is accepted that the variables of which the activity is ultimately a function are located intra-personally in the form of subjectively experienced emotional feelings.[6] So what this question is really asking is: is there a "person" who can make independent decisions that guide behavior? In what sense is there a "person," motivated by optimal levels of pleasure, arousal, and dominance within a context of desires, beliefs, emotions, and perceptions, who takes autonomous decisions to act in a particular way? Is this person aware of the contingencies in operation? Can he or she ignore them in deciding how to act?[7]

Implications of Action: Agency Incompatibilism

This discussion of action as activity at the heart of intention-based explanation leads naturally to consideration of the relationship between action and agency. The viewpoint of the philosopher, Helen Steward, which she terms *agency incompatibilism*, is relevant here. Steward (2012) argues forcefully against the universal determinism that marks many accounts of behavior that portray human activity, like everything else that occurs in the universe, as entirely explicable in terms of a closed physical system.

---

[5] Though not necessarily those of Skinner and some other radical behaviorists, for whom an independent science of behavior requires that the variables of which behavior is a function be restricted to elements of the extra-personal environment. In saying "even in operant terms" here, I mean for operant psychologists who accept that the ultimate reinforcers are to be found in the emotional feelings engendered by the reinforcing stimuli acting, in a process of respondent conditioning, to effect emotional responses.

[6] Radical behaviorism is of course amenable to the idea that private events in the form of feelings form part of a functional analysis, though radical behaviorists like Skinner have traditionally insisted that the feelings are responses rather than discriminative or reinforcing stimuli. Other radical behaviorists have been more open to the view that any element of the three-term contingency can be understood as a private event.

[7] Does moving the utility function from environmental causation to intra-personal causation mean that the behavior is no longer determined? It may not be environmentally determined but it could be biologically determined even so. All we have done by shifting the utility function is suggest an identity for the neurophysiological basis of reinforcement that Skinner predicted would come.

Contra Determinism

Agency incompatibilism closely relates action and agency: "…an agent is an entity that has a body and can make that body move in various ways and, correlatively, an action is an exercise of this power to make the body…move" (Steward 2012, p. 32). Action, as the term is used here, includes mental actions, and so is not confined to "bodily movement" in a narrow sense.[8] Building on Hornsby's (1981) understanding of action, Steward (2012) proposes as the basis of her metaphysics for freedom the observation that universal determinism would be undermined by—in fact, is wholly incompatible with—an organism having the capacity to move its body, that is, to engage in activities$_T$. Universal determinism, the view that everything that has ever happened and that will happen henceforth was determined by the Big Bang, precludes action explanations of human activity: a universe in which everything is pre-determined and fully explicable in terms of the laws of physics has no need of organisms capable of settling matters for themselves. Steward's (2012) argument against this view comprises four steps.

First, *if universal determinism is correct, then the future is not open*, that is, there is, physically, only one future, every detail of which has been settled. If determinism were the case, then every detail of an animal's behavior must have been settled by physical forces and there is no room for any exception to this rule. Agency is incompatible with determinism.

Second, *the existence of self-moving animals would mean that the future was open*. Self-movement can only be a feature of a creature that is able to make itself move. We can make an owner-body distinction of a creature such as this: indeed, owning one's body is the essence of agency. If there are in fact animals that can make their bodies move—that is, agents—then the future must be accounted open, unsettled. Such a creature would also have to have a mind—to have certain mental predicates.

---

[8] Moreover, "the capacity for discretion which I shall be maintaining is the hallmark of true agency is an *evolved* capacity, crucially important for creatures which need to make decisions based on a very large number of complex and often incommensurable factors, about how to distribute their efforts through space and across time, and how to respond as they move to a constantly changing environment" (Steward 2012, pp. 18–19). Note that this brings thinking and feeling, which Skinner calls "private events," into the realm of action explanation.

Another way of putting this is that it would be "up to" a creature of this ilk what it did, at least some of the time; hence, it would have to be capable of settling matters. If this could be shown to be the case, universal determinism would fail.

Third, *some animals can move their bodies.* They *contribute* to the mechanisms of movement production that they contain. While a paramecium is simply an "arena" for certain bodily functions to take place in response to environmental stimulation, other creatures can make their bodies move by means over and above the chemically induced movements of this kind.[9] These are self-moving animals and their existence means the future is open. Such self-movers are agents. "The capacity for discretion is the hallmark of true agency... This discretion is an evolved entity. Animals are authors of their actions – not mere loci" (Steward 2012, p. 18, p. 20). The key difference is between *having* a body and *being* one's body: crucially, "Agents are entities that things can be up to" (p. 25). The essence of Steward's argument is that the details of a behavior pattern cannot be determined in advance of the entity's acting: whether an animal shakes some of its tail feathers when moving off toward prey, whether a human moves his or her neck first to the right or the left when overcoming stiffness, whether a consumer buys Brand A or Brand B. These matters, small as they may be, are *up to* the individual. The alternative is to subscribe to the idea that such matters are fixed and already settled by the Big Bang and the laws of nature: "but I find myself quite unable to believe that this is so—it is literally incredible. It seems to me to be an utterly basic part of our everyday commonsense metaphysics that the universe is, as it were, loose at those places in it where animals act—that they are free, within limits, at those junctures, to make it unfold as they will" (p. 21).

Fourth, *determinism cannot therefore be the case.* Agency itself is incompatible with determinism. We can, therefore, reject traditional concepts of both freedom and determinism as they have featured in the freewill

---

[9] Steward's use of the term "arena" here is reminiscent of Skinner's (1999) lecture on "having" a poem, in which the poet is viewed as no more than the *locus* of a poem, a lecturer as no more than the place where the lecture occurs. He concluded this lecture with the words, "And now my labor is over. I have had my lecture. I have no sense of fatherhood. If my genetic and personal histories had been different, I should have come into possession of a different lecture. If I deserve any credit at all, it is simply for having served as a place in which certain processes could take place. I shall interpret your applause in that light" (Skinner 1999, p. 401).

debate. The true emphasis should be on how *actions* can be accommodated within nature. *Freedom* is often assumed to be the capacity of an agent to have done otherwise. "*Animals* make trouble for determinism" (Steward 2012, p. 3, emphasis in original). *Agency* is "the capacity to move oneself about the world in purposive ways, ways that are in at least some respects up to oneself... The falsity of universal determinism is a necessary condition of the possibility of any freedom or moral responsibility there might be..." This is because "the falsity of universal determinism is a necessary condition of *agency* – and agency is, in turn, a necessary condition of both free action and moral responsibility" (Steward 2012, pp. 4–6). Much rests, however, on the ability to demonstrate that some things are indeed up-to the creature.

Up-to-Usness and the Settling of Matters

"Actions... are the particular engagements with the world by means of which, at the time of action, I typically settle such matters as whether or not I shall φ and, if I do, when, how, and where I shall do so" (Steward 2012, pp. 38–9). An agent is not the cause of a particular instance of an action but an entity that *settles* matters such as whether, when, how, etc. he or she will φ, these remaining open questions until he or she settles them by φ-ing. The answers are up to the individual. If determinism were true, it would not be up to the individual to settle any of these matters. Rather, they would have been settled already, before it even occurred to the individual to φ. If determinism were the case, therefore, there would be no agents and no actions. This is the core of the argument that agency is not consistent with determinism.

Consumers settle matters in numerous ways. While the fundamental components of their utility functions have been set in the course of their phylogenetic histories—the levels of utilitarian and informational reinforcement necessary for their biological well-being and fitness—the particular components of their consideration and consumptions sets are shaped and maintained in the course of an ontogenetic life-story based on operant conditioning. However, the timing of their purchasing and consumption activities, the precise brands that are purchased, the amount they will pay, and the source of rewards are all largely decided by individual consumers for themselves. These factors, notably brand choice on specific purchase occasions, are unpredictable, apparently random within the consumer's subset of available brands that comprises the relatively small group of tried and tested alternatives that are the buyer's consideration set. The lesson of multiattribute modeling of consumers' attitudes and intentions in relation to their manifest purchasing behavior is that these decisions are unknowable in advance. The consumer's intentionality is inchoate prior to the opportunity to purchase.

The point about these decisions is that they are trivial both in evolutionary terms and from the point of view of most consumers' personal experience. Most consumers exhibit multibrand purchasing and although they are sensitive to price differentials among brands they perceive the alternatives that compose their consideration sets as identical in function. These brands are therefore perceived as offering similar utilitarian reinforcement. Moreover, since most consumers purchase within a given band of informational reinforcement they are all the more likely to see the brands that make up their consideration set as interchangeable. Most consumers will settle these matters instore. The exceptions are the relatively few brand loyal consumers for whom informational reinforcement is more likely to exert a crucial effect on purchasing: nonavailability of the favored brand will be discomfiting to them. In this case they may seek alternative retail outlets, try a different brand, or in some other way settle the matter for themselves. In sum, while the levels of utilitarian and informational reinforcement optimal for consumer well-being may be laid down by evolutionary considerations, and while the products and brands supply the particular patterns of reinforcement that consumers are guided toward by both evolutionary and contemporary considerations, the specific ways in which they fulfill these requirements are a matter that is settled by consumers for themselves. Consumer brand choice is predictable in the aggregate but this is dependent on the settling decisions made by millions of individuals exercising their up-to-usness.

Agency and Intentionality

The "mature conception" of agency that Steward (2012, pp. 71–2) advances has four components. An agent is (i) able to move some or all of its body: that is, perform activity$_T$; (ii) capable of subjective experience: it is consciously aware; (iii) capable of having intentional states (desires, beliefs, emotions, and perceptions) ascribed to it; and (iv) able to settle matters for itself, that is, not simply be an instrument through which something else settles them by moving it. The idea of an agent, as described by these considerations, is richer than Dennett's of an intentional system. But Steward admits that deciding what is an agent cannot be done by any independent means: there is no way of telling whether an agent fulfills any of these four conditions. She therefore adopts Dennett's intentional strategy to the extent that she argues that it is possible to decide if an entity is an agent by "by deciding whether or not it is a creature or system with respect to which it is *necessary*, if we are to explain its behavior, to utilize at least the teleological stance" (Steward 2012, p. 105). *The teleological stance* (Gergely and Csibra 2003; Gergely et al. 1995) is based on interactions of three representational elements: the action itself, a possible future state (the goal), and the relevant situational constraints. (There is no intentional content necessary: the stance is non-mentalistic and does not, therefore, require the ascription of intentionality.) Given two of these elements, an infant can make inferences about the third based on the rationality principle: "This principle supposes that agents will in general take the most efficient action for achieving their goals given the situational constraints *as these are perceived by the infant herself*" (Steward 2012, p. 87).

However, Steward points out that this approach differs from Dennett's in two ways. The first is her suspicion of the *necessity* of taking this stance for entities that are not agents in the sense she defines, which we have already noted. The second is her argument that adopting either the teleological stance or the intentional stance involves more than treating the system as an instantiator of desires and beliefs: it is to say that the system meets the requirements of points (i)–(iv) above. The only way to ascertain whether a system is an agent is to decide whether there is an alternative to the folk psychology—that is, the agency scheme—that accounts satisfactorily for its behavior. If there is, then the system is not an agent. If not, however, it is. Moreover, and this marks an important distinction from Dennett's instrumental approach, the explanation of the agent's behavior in terms of the teleological stance and the intentional stance, when one of these is inevitable, works *because there is a reason for its doing so*, namely the actual mode of functioning of the entity. The reason is that the agent actually has cognitive capacities as a result of an evolutionary history that developed these powers in order that the agent could be a settler of matters. This settling of matters is "a very special form of causation indeed" (Steward 2012, p. 106). So, the reason the teleological stance and intentional stance work is that they are predicated on the very real causal role played by the organism "and its assessment of its options in the light of its knowledge, experience, and desires in the generation of its own behavior" (Steward 2012, p. 106). This role cannot be captured by a deterministic account of the causation of behavior since the biologically based capacity of an agent to act introduces "a real source of indeterminism" (Steward 2012, p. 107) into the world.

The real import of this objection to Dennett is the reversal of his explanatory mode in the intentional stance: "My anti-Dennettian suggestion, then, will be that we have to treat certain things as agents, roughly speaking, because that is what they are, and not the other way around" (Steward 2012, p.107). The view that *all there is* to being an intentional system is to be predictable in terms of ascribed desires and beliefs is a form of instrumentalism that is not compatible with the view Steward is putting forward here. Desires and beliefs are real, it is often argued, and should not be assumed of a system just for the sake of explanatory or predictive convenience.[10] There is a clear distinction to be made between true agents, those that can settle things for themselves, and other systems/creatures that simply test our theory of agency.[11]

---

[10] This rejection of Dennett's instrumentalism should not lead simply to token physicalism. The philosophers who have argued against Dennett—Steward cites Pylyshyn (1984), Fodor (1987), and Lycan (1988)—have concentrated on the intentional states themselves rather than on the powers available to their possessors.

[11] Whether this indeterminacy amounts to what is commonly called "freewill" may be disputed. Within an enormous literature on freewill, see, as indicative of a skeptical view, Strawson (1986).

Summing-Up

Consideration of knowledge by acquaintance provides a rationale for the origin of desires and beliefs but it rests ultimately on each individual's reported private experience and the faith that others' reported experience is of the same nature. The agent proposed by Steward can, however, *settle things* that we cannot show to be settled by other means. To do so, the agent requires intentional experience: not just the ascription of intentionality to explicate or predict their behavior but actual conscious cognitive functioning.

Ascribing Consumer Intentionality

The Continuum of Consumer Choice

The content of the intentionality we might reconstruct for a consumer is potentially vast, depending on the specific situation he or she is facing. All manner of brand, product, and retailer beliefs, attitudes, and intentions may be appropriate given the consumer's consumption history and the reinforcement possibilities signaled by the setting stimuli. This exposition concentrates on a single source of attitudes, namely those concerned with temporal preference for consumption of goods that become available at different times. This allows us to discuss a whole range of consumer behaviors in similar terms. On the basis of the findings generated by the behavioral perspective of the BPM, we can assume that the consumer behaves according to certain customary principles, for example, that he or she maximizes a combination of utilitarian and informational reinforcement within his or her budget. But we need to confine our discussion if it is to be meaningful. In particular, it is necessary to employ an intentional observation of consumer choice that applies to the widest range of consumer activities and which is necessary to render those activities intelligible given the absence of a sufficient stimulus field.

A framework for accomplishing this is provided by the observation that consumer behaviors range from the routine, of which the exemplar is everyday product, brand, or store choice for consumer nondurables, to the extreme, exemplified by compulsion and addiction. These behaviors differ in terms of the consumer situations in which they arise and the pattern of reinforcement by which they are sustained. They can therefore be analyzed by the behavioral perspective of the BPM. But there are aspects of these behaviors that are amenable only to an Intentional Interpretation because they involve continuities and discontinuities for which a stimulus field cannot be adequately identified, if identified at all; because they require a personal-level exposition if they are to be fully understood; and because it is necessary to delimit behavioral interpretations of them by restricting the possible range of reinforcers that could account for them.

The principal dimension on which consumer behaviors may be arrayed displays them as differing in the extent to which consumers discount the future in the course of their purchase and consumption activities. The

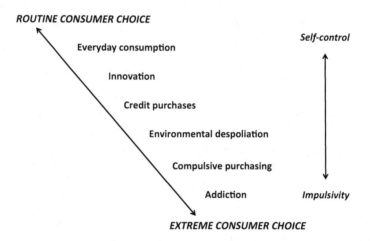

Fig. 7.2 *The continuum of consumer choice: From self-control to impulsivity.* Modes of consumer choice vary according to the degree to which they entail temporal discounting. For further exposition, see Foxall (2010a, 2016a) (Adapted from Foxall (2010b). Accounting for consumer choice: Intertemporal decision-making in behavioural perspective, *Marketing Theory*, 10, 315–345)

Box 7.2 Temporal Discounting and Preference Reversal

A reward that is to be received at some time in the future—say, $100 in a year's time—does not seem right now to be worth waiting that long for unless there is some extra bonus attached to it. If someone owes me this amount and offers to let me have it in 12 months, I am inclined to say that I will require, say, $110 at that time. Rewards for which one has to wait are devalued or discounted. We say that temporal discounting is concerned with the *current subjective value* of a reward that will be received in the future, that is, the value of that future reward rated in the present moment.

Rational decision makers, like bankers, discount exponentially, that is, at a constant rate regardless of the time elapsed. Their behavior can be expressed as $Vi = A_i e^{-kDi}$ where Vi is the present value of a delayed reward, Ai the amount of a delayed reward, k a constant proportional to the degree of temporal discounting, Di the delay of the reward, and e the base of natural logarithms. Because this behavior is based on a constant rate of discounting, a larger, later reward (the LLR, available at t_2) *always* has a value greater than that of a smaller reward available sooner (the SSR, available at t_1). This is shown in the first segment (a) of the figure, where the two lines, representing the relative values of the rewards, never cross.

Much human behavior, however, is marked by a style of discounting in which the value of a reward changes radically as the time remaining before it becomes available is reduced. While the LLR is preferred at t_0, indicated by the initially higher line in segment (b) of the figure, just prior to t_1, *when* the SSR will becomes available, its value markedly increases, the curves cross, and the individual opts for the objectively poorer reward.

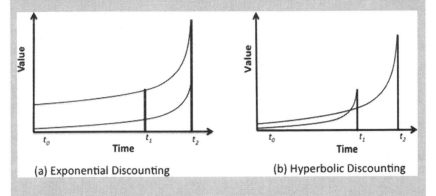

(a) Exponential Discounting   (b) Hyperbolic Discounting

This form of temporal discounting and the preference reversal it involves are described by a hyperbolic function: $V_d = A / (1 + kD)$ in which V_d is the discounted value of a reward of a particular magnitude or amount, A, received after a delay, D (Mazur 1987; Madden and Bickel 2010). In summary, the rate of discounting now varies with the amount of delay (Ainslie 1992, 2001; Rick and Loewenstein 2008).

Adapted from Foxall (2016b). Metacognitive control of categorial neurobehavioral decision systems, *Frontiers in Psychology* (*Theoretical and Philosophical Psychology*), 7: 170, pp. 1–18.

resulting Continuum of Consumer Choice is shown in Fig. 7.2, and temporal discounting and preference reversal are described in Box 7.2.

Everyday brand choice involves established products, for which the consumer has a stable consideration set. The outcomes of purchasing and consuming these items are predictable because they are tried and tested; the consumer is something of an expert on them. We can surmise that the principal operant class involved is maintenance, though it might be accumulation or hedonism. The consumer behavior setting is predominantly open since numerous brands are available in each product category. But because brands in the consideration set are functionally similar they are in any case substitutes; therefore, the unavailability of one brand or another scarcely restricts the scope of the consumer behavior setting since there will always be an alternative version of the product available. Discounting of the future, if there is any, is shallow: the typical consumer feels no pressure to hoard goods of this kind under normal circumstances, and there is no advantage generally in having a stock of them that exceeds one's weekly or monthly consumption requirements. The same brands will in all likelihood be available on each shopping occasion in the future and at similar prices. The value of any one of the brands that comprise the consumer's consideration set is much the same as that of any other, and it is the same now as it will be next week, next month, or next year. We would expect deviations from this pattern of consumer behavior should there be a general shortage of the product category on the horizon, should one brand be offered as part of a price promotion, or should the consumer be planning to hole up for several months to write a monograph on consumer cognition. And this general analysis will not apply exactly to those relatively few consumers who are sole purchasers of just one brand in any product category. But we are speaking here of routine consumption in terms of what is the general pattern of behavior and reward for the predominant proportion of consumers. Many aspects of routine consumer choice are reliably predictable on the basis of the variables contained in the behavioral perspective of the BPM.

This routine behavior pattern is disturbed somewhat when the consumer includes an innovative brand in his or her consideration set. Innovative buying, the action of the by-now very familiar consumer who adds brand E to their consideration set consisting of brands A, B, C, and D, is an act of initiation. The consumer expands this consideration set only in the expectation that the new brand being bought for the first time will provide similar functional outcomes to those delivered by the existing members of the set. But there is still the hint of an uncertain future, marked by less predictable outcomes that will need to be evaluated. Innovative items may become available in any of the operant classes but the setting is predominantly open because the trialed brand can be dropped at any time without loss. The consumer can be depicted as discounting the future, if only to a minimal degree.

Discounting is evident, however, when the consumer embarks on credit purchases of any kind for this involves obtaining utility immediately that would otherwise require patience. Gaining temporal advantage through speedier ownership and acquisition of consumption benefits must eventually be offset by the aversive consequences felt by the individual alone or his or her near family as interest must be paid. The operant class of consumer behavior will vary, and although entering into a credit agreement extends the scope of the consumer behavior setting (by making an additional purchase available), the subsequent effect of incurring higher payments may restrict it (by precluding alternative purchases). The degree of temporal discounting is variable depending on the magnitude of the credit obtained, the repayment arrangements including annualized interest rate, the consumer's income, and his or her other commitments and wants.

Consumers may enact numerous kinds of environmental despoliation through the accrual of economic and social goods and their casting aside. The tragedy of the commons arises because a single person's consumption makes a negligible difference while the cumulated effects of everyone's consumption behaviors are highly damaging. There is a temporal advantage for the busy individual in disposing of waste items where it is convenient, especially when any aversive consequences are widely shared throughout the community and perhaps distant in any case in time and place. The overconsumption of fossil fuels is not only polluting but also may reduce their future availability. All operant classes of consumer behavior are involved; the consumer behavior setting is open when these types of consumption or disconsumption occur but closes when their adverse effects are incurred. Environmental despoliation is therefore an activity that involves steepening discounting.

Compulsive purchasing encompassing the immediate acquisition of a magnitude of goods beyond the capability of the individual to consume involves very steep discounting, however (Faber and Vohs 2013; Müller and Mitchell 2011; Ridgway et al. 2008). The operant classes of consumer behavior that are predominantly involved are likely to be accomplishment and accumulation, though all could be relevant. The open consumer behavior setting during the acquisition of goods gives way to a very closed setting when the goods must be paid for.

Finally, at the most extreme comes addiction, a mode of consumption marked by steep temporal discounting and preference reversal, involving the pursuit of a substance or behavior pattern to the point of economic irrationality, where it fundamentally disrupts the individual's lifestyle (Foxall 2016a, b).

Summing-Up: Bounds of Behaviorism, Imperatives of Intentionality

What is the connection between the imperatives of intentionality on the one hand and the Intentional Interpretation and the Cognitive Interpretation on the other? How do Intentional Interpretation and Cognitive Interpretation overcome the bounds of behaviorism? I will seek answers to these questions by considering anew the by-now familiar context of consumer choices that differ in the degree of temporal discounting they entail, represented by the range of options from routine brand selection through the trial of an innovation or buying on credit to behaviors marked by compulsion or addiction. In each case, as we have noted, there is a conflict between a more immediate reward of lesser magnitude (the SSR) and a more long-term reward that is larger. Consider in each case of consumer choice an individual who resolves at t_0 to be patient but succumbs at t_1 to the SSR rather than endure until t_2. The explanation of each of the instances of consumer choice that involves issues of temporal discounting in this manner encounters the bounds of behaviorism.

Most frequently, the predominant problem for the behaviorist in contemplating the effects of temporal discounting on consumer choice is to account for the discontinuity of the observed behavior in the absence of a consumer situation that specifies how the observed behavior is related to environmental stimuli. There cannot be other than a rudimentary stimulus field to explain the choice of SSR at t_1, following a resolution at t_0 to avoid the SSR and wait for the LLR, because we can only explain this as a devaluing of the LLR shortly before t_1. This LLR only exists, however, in the mind of the consumer. If the radical behaviorist should argue that the imminence of the SSR is the causal stimulus we can answer that he or she must therefore explain how this overcomes the resolve of the consumer at t_0 to avoid the SSR.

But let us suppose that the consumer shows resolution on the basis of bundling the sequences of SSR and LLR and being strengthened thereby to show self-control.

We cannot explain this consumer's ignoring the SSR at t_1 and his or her waiting for the LLR when it appears at t_2 in terms of a stimulus field (again, other than one of the most rudimentary kind that consists in our interpretation of the consumer's experience of temporality) because the only reason the consumer avoids the SSR is a mental image of the superiority of the LLR at a future time. What contingencies there are (the imminence of the SSR) are exactly the same as in the first example: the only reason they are not effective is that the consumer has undertaken a bundling exercise that has led to a belief in the superiority of the LLR at a later time. It is the consumer's first-personal valuation of the alternatives available (insofar as they are known to him or her) that must account for his or her observed behavior. This has brought us to the second bound of behaviorism, the need to give an explanation of behavior that entails the consumer's phenomenology, his or her knowledge by acquaintance of the situation. The consumer's valuations of the SSR and LLR are intentional ascriptions that explain his or her behavior in the absence of any stimuli that would support an extensional account. This following of the imperatives of intentionality overcomes the bounds of behaviorism by making the behavior intelligible.[12] Crucially, we must conclude that the explanation of behavior in terms of the intertemporal valuation of alternatives is dependent on the imputation to the consumer of mental objects and the mental operations required for their comparative appraisal prior to action.

The initial imperative of intentionality (see Fig. 3.2) requires the *establishment of the intentional grounds of behavioral continuity and discontinuity*. This is precisely what we have done by giving intentional descriptions of the determinants of the observed behavior, notably in terms of desires and beliefs. Having reached a point where the contingencies of reinforcement, such as they are, are inadequate for us to speak of the phenomenology of the consumer in this situation, the behaviorist explanation must yield to an intentional account at the personal level of exposition. Hence, the second imperative of intentionality is the *Provision of an account of first-personal experience* and this takes the form of a description of the consumer's likely experience of mental conflict as his or her desires for long-term benefit and welfare are felt to be dissonant with the desire for immediate gratification. The third imperative of intentionality requires that we confine our interpretation to *proximate stimuli* rather than imagined future stimulus fields. We have confined our account to the stimuli presented by the SSR and LLR and the consumer's previous experience of them, and from these alone have we constructed a phenomenology to account for his or her choice.

The Cognitive Interpretation shows how the structure and functioning of a mental apparatus could allow the individual to undertake the operations that are required by the Intentional Interpretation. This reinforces the pursuit of the imperatives of intentionality and their remedying of

---

[12] I am here regarding an explanation in Boden's terms as "any answer to a why question that is accepted by the questioner as making the event in question somehow more intelligible" and a scientific explanation "as an explanation that is justified by reference to publicly observable facts, and which is rationally linked to other, similar explanations in a reasonably systematic manner" (Boden 1972, p. 32).

the limitations of extensional explanation revealed by the identification of the bounds of behaviorism.

Toward Cognitive Interpretation

The Intentional Interpretation ascribes to consumers whose behavior ranges from the routine to the extreme a pattern of intentionality based on their valuation of alternative purchase or consumption opportunities that are temporally separated. Their behaviors are characterized by varying degrees of preference reversal. In the case of the routine purchaser preference reversal is almost absent as long as the steady state circumstances described above obtain. In the case of extreme consumer choice such as addiction, preferences shift dramatically in the course of the timeframe depicted in Box 7.2 for hyperbolic discounting. At t_0, when both reward options are at some temporal distance, it is common to opt for the LLR; but as t_1 approaches, and especially just before the SSR becomes available, its value increases considerably until it exceeds that of the LLR. Having chosen the SSR, the addict is likely to reverse his or her preferences again, resolving in future to choose the LLR. The extent to which we can explain the addict's behavior in operant terms is limited; the objective contingencies do not change between t_0 and t_2. We can predict the behavior of the addict on the basis of the time elapsed since t_0 and the temporal closeness of the SSR, but this is not a comprehensive explanation. The behavior of the addict depends on a subjective valuation of the SSR and LLR, first at t_0, then at t_1, and finally at t_2. This evocation and comparison of alternative outcomes in terms of their value is entirely a cognitive affair: there is no stimulus field to show how this state of affairs can be predicted or controlled. We therefore ascribe intentionality in terms of valuation and preference formation and reversal in order to render the behavior intelligible. This is Intentional Interpretation (for a detailed account, see Foxall 2016a).

Having established the form that the intentional consumer situation takes and suggesting how it can be used to interpret behavior for which no stimulus field is identifiable, the next stage of psychological explanation is to show how this situation could have come about as a result of the cognitive functioning of the consumer. The micro-cognitive psychology (MiCP) and macro-cognitive psychology (MaCP) to which we now turn are not intended to justify any particular interpretation of behavior but to show how the Intentional Interpretation of the consumer situation itself is supported by cognitive psychologies that lean respectively to neurophysiology and operancy. Importantly, the cognitive psychologies employed for this purpose are preexisting and not invented specifically for the purpose of justifying the Intentional Interpretation.

MiCP and MaCP are concerned to demonstrate how the idealized Intentional Interpretation of behavior could result from a process of cognitive decision making, and how these in turn are respectively related to explanation at the sub-personal level (of neurophysiology) and the super-personal level of environmental contingencies. There is a need to show how the cognitive processing that we understand as MiCP and MaCP generates the desires, beliefs, emotions, and perceptions which figure causatively in the Intentional Interpretation, how these become implemented at the level of action, how their functioning is evaluated, and how they are modified in light of experience and changing circumstances. This is the task of Cognitive Interpretation.

Micro-cognitive psychology is concerned to develop a theory of human decision making that grounds it primarily in neurophysiology, while acknowledging that operancy plays a vital part in shaping neurophysiological readiness to respond. The starting point is the range of types of decision making that accompany the various modes of consumer choice that comprise the Continuum of Consumer Choice, from familiar everyday consumption to addiction. The aim is to show how these can be accounted for in terms of a similar range of operant and neurophysiological events.

Macro-cognitive psychology is concerned with theories of human decision making that relies on the competing demands of alternative patterns of contingency that maintain behaviors that may be incompatible. This is far from denying the neurophysiological basis of intra-personal strategic conflicts such as those described by picoeconomics (Ainslie 1992) but it is principally concerned with the interests that compose them and which are the outcome of operancy.

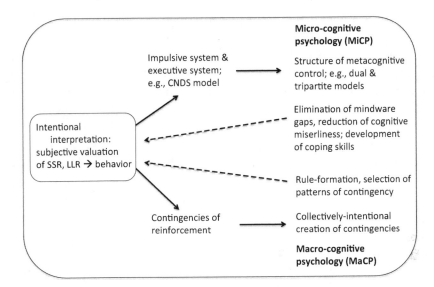

Fig. 7.3 *Micro- and macro-cognitive psychologies.* The MiCP agenda seeks to determine whether the Intentional Interpretation is consistent with sub-personal neuroscience and to link it to a cognitive psychology that is similarly consistent with neuroscience. The MaCP agenda seeks to determine whether the Intentional Interpretation is consistent with super-personal behavioral science and to link it to a cognitive psychology that is similarly consistent with behavioral science. See text for further elaboration

Figure 7.3 proposes the form that the second stage of psychological explanation, Cognitive Interpretation, takes. MiCP relates the personal level of exposition to the sub-personal neurophysiological events that are correlated with observed behavior at the personal level. The purpose is to show how the substance of the Intentional Interpretation, namely the subjective valuation of rewards that become available at different times, is reflected in both neurophysiology and an appropriate cognitive psychology. The former is well-illustrated by the CNDS model (Bickel and Yi 2008); the latter, by dual and tripartite models of metacognitive structure and functioning (e.g., Evans 2010; Evans and Stanovich 2013; Shea et al. 2014; Stanovich 2009a, b, 2011). While all of these models are open to the effects of super-personal considerations on behavior, neurophysiology, and cognition, they deal principally with the sub-personal level in relationship to behavior. MaCP relates the personal level of exposition to the super-personal events summarized by the contingencies of reinforcement and their influence on observed behavior at the personal level. Its purpose is to demonstrate how the substance of the Intentional Interpretation, the subjective valuation of rewards that become available at different times, stands in relation to the objective contingencies that govern the availability of these competing reinforcers. It seeks also to relate the actual behavior of consumers faced with such a set of circumstances to an appropriate cognitive psychology. The actual contingencies can be ascertained by observation and, where it obtains, experimental design, that is, by the standard procedures of behavior analysis. An appropriate cognitive psychology is provided by picoeconomic analysis (Ainslie 1992, 2001), which may form a cognitive component for the CNDS model (Foxall 2014a, b, 2016a, b). While all of these frameworks of conceptualization and analysis are open to the considerations raised by sub-personal neuroscience and its influence on behavior and cognition, they are principally concerned with the effects of the super-personal contingencies of reinforcement on cognition, neurophysiology, and choice.

Micro- and macro-cognitive psychologies, therefore, give rise to different agendas, each of which seeks to clarify and contextualize the Intentional Interpretation.

The MiCP agenda seeks to determine how far the Intentional Interpretation is consistent with sub-personal neuroscience and to link it to a cognitive psychology that is similarly consistent with neuroscience. It then seeks to determine whether the observed degree of similarity between the Intentional Interpretation and the sub-personal basis of behavior is explicable in terms of a generally accepted source of MiCP such as dual and tripartite models of metacognitive structure and function. The MaCP agenda seeks to determine how far the Intentional Interpretation is consistent with super-personal behavioral science and to link it to a cognitive psychology that is similarly consistent with behavioral science. It then seeks to determine whether the observed degree of similarity between the Intentional Interpretation and the super-personal basis of behavior is explicable in terms of a generally accepted source of MaCP such as picoeconomic theory.

While prediction based on the Intentional Interpretation is too general to be other than trivial, prediction based on Cognitive Interpretation can be sufficiently specific to allow testing of the cognitive account in relation to the Intentional Interpretation. that is, changes in cognition → changes in subjective intentionality → changes in behavior. It is instructive, therefore, to inquire whether the considerations raised by micro- and macro-cognitive psychologies can be employed in an attempt to change behavior by modifying the subjective valuation of the rewards. In the case of MiCP, it is possible to attempt to reduce dysrationalia by eliminating mindware gaps and decreasing cognitive miserliness, and to correct excesses in cognitive style by the development of coping skills (Stanovich 2011; see also Foxall 2016a). In the case of MaCP, it is possible to employ picoeconomic strategies to affect the valuation of future outcomes of behavior. An implication of this is that the micro- and macro-cognitive psychologies can be tested through prediction of how these modifications in the verbal behaviors of consumers will affect their behavior.

Requirements of the Cognitive Interpretation

Numerous complicated details of intentionality would have to be specified to account for the behavior of an individual pursuing a particular pattern of choice for which the stimulus field for an extensional explanation was not empirically available. The consequences of embarking on such an intellectual exercise would ramify endlessly. With some simplification, therefore, Chapter 7 proposed an Intentional Interpretation leading to the broad conclusion that consumer behaviors differ in the extent to which they entail discounting the future. Even this simplified intentional account of consumer choice entails a complex cognitive framework to explain how the intentionality required of the consumer could come about. At a minimum, the following cognitive capacities are essential to the formulation of an intentionality couched in terms of the differential discounting of alternative choices. The consumer must be able to

(i) formulate a structure of desires, positive outcomes that his or her choice is expected to achieve, costs that it is intended to avoid. We can assume, on the basis of the extensional explanation of consumer choice, that the overall goal is the maximization of the utilitarian and informational reinforcement obtainable by acting in a particular manner. This maximizing of utility might be achieved moment by moment rather than globally; the processes of matching and melioration mentioned in Chapter 3 (for elaboration in the current context, see Foxall 2016a, Chapter 3) would lead us to expect local rather than overall maximization. However, in an intentional account, what is considered as reinforcement differs from consumer to consumer. This is especially so in the case of informational reinforcement, that which leads ultimately to self-esteem or pride and avoids self-disappointment or shame (as depicted in the BPM Pride-Shame Continuum, Fig. 2.5). Moreover, the individual's preference function is determined in part by his or her cognitive style (see, e.g., Foxall 2016a).

(ii) imagine future choice scenarios that will likely be available. This draws on information (beliefs) one has about what will be available and its likely results; it involves memory as well as mental projection—forward and backward time travel. The exercise of this sort of imagination requires placing normal mental functioning in abeyance while the mental operations required for future imagination and planning can take place.

(iii) undertake the evaluation of imagined future contingencies. This too entails forward and backward mental time travel. In particular, it requires personal judgments of the utilitarian and informational reinforcement and punishment that will ensue from the performance of alternative patterns of choice.

(iv) compare these choice scenarios, and their outcomes (i.e., their costs and benefits) both with one another and with an overall system of goals; this requires flexibility in changing goals at this point, substituting those beneficial goals and outcomes that emerge as more probable and relegating those that appear less so. This flexibility may require the abandonment of some goals even during the decision process and the substitution of alternatives.

The mental context of the configuration involved in these stages, a system of relevant desires, beliefs, emotions, and perceptions, composes the intentional consumer situation. The final stage comprises the action output of the intentional consumer situation, which consists in action, in fact mental action:

(v) select, intend, and work toward one particular goal, possibly keeping other(s) in reserve in case the first cannot be realized. This procedure requires perseverance toward the specified goal.

These elements of decision making require the proposal of theories of cognitive processing which can account for the initiation and maintenance of the intentionality of the idealized consumer advanced in this chapter. Chapters 8, 9, and 10, therefore, address the capacity of well-formulated and empirically supported models of cognitive structure and functioning to show how such intentionality would be brought about and sustained.

Bibliography

Ainslie, G. (1992). *Picoeconomics: The strategic interaction of successive motivational states within the person.* Cambridge: Cambridge University Press.

Ainslie, G. (2001). *Breakdown of will.* Cambridge: Cambridge University Press.

Bickel, W. R., & Yi, R. (2008). Temporal discounting as a measure of executive function: Insights from the competing neuro-behavioral decisions systems hypothesis of addiction. *Advances in Health Economics and Health Services Research, 20,* 289–309.

Boden, M. A. (1972). *Purposive explanation in psychology.* Cambridge, MA: Harvard University Press.

Dennett, D. C. (1991a). *Consciousness explained.* London: Penguin Books.

Dennett, D. C. (1991b). Real patterns. *Journal of Philosophy, 88,* 27–51.

Dretsky, F. (1988). *Explaining behavior: Reasons in a world of causes.* Cambridge, MA: MIT Press.

Evans, J. S. B. (2010). *Thinking twice: Two minds in one brain.* Oxford: Oxford University Press.

Evans, J. S. B. T., & Stanovich, K. E. (2013). Dual-process theories of higher cognition: Advancing the debate. *Perspectives on Psychological Science, 8,* 223–241.

Faber, R. J., & Vohs, K. D. (2013). Self-regulation and spending: Evidence from impulsive and compulsive buying. In K. D. Vohs & R. F. Baumeister (Eds.), *Handbook of self-regulation: Research, theory, and applications* (2nd ed., pp. 537–550). New York: The Guilford Press.

Fodor, J. A. (1987). *Psychosemantics*. Cambridge, MA: MIT Press.

Foxall, G. R. (2010a). *Interpreting consumer choice: The behavioral perspective model*. New York: Routledge.

Foxall, G. R. (2010b). Accounting for consumer choice: Inter-temporal decision-making in behavioral perspective. *Marketing Theory, 10,* 315–345.

Foxall, G. R. (2014a). Neurophilosophy of explanation in economic psychology: An exposition in terms of neuro-behavioral decision systems. In L. Moutinho et al. (Eds.), *Routledge companion to the future of marketing* (pp. 134–150). London/New York: Routledge.

Foxall, G. R. (2015c). Consumers in context: The BPM research program. London/New York: Routledge

Foxall, G. R. (2016a). *Addiction as consumer choice: Exploring the cognitive dimension*. London/New York: Routledge.

Foxall, G. R. (2016b). Metacognitive control of categorial neurobehavioral decision systems. *Frontiers in Psychology, 7,* 170.

Geertz, C. (1973). *The interpretation of cultures: Selected essays*. New York: Basic Books.

Gergely, G., & Csibra, G. (2003). Teleological reasoning in infancy: The naïve theory of rational action. *Trends in Cognitive Sciences, 7,* 287–292.

Gergely, G., Nidasdy, Z., Csibra, G., & Bíró, S. (1995). Taking the intentional stance at 12 months of age. *Cognition, 56,* 165–193.

Hornsby, J. (1981). *Actions*. London: Routledge and Kegan Paul.

Lycan, W. (1988). Dennett's instrumentalism. *Behavioral and Brain Sciences, 11,* 518–519.

Madden, G. J., & Bickel, W. K. (Eds.). (2010). *Impulsivity: The behavioral and neurological science of discounting*. Washington, DC: American Psychological Association.

Mazur, J. (1987). An adjusting procedure for studying delayed reinforcement. In M. Commons, J. Mazur, J. Nevin, & H. Rachlin (Eds.), *Quantitative analysis of behavior* (The effect of delay and of intervening events on reinforcement value, Vol. 5, pp. 55–73). Hillsdale: Erlbaum.

Pylyshyn, Z. W. (1984). *Computation and cognition: Toward a foundation for cognitive science*. Cambridge, MA: MIT Press.

Rick, S., & Loewenstein, G. (2008). Hypermotivation. *Journal of Marketing Research, 45,* 645–648.

Ridgway, N., Kukar-Kinney, M., & Monroe, K. B. (2008). An expanded conceptualization and a new measure of compulsive buying. *Journal of Consumer Research, 35,* 622–639.

Ryle, G. (1971). The thinking of thoughts: What *is Le Penseur* doing? In G. Ryle (Ed.) *Collected papers.* II: *Collected essays 1929–1968.* London: Hutchinson.

Shea, N., Boldt, A., Bang, D., Yeung, N., Heyes, C., & Frith, C. D. (2014). Supra-personal cognitive control and metacognition. *Trends in Cognitive Sciences, 18,* 186–193.

Skinner, B. F. (1953a). *Science and human behavior.* New York: Macmillan.

Skinner, B. F. (1957). *Verbal behavior.* New York: Century.

Skinner, B. F. (1999). A lecture on "having" a poem. In B. F. Skinner (Ed.), *Cumulative record* (Definitiveth ed., pp. 391–401). Acton: Copley.

Smith, T. L. (1994). *Behavior and its causes: Philosophical foundations of operant psychology.* Dordrecht: Kluwer.

Stanovich, K. E. (2009a). Distinguishing the reflective, algorithmic, and autonomous minds: Is it time for a tri-process theory? In J. S. B. T. Evans & K. Frankish (Eds.), *In two minds: Dual processes and beyond* (pp. 55–88). Oxford: Oxford University Press.

Stanovich, K. E. (2009b). *What intelligence tests miss: The psychology of rational thought.* New Haven/London: Yale University Press.

Stanovich, K. E. (2011). *Rationality and the reflective mind.* Oxford: Oxford University Press.

Steward, H. (2012). *A metaphysics for freedom.* Oxford: Oxford University Press.

Strawson, G. (1986). *Freedom and belief.* Oxford: Oxford University Press.

Taylor, C. (1964). *The explanation of behaviour.* London: Routledge and Kegan Paul.

8

Consumer Choice as Decision: Micro-Cognitive Psychology

Introduction

In this chapter Cognitive Interpretation is explored in terms of a micro-cognitive psychology (MiCP). This relates the Intentional Interpretation to neuroscience and metacognitive functioning in which a rapidly operating impulsive mode of decision making must be brought into balance by a slower executive mode. At least it must if the problems associated with impetuous and imprudent consumption are to be avoided. This chapter identifies the need for a cognitive interpretation as the explication of intra-personal, inter-agent communication and cooperation. Its mission is to show how this can be effected in the individual in a manner that is consistent with neurophysiological functioning while remaining sensitive to the influence of environmental stimulation on behavior.

© The Editor(s) (if applicable) and The Author(s) 2016   **211**
G.R. Foxall, *Perspectives on Consumer Choice*,
DOI 10.1057/978-1-137-50121-9_8

Micro-Cognitive Psychology

Linking Personal Level Cognition with Sub-Personal Neurophysiology

All rewarded behavior is associated with a particular set of neural circuits and events, principally what is known as the limbic and paralimbic dopamine system. Reinforcing events, whether they occur as a result of everyday routine consumption, the administration of drugs of abuse, or engagement in potentially addictive behaviors such as slot machine gambling, all recruit this machinery (see, e.g., McKim and Boettiger 2015; see also Foxall 2016a). The dopamine system, which enables rapid reactions to environmental opportunities and threats, developed in the course of evolution by natural selection. The rapid responses that this system causes to occur with a high degree of automaticity are essential to activities such as the securing of prey and the escape from predators. However, the responses made possible by this system may or may not be appropriate in the everyday modern life of the consumer. Being able to respond quickly to unexpected oncoming traffic ensures the safety and possibly the survival of the driver. But acceptance without thoughtful consideration to the offer of another drink may well be disastrous. The capacity of executive functions, associated with prefrontal cortical activity, to overcome such impulsiveness by means of a process of considered decision making can counter the innate tendency to satisfy consumption demands without thought of the future.

The discussion of MiCP begins with the recognition that human decision making is characterized by a number of different modes from reflex responses through classical and operant conditioning, to deliberative planning. Each of these is a method of decision making because it is a process of *action selection*, as Redish (2013, 2015) defines decision making. Each of these decision methods is associated with a specific pattern of behavior and a neurophysiological substrate and is also explicable in terms of an appropriate range of intentionality. Each seems appropriate to a particular set of circumstances that would have been encountered in the course of evolution and/or ontogenetic development. In general, two broad categories of decision making form the basis of the models of cognitive processing with which MiCP is concerned: the rapid and inflexible responding to immediate circumstances that is often described as impulsivity, and the deliberative planning of future behaviors and their outcomes that is generally attributed to an executive system (Fig. 8.1.) The *impulsive decision mode* is that which is based on neurophysiological events in the limbic and paralimbic systems, while the *executive decision mode* is that which is dependent on the functioning of the prefrontal cortex (PFC). The former is appropriate to the production of rapid responses occasioned by a fast-moving environment such as that in which the prey become intermittently available and must be caught with accuracy and speed. The latter is relevant to a more predictable environment in which time and other resources are available for the consideration of alternative futures and their evaluation in terms of the individual's goals

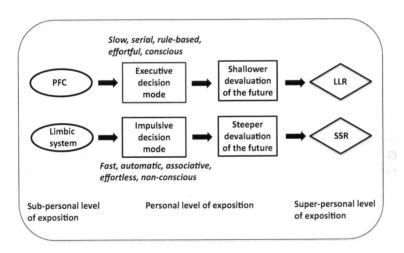

Fig. 8.1 *Summative dual process depiction of metacognitive control.* This depiction of a dual system of cognitive control maintains the separation of the sub-personal, personal, and super-personal levels of exposition, a detail which is overlooked in many models of this type. The sub-personal level of exposition links Cognitive Interpretation to its neurophysiological basis; the super-personal level of exposition, to its operant basis. The diagram also shows the cognitive conclusion of each of the decision modes: steeper vs. shallower devaluation of the future, and the behavioral outcomes to which each of these leads (choice of SSR vs. choice of LLR). See text for further exposition. For further exposition, see Foxall (2016a, b)

and capabilities. The first entails the kind of reflexive responses that may be innate as well as learned responses that arise in the course of behavioral conditioning; the second the kinds of mental responding that can inhibit immediate reaction in favor of the informed pondering of alternative future scenarios. Of course, many consumer decisions depend on less extreme approaches than these, or on a combination of aspects of both. Problems may occur when the decision mode appropriate to one particular set of environmental circumstances is employed in action selection for an incompatible set of circumstances or when one approach interferes with the execution of the other. Problems are also evident when one set of decision procedures malfunctions as a result of neurophysiological damage. This situation is often implicated in overconsumption to the point of addiction.

The impulsive decision mode is marked by such rapidity as to make its operations appear automatic, though this does not of course imply that they are spontaneous or uncaused. The point about this mode of decision making is that it is informed principally by a subset of the consequences of prior behavior, those that have achieved ends in a competitive environment with the least expenditure of effort or resource. Such responses are effective because they are not delayed by deliberation; they work because their immediacy forestalls counter actions by a predator or some other aspect of a quickly changing environment.

The episodic future-oriented thinking required for deliberative decision making entails the capacity to imagine one's future behaviors and their consequences, both reinforcing and punishing; it also depends on the ability to draw upon memories of past behavior and its outcomes, the subjective internal representation of one's learning history, which is necessarily selective and partial. This executive decision mode relies therefore on an internalized model of behavior-environment relationships as they have occurred in the past, but also the capacity to override these considerations in order that novel situations can be imagined and evaluated.

These evaluation procedures conspicuously demand cognitive abilities: to hold current states and future events in imagination, to compute their worth at different times, to compare their outcomes with one another and with those of one's usual courses of action, to evaluate all in terms of one's objectives, to assess the costs of implanting each, and having chosen among them to formulate an action plan. The description of these operations requires a cognitive framework. Behaviorists who propose that these activities are simply behaviors, just like their overt counterparts, apart from being private and uniquely observable by the individuals to whom they belong, make sense only if they can point convincingly to the reinforcing and punishing consequences of such "behavior" that shape and maintain it; if, alternatively, they argue that the "behavior" is classically conditioned, they must identify the US and CS by means of which it was learned. There is no room in behaviorism for speculative ascription of stimuli and responses.

Dual Systems Approaches

Dual systems theories of decision making and behavior have received considerable theoretical and empirical support among cognitive psychologists and cognitive neuroscientists as a means of coming to terms with the differing cognitive styles that the impulsive and executive decision modes portray (see, for instance, Evans 2010; Kahneman 2011). Norman and Shallice (1986; Shallice and Cooper 2011) argue that behavior is cognitively controlled in two ways. The first is by "overlearned cognitive schemata" on one hand (Baddeley 2007, p. 120) which in the process of conditioning lead to habits that are automatic and fast, driven by schemata that take control of behavior with immediacy. The second is a *supervisory attention system* (SAS) that is able to override the stimulus-bound habitual behavior generated in the first case if its outcomes are detrimental to the individual. The production of novel behavior thus relies on the SAS which has the capacity to engender search for solutions to problems which are not amenable to tried and tested means.

The view that the cognitive components of the impulsive and executive decision modes are instantiated in specific neural regions is corroborated by experiments incorporating fMRI scans of humans choosing between SSR and LLR (McClure et al. 2004). Student participants in this experiment made a choice between reinforcers that varied in terms of both their magnitude and the temporal delay incurred before receiving them. In the course of decision making about the immediate reinforcers, the limbic and paralimbic regions of the students' brains were highly activated. These regions include the ventral striatum, the medial orbito-frontal cortex, medial prefrontal cortex, and posterior cingulate cortex. By contrast, when they were making decisions about delayed reinforcers, the activated brain regions were in lateral prefrontal parts of the brain. These regions include the dorsolateral prefrontal cortex, the ventrolateral prefrontal cortex, and the lateral orbitofrontal cortex.

Dual process theories can easily fail to maintain the essential distinction between the sub-personal and personal levels of exposition. The generalized depiction shown in Fig. 8.1 makes clear this difference and also includes the super-personal level of exposition. The main cognitive skills that compose each of the decision modes are depicted in Fig. 8.2. The executive decision mode is marked by relative high levels of: *behavioral flexibility* (including *capacity to switch tasks*), *behavioral inhibition*, *attentional control* (including the maintenance and division of attention), *planning ability*, *valuation of future events*, *recruitment of working memory*, and *reflective ability* including the capacity to imagine future behavioral scenarios and their outcomes. The impulsive decision mode is correspondingly weak in these respects, and some of these cognitive capacities (e.g., engagement of working memory) may be entirely absent.

Fig. 8.2 *Dimensions of difference between impulsive and executive decision modes.* This figure indicates the principal areas of mental functioning that distinguish the executive and impulsive modes identified. Each dimension is represented to a greater extent in the case of the executive decision mode (+) than that of the impulsive decision mode (–). These dimensions are chosen for their summative nature: for instance, valuation of future events includes considerations of sensation seeking and reinforcement sensitivity. They also enjoy well-founded empirical support (Bickel et al. 2012). For further exposition in the current context, see Foxall (2016a, b)

This dichotomy of the cognitive skills reflected in the impulsive and executive decision modes is derived from an extensive study undertaken in the context of one of the most elaborated and successful of dual-process models, the Competing Neurobehavioral Decisions Systems (CNDS) model (Bickel et al. 2012).[1]

The CNDS hypothesis seeks to explain normal and addictive behaviors in terms of differences in rates of temporal discounting that reflect the degree of balance between an individual's "impulsive" and "executive" systems. The neurophysiological substrates of the impulsive system are located in the limbic and paralimbic brain regions, while those of the executive system are found in the prefrontal cortex (PFC). Hyperactivity of the impulsive system, coupled with hypoactivity of the executive system is hypothesized to eventuate in steep discounting of the future and to increase the individual's tendency toward addictive behavior (Bickel and Yi 2008).

Temporal discounting provides a measure of the degree of executive functional control reflected in behavior (Bickel and Yi 2008); addicts, and others who consume to excess, discount more steeply than nonaddicted consumers (Madden and Bickel 2010). The competing neuro-behavioral decision systems model links addiction to the hypoactivity of the executive system, based in PFC, and the hyperactivity of the impulsive system, based in the limbic and paralimbic regions. This chapter is concerned to clarify the use of cognitive language which is inevitable in this endeavor to specify *decision* systems: the authors of the CNDS model speak for instance of metacognition while the exposition of picoeconomics, which has been proposed as a cognitive level of analysis for the CNDS model (Foxall 2014a, b), involves the intra-personal interaction of strategic interests (Ainslie 1992).

Intra-personal, Intra-agent Communication, and Cooperation

If the first task on the MiCP agenda is to link the Intentional Interpretation with neuroscience, then the second is to link both to an appropriate theory of metacognitive control. Recent theoretical work on cognitive and

---

[1] Bickel et al. (2012) provide an informative summary of the CNDS model. For further discussion in the context of consumer choice and decision making, see Foxall (2016a, b).

metacognitive control as a mechanism for *supra-personal* communication and cooperation by Shea et al. (2014) suggests a means of conceptualizing *intra-personal* interactions between the impulsive and executive systems and sets out necessary functions of systems of metacognitive control. These authors propose a dual systems model of metacognition in which a "cognitively lean" system, designated *system 1* (hereafter, S1) *metacognition*, accounts for intra-personal cognitive control, while "cognitively rich" *system 2* (S2) *metacognition* is responsible for supra-personal cognitive control, that is, cognitive control among a plurality of agents, conceived as separate individuals. S1 metacognition, which is common to many animals, functions in the absence of working memory and is "typically fast, automatic, associative, effortless, and non-conscious"; by contrast, S2 metacognitive systems rely on working memory, are "typically slower, serial, rule-based, more effortful, and conscious," and are probably exclusive to humans (Shea et al. 2014, p. 186). Although Shea et al. (2014) allude to the possibility that S2 metacognitive processes are implicated in the intra-personal regulation of behavior, their emphasis is on inter-personal inter-agent cooperation. They argue that S2 metacognitive systems enhance such cooperation in three ways:

1. by distributing metacognitive representations for verbal communication;
2. by evaluating metacognitive representations to motivate appropriate action; and
3. by extricating metacognitive representations from weak metacognitive information.[2]

S2 systems also exert synchronic (enhancing the performance of multiple agents simultaneously engaged in a common task) and diachronic

---

[2] Although supra-personal metacognition is compatible with intra-personal, inter-agent metacognition, it is not obvious that it is historically or logically prior to it; nor is intra-personal metacognition necessarily a side effect. However, it is probable that cultural evolution played a dominant role in the development of S2 metacognition as a cognitive control mechanism that overcomes impulsiveness by engendering cooperation between short- and longer-term interests. The modification of temporal horizon from that predisposing toward impulsiveness to that in which consumption can be delayed is traceable to the transition from hunter-gathering to agriculture and more recent religiously based community, hence from early hominins to modern humans (Bickel and Marsch 2000).

(influencing how other agents later think and act and so enhancing joint performance) supra-personal cognitive control (Shea et al. 2014, p. 190.) While economic models[3] indicate the options available to the agent, System 2 metacognitive models suggest how choice (cooperation rather than conflict) would be exerted at an overarching cognitive level. It is necessary that CNDS and picoeconomics offer an explanation at this level to account for the selection of one or other response in a given situation. This requires understanding of how metacognitive representations of patterns of reinforcement that have previously shaped and maintained patterns of choice (i.e., super-personal metacognition) or reward prediction errors based on neuronal firing rates (sub-personal metacognition) are acted upon by S2 metacognition in the course of decision-making and action outputs.

Cognitive control effected at the supra-personal level by S2 metacognition to facilitate inter-personal communication and cooperation may account also for coordination between the intra-personal agents portrayed by picoeconomics (Ainslie 1992; see also Elster 2015) as incompatible intertemporal interests. Picoeconomic analysis accords with the competing neuro-behavioral decisions systems (CNDS) hypothesis (Bickel et al. 2012) in which addiction results from imbalance, reflected in exaggerated temporal discounting, between a hyperactive *impulsive system* based on the limbic and paralimbic systems and a hypoactive *executive system* based on OFC (Bickel and Yi 2008; see also Foxall 2014b). The *competing neuro-behavioral decision systems* (CNDS) hypothesis seeks to explain normal and addictive behaviors in terms of differences in rates of temporal discounting that reflect the degree of balance between an individual's "impulsive" and "executive" systems. These systems are akin to the S1 and S2 systems, respectively, that we have been considering. The

---

[3] The economic modeling of the interests proposed by picoeconomics (Ainslie 1992) reaches similar conclusions. These interests or subagents may behave synchronously on the basis of either their contradictory utility functions or their incompatible temporal preferences (Ross 2012). The hyperbolic time preference in the second case reflects rivalry between "limbic regions" exhibiting steep, exponential discounting and "cognitive regions" showing less steep exponential discounting (Ross 2012, p. 720). Alternatively, the interests may be understood as residing in a person who is "diachronically composed of multiple selves" that have varying utility functions and incomplete knowledge of one another. Consideration of supra-personal cognitive control and metacognition emphasizes reconciliation and cooperation; the economic portrayal, conflicting interests.

neurophysiological substrates of the impulsive system are located in the limbic and paralimbic brain regions, while those of the executive system are found in the PFC. Hyperactivity of the impulsive system, coupled with hypoactivity of the executive system is hypothesized to eventuate in steep discounting of the future and to increase the individual's tendency toward addictive behavior (Bickel and Yi 2008). Between the extremes of balanced and imbalanced interactions of these systems lie the possibilities of a diversity of levels of temporal discounting and of consumer behaviors that reflect varying degrees of preference reversal. The Intentional Interpretation, which concentrated on the subjective intertemporal valuations of alternative choices, receives support from this reasoning about the neurophysiological bases of impulsivity and self-control. However, we may inquire whether this simple dichotomy is sufficient to capture the cognitive complexities of decision making in those circumstances that present us with such alternatives.

Adequacy of Dual Process Depiction

Two considerations suggest that a dual process depiction may be inadequate: the demands on rationality made by decision strategies, and the consequent need of a superordinate forum for decision control.

Rationality Requirements of Decision Strategies The first alludes to functional factors: decision making that overcomes the impulse toward immediate gratification may require a level of rationality not accounted for in the dual process models. The conflicting interests with which the individual has to contend must communicate in order for decisions to be reached. First, the metacognitive representations required for communication between interests require a mechanism for their distribution. Second, they require a mechanism for the generation and comparative evaluation of possible future courses of action. And, third, weak metacognition information must be amplified by some mechanism so that it can be taken into consideration in the decision process. Each interest's ignorance of the other, pointed out by Ross (2012) means that the information it encapsulates will remain weak unless some additional mental component augments it and makes it more generally available. Neither of the interests depicted by picoeconomics or the CNDS model can undertake these functions. The list of components of the impulsive and executive systems provided by Bickel et al. (2012) do not provide for this except in the possible metacognitive function and emotional memory they assign to the executive system. Yet it is not feasible to justify the inclusion of these functions in the system of antipodal components they seek to establish. They include them in the executive system but they have no antipodal echo in the impulsive system. It is reasonable therefore to argue that these components belong in a mental system that is beyond the impulsive or executive systems. Stanovich's (2009b, 2011) tripartite model provides a natural resting place for these elements. Algorithmic Mind contains some of the executive functions which Bickel et al. (2012) ascribe to the executive system. But Stanovich's model also incorporates Reflective Mind as an additional Type 2 system.

The Need for a Superordinate Forum for Decision Control The second consideration alludes to topographical factors: the evaluation of alternative futures and deciding among them requires a forum not evident in descriptions of the S1 system or the impulsive decision mode, on the one hand, the S2 or the executive decision mode, on the other. Neither of these provides a *forum* for the conduct of the three metacognitive functions identified by Shea et al. (2014). This forum must be independent of both the impulsive and executive systems if it is to distribute information from each that the other can respond to, if there is to be evaluation of the claims of each in light of the environmental threats and opportunities with which the individual is presented, and if adjudication can take place leading to appropriate decision making. A mental region or additional metacognitive system is required to undertake these operations. Moreover, if the impulsive and executive systems proposed by the CNDS model are truly antipodal then metacognition and emotional activation and self-regulation need to be removed from the executive system since they have no counterpart in the impulsive system. The remaining impulsive and executive elements cannot account for the kinds of rational formulation of goals appropriate to the organism and its environment.

A useful working hypothesis at this point is that these considerations may justify a tripartite theory. The following section therefore discusses the tripartite model of Stanovich (2009a, b) which is probably the most comprehensively and closely argued of its type.

Tripartite Modeling

Stanovich's Tripartite Model Stanovich's (2009a, b) tripartite model then consists of an Automatic Mind, which has much in common with the S1 system,[4] conceptualized not as a single entity but rather a series of brain systems that operate spontaneously, each in response to a cluster of stimuli that are peculiar to it. Collectively, these S1-*type* systems are known as *the autonomous set of systems* (TASS). As was suggested above, the S2 system is reminiscent of what Stanovich terms Analytic Mind, a composite of the Reflective Mind and the Algorithmic Mind. While the Algorithmic Mind is shaped by individual differences in IQ, the operation of the Reflective Mind reflects individual differences in rational thinking dispositions or cognitive styles. Rationality encompasses a broader purview than intelligence, depending on strongly formulated desires (goals) and beliefs, plus a capacity to act in accordance with them.[5]

TASS works relentlessly toward the realization of short-range interests as long as these are not overruled by the Algorithmic Mind, which promotes long-range interests. The signal to overrule is initiated by the Reflective Mind, and depends on the cognitive style it embodies, but implemented by the Algorithmic Mind, which reflects the fluid intelligence of the individual. The operations of these two elements of Analytical Mind are determined by individual differences, differences from person to person in intellectual style and level in the case of Reflective Mind,

---

[4] I am tempted to make the assumption that the Type 1 and Type 2 processing to which Stanovich refers correspond broadly to S1 and S2 metacognitive systems especially functionally. This suggestion of correspondence, however tentatively it is made, must be viewed with a critical eye. While there may be some functional similarity, it is not clear that the systems involved are identical (Evans 2010).

[5] Stanovich (2009a, 2011) provides the most informative and comprehensive accounts of his tripartite model. For a more complete discussion in the present context than is possible in Chapter 8, see Foxall (2016a, b).

and in intellectual level in that of Algorithmic Mind. Individuals respond differently to environmental stimuli, therefore, depending on their overall capacity to respond rationally to stimuli and their level of intelligence which determines their ability to respond to the cues put out by Reflective Mind, successfully override Automatic Mind over a period to time so that cognitive rehearsal of alternative future action patterns can take place. Failure to countermand TASS might, therefore, reflect a cognitive style at the level of Reflective Mind that encouraged the pursuit of LRI, or an inability of Algorithmic Mind to respond to Reflective Mind's instruction to place Automatic Mind in abeyance and inaugurate cognitive rehearsal, or the incapacity of Algorithmic Mind to maintain the necessary detachment while this work of imagination proceeds. Unless it is effectively checked by Algorithmic Mind, Automatic Mind will have free reign to react with immediacy to environmental conditions. As we have noted, on this basis, Stanovich (2009a) argues for the superordinate level of cognitive processing that he terms the Reflective Mind.

Another consideration is that, in order to effect a balance between the SRI and the LRI, there is need for a forum in which personal-level goals and strategic procedures that are beyond the influence of either Automatic Mind or Algorithmic Mind can influence decisions and behavior, a level of processing that is superior to both of them. This provides a further rationale for the inclusion of Reflective Mind. There is of course no way of knowing precisely if and how human mentality works on a tripartite basis in this way. However, the genius of the tripartite model lies in its delineating the necessary functions of mind that would be logically involved in the pre-behavioral guidance of a rational being. In this competence theory, Reflective Mind inaugurates a call to Algorithmic Mind to begin the process of cognitive simulation or hypothetical reasoning. Algorithmic Mind in turn accomplishes within the scope of its individual capacity the procedure of *decoupling*, disengaging itself from mental construal of the current situation so that possible courses of future action can be imagined unambiguously and without confusion. This *simulation* of future events entails the metacognitive representation of scenarios in relation to the organism's immediate goals and its long-term welfare. These functions of Analytic Mind are similar to S2 functions, entailing serially instantiated operations and specialized computation, which require numerous components we have associated with the executive decision mode like behavioral flexibility and inhibition, planning skills, the valuation of future events, and working memory.

Making Room for Executive Function Recall that Analytic Mind contains two metacognitive processes, namely, the *Algorithmic* level and the *Reflective* level. However, the executive functions—principally including the decoupling abilities ascribed to the Algorithmic Mind, and which we may see as essentially tactical—differ conceptually from the more strategically oriented epistemic regulation and cognitive allocation that lie within the domain of Reflective Mind. Stanovich (2009a) argues that the term "executive functions" is therefore a misnomer. What Algorithmic Mind does can be better described as the execution of *supervisory processes*, based on as they are on rules that are externally provided rather than through internally inaugurated decision processes. It is Reflective Mind that determines "the goal agenda" and operates at the level of epistemic regulation which he defines as "directing the sequence of information pickup." Stanovich's point is that this work of Reflective Mind, this strategic directing, is not what is generally thought of as comprising "executive functions" as this term is understood in cognitive psychology. Better, therefore, to describe the generally understood operations of Algorithmic Mind as "supervisory tasks," retaining "executive functions" for the work of Reflective Mind.

The purpose of raising this point in the present context is to draw attention to the duality of function involved. The restraining activities of Algorithmic Mind and the insistent activities of TASS as impulsive drives are overcome by the exercise of executive functions. The interaction of Algorithmic Mind and TASS is governed not by external rules but by policies determined by a process of strategic decision making that reflects the broad approaches to the conduct of behavior set by an overarching cognitive style. This genuinely managerial (executive) activity determines overall objectives for the individual and the ways in which they are to be achieved. It requires a mind (a mental system) that is global in its reach rather than being confined to the resolution of a particular set of external environmental circumstances. The determination and implementation of ways of working at this level has implications for the way in which the individual responds to a particular stimulus field when it presents itself but it does so by operating at a broader level of consideration. The parallel is with Roll's (2014) theory of emotion in which the goals of behavior, rather than the specific behaviors that achieve them, are set genetically: here the goals of behavior are set in cognitive terms, leaving the resolution of how to behave in particular situations to the interaction of impulsive and executive decision modes at a quite different level of conceptualization and operation. These broader functions do not fall within the operational purview of either Automatic Mind or Algorithmic Mind: they require the third tier, that of Reflective Mind.

How the Tripartite Model Meets the Requirements of Metacognitive Control

The metacognitive requirements for intra-personal, inter-agent communication and cooperation, exemplified by the conditions needed for bundling to work, are those suggested by Shea et al. (2014) for supra-personal inter-agent interaction: first, distributing metacognitive representations for verbal communication; second, evaluating metacognitive representations to motivate appropriate action; and, third, extricating metacognitive representations from weak metacognitive information—before discussing their relevance to the interaction of picoeconomic interests.

Figure 8.3 shows these three metacognitive functions identified by Shea et al. (2014) in relation to the tripartite model advanced by Stanovich (2009a, b). Discussing them in reverse order makes their relevance to the present discussion more apparent.

Extricating Metacognitive Representations from Weak Metacognitive Information Where is metacognitive information likely to be weak within this framework? Insofar as metacognition is thinking about thinking it is S1 that is likely to convey relatively little deliberative reflection on what is happening to the individual. This extraction of metacognitive representations from weak metacognitive information can only be accomplished by Reflective Mind which cumulates the experience of operant behavior and its outcomes into learning histories that impinge on further responding. It is through this cumulation of information that the decoupling of

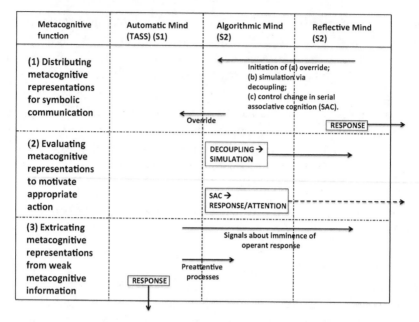

Metacognitive function	Automatic Mind (TASS) (S1)	Algorithmic Mind (S2)	Reflective Mind (S2)

Fig. 8.3 *Metacognitive functions in relation to tripartite theory.* The three metacognitive functions identified by Shea et al. (2014) are shown in relation to Stanovich's (2009a) tripartite theory of cognitive functioning. The relationships proposed by the latter entail, in the intra-personal cognitive environment, the kinds of metacognitive function to which Shea et al. draw attention in the context of inter-personal interaction. Picoeconomic understanding of conflicting intra-personal interests is enhanced through its consideration within this framework. For further explication, see Foxall (2016a, b) (Adapted from Foxall (2016b). Metacognitive control of categorial neurobehavioral decision systems, *Frontiers in Psychology* (*Theoretical and Philosophical Psychology*), 7: 170, pp. 1–18)

Automatic Mind and the simulation of alternative futures can be initiated. The process of cumulation and extraction will be guided by the individual's cognitive style: an adaptive style is more sensitive to reinforcement contingencies than an innovative style.

The communication this requires is understood in the context of intra-personal bargaining as the symbolic deliberation among alternative courses of action, their likely consequences, and choice between/among them. This clearly entails laying out the alternatives so that they and their implications can be assessed, their future values computed and compared in the present moment. The selection of the shorter- or longer-range behavior requires their comparative intertemporal valuation. The intensification of the signals presented by the experienced and promised outcomes of self-control is necessary for the individual to become aware of the likely outcomes of each of the behaviors available to him or her, and crucially of the values he or she attaches to each of them.

The steep discounter may be unaware of or pay only cursory attention to the effects of patience: he or she may have little learning history from which sensitivity to the superior outcomes of waiting would become apparent; or there may be inherent tendencies to devalue future outcomes as a matter of course. The power of this influence on behavior is evident from the fact that at every t_1 thus far encountered SSR>LLR, and the expectation is that this state of affairs will continue. There is little reason to believe that a person who has been motivated by the choice of SSRs over a period would become convinced that awaiting the LLR on the next occasion would be sensible. It requires mental effort to bring forth the two streams of future rewards and to compare them, and there are countervailing forces at work. First, the tendency toward cognitive miserliness might easily prevail, favoring sticking with tried and tested approaches to behavioral decision making and avoiding the cognitive costs of learning to think in new ways. Second, the individual may simply not have access to the mindware necessary to make the logic of bundling apparent to him or her. The intellectual ability and/or knowledge to comprehend the processes involved in bundling, which he or she must not only initiate but carry through, may be lacking. Explanation of the behavior of a person who both avoids cognitive miserliness and possesses necessary mindware still requires a psychological mechanism which brings together the advantages of selecting LLR over SSR for a sustained period, that enables comparison of what at the decision point are mentally entertained hypothetical alternatives, and that makes possible selection of the "road less travelled." If weak information requires cumulation, consolidation, and synthesis to become effective in decision making, there must be a forum in which the necessary processing can occur, especially if there is a tendency toward economizing mental exertion.

The generation of metacognitive representations is depicted initially as a function of Reflective Mind which extricates relatively weak metacognitive information via its monitoring of the environment and Automatic Mind's potential responses to it. The weak perspective metacognitive signals generated by Automatic Mind are extricated and cumulated by Reflective Mind which is involved in their evaluation and a decision whether to initiate override of Automatic Mind by Algorithmic Mind. The information so generated by Automatic Mind is considered meta-cognitively weak because, first, it is questionable how far it is information about cognition, that is, whether it is *meta*cognitive at all. One possi-bility is that it must be based predominantly in the neurophysiologi-cal remnants of a learning history rather than intentional cognitions. It is this neurophysiological readiness that promotes the automaticity of TASS. Another view is that this learning history is encapsulated some-how in affective somatic markers lodged in PFC which would also guar-antee a rapid positive or negative response to environmental stimulation (Damasio 1994). In this case, Automatic Mind *could* be considered meta-cognitive in its operation. Second, Automatic Mind is geared toward immediate action rather than the proliferation and evaluation of details concerning it. What it is "going to do" is therefore not necessarily an explicit given. Only in the light of the individual's learning history and an assessment of the possible outcomes of precipitate action generated by Automatic Mind can a decision be made about whether to override it and initiate a deeper evaluation of alternative actions. All in all, even if we consider Automatic Mind to involve metacognition, this is very shallow, consisting in registered emotional reactions to previous behavior rather than considered cognitive deliberations.

Evaluation of the Resulting Metacognitive Information to Motivate Appropriate Action The second metacognitive function highlighted by Shea et al. (2014), evaluation metacognitive representations to motivate appropriate action, belongs to Algorithmic Mind which is responsible for the anthologizing and comparative appraisal of behavioral alterna-tives. The range of possibilities must arise from (a) prior behavior and its outcomes, through the representation of previous operant functioning, and these must be present in the form of beliefs about the range of fea-sible actions amenable to the individual, the possibility of their produc-ing particular outcomes, the likely probability of each outcome; (b) the source of these metacognitive representations and their distribution will be strongly influenced by Reflective Mind and the prevailing cognitive style that dominates it.

The evaluative process is accomplished by Algorithmic Mind but within the scope of the cognitive style that partly defines the nature/tone of Reflective Mind. Cognitive style determines the kinds of goals the individual pursues, the means he or she adopts or repudiates in order to achieve goals, the beliefs that guide his or her values and therefore permissible behaviors. An innovative cognitive style is broadly defined by the tendency to proliferate ideas in seeking to solve a problem, and the lack of rule conformity in the process of finding and implementing solutions (Kirton 2003). The problem itself is conceptualized as an opportunity to break free of previous conventions and behaviors, to *do differently*. The adaptive cognitive style by contrast is marked by a reliance on tried and tested methods, a more restricted (but usually more practicable) range of ideas for the solution of a problem, the conceptualization of the problem as an opportunity to *do better* than has hitherto been accomplished. Cognitive style therefore determines what is seen as a problem. The extreme innovator is far less likely to try to constrain the operation of Automatic Mind than is the extreme adaptor who is more likely to pick up weak metacognitive information and transform it into metacognitive representations that quickly initiate decoupling and simulation.

Should the innovator reach this stage, his or her proliferation of ideas in the course of cognitive rehearsal leads to the consideration of more (though not necessarily better or more appropriate or more relevant) alternatives being considered but their comparative evaluation may be made more on the basis of the sensation seeking and reinforcement sensitivity proclivities of the decision maker than if he or she were an adaptor (Kirton 2003; see also Foxall 2016a).

As necessary, on the basis of its extrication and organization of the weak metacognitive information thus gleaned from Automatic Mind, Reflective Mind manifests the second metacognitive function, the evaluation of the resulting metacognitive information to motivate appropriate action. This consists in initiating override via Algorithmic Mind, instructs Algorithmic Mind to decouple and initiate simulation (cognitive rehearsal). The overriding of Automatic Mind puts the automatic operant response on hold, and the results of the evaluation of simulated alternative behaviors which promise more beneficial outcomes are relayed to Reflective Mind so that a response is available. Overriding may be thought of as taking Automatic Mind offline, enabling Algorithmic Mind to undertake the decoupling from its understanding of how things are so that cognitive simulation, the rehearsal of alternative futures, can occur without ambiguity or confusion.

The hypothetical thinking involved in simulation entails *reasoning*, in which both the algorithmic and the reflective processes of the Analytic Mind function crucially. Hypothetical thinking is needed if the TASS-initiated tendencies are surmounted and superseded by responses that are more appropriate to the individual's long-term welfare or superordinate goals. This relies on the Algorithmic Mind's engaging in cognitive simulation, in which such strategies are tested in a way that ensures their survival or demise. Reflective Mind reviews the products of such simulation and brings about changes in serial associative cognition (SAC), which prompts Algorithmic Mind to develop and inaugurate an appropriate response. Hence, not all of the actions of Analytic Mind involve hypothetical thinking: SAC is, by contrast with simulation, a rather shallow kind of thinking. It does not evince the rapidity and parallel processing which characterize the Automatic Mind. It "is nonetheless inflexibly locked into an associative mode that takes as its starting point a model of the world that is *given* to the subject" (Stanovich 2009a, p. 68). Serial associative cognition "is serial and analytic ... in style, but it relies on a single focal model that triggers all subsequent thought" (p. 70).

Distribution of Metacognitive Representations to Facilitate Symbolic Communication Automatic Mind, motivated by SRI, does not actively communicate prior to acting. Impulsive and fast, it has often motivated action before any deliberation has had time to occur. Yet the SRI can be overridden. In tripartite theory this is accomplished by the signal from Reflective Mind to Algorithmic Mind to override the Automatic Mind. In order for this to occur, Reflective Mind must become aware of the imminent likelihood of Automatic Mind's responding to an environmental stimulus. This does not consist in active communication on the part of Automatic Mind, but of Reflective Mind's extricating weak metacognitive information and transforming it into metacognitive representations that can, if required, lead to the disengagement of Automatic Mind so that appropriate deliberation (cognitive rehearsal) can be undertaken by Algorithmic Mind (so that Reflective Mind can initiate simulation via decoupling). If it is not overridden, TASS will communicate with action components and the individual will act impulsively.

Reflective Mind, having obtained communication from Automatic Mind, must then initiate decoupling of Automatic Mind by communicating with Algorithmic Mind. It must also instruct Algorithmic Mind to inaugurate cognitive rehearsal, the contemplation of alternative points of view, possible future actions, and their likely consequences. This is the source of the Popperian mind. Algorithmic Mind must communicate with Automatic Mind to override its functioning. It must also communicate with action-effecting elements to initiate an alternative course of action to that to which Automatic Mind's uninhibited processing will lead.

The implication of the ability of Reflective Mind to initiate override of the TASS is that the metacognitive representations that originate with S1 are *distributed* such that (i) Reflective Mind can *become aware of* the behavior that will be elicited if TASS is not overridden, (ii) Reflective Mind can instruct Algorithmic Mind to override Automatic Mind, and (iii) inaugurate cognitive simulation to identify alternative courses of action that are less costly/more beneficial than that which will eventuate if the Automatic Mind proceeds unhindered.

In inaugurating these procedures of Algorithmic Mind, Reflective Mind fulfills the first metacognitive function mentioned by Shea et al. (2014): the distribution of metacognitive representations to facilitate symbolic communication (verbal and nonverbal). In fact, by initiating decoupling and simulation in Algorithmic Mind, Reflective Mind's actions have a twin influence on the metacognitive activity of Algorithmic Mind. First, it distributes the import of the weak metacognitive information it has gathered from Automatic Mind and synthesizes them into stronger metacognitive symbols by making its conclusions available to Algorithmic Mind. Second, it thereby stimulates Algorithmic Mind to clarify and make use of the (*relatively weak*) metacognitive information it has access to by promoting the formation of alternative future actions in the process of simulation.

Conclusion

The conclusion to which these considerations point is that the tripartite model embraces the three functions of metacognitive control suggested by Shea et al. (2014) more comprehensively than do dual process models. It seems particularly apparent that level of metacognitive processing that transcends the specific demands of the impulsive and executive decision modes and that lays out the general "policy framework" within which decisions are to be reached is necessary. Among other things, this will be a repository of the cognitive styles that influence general susceptibility to reinforcement sensitivity, sensation seeking, and, therefore, impulsivity and self-control (Foxall 2014a, b). Having discussed aspects of the metacognitive mechanisms that foster *intra-personal* communication and cooperation to attain the organism's superordinate goals set by this cognitive style, we turn in Chapter 9 to the social mechanisms that influence *supra-personal* decision making.

Bibliography

Ainslie, G. (1992). *Picoeconomics: The strategic interaction of successive motivational states within the person.* Cambridge: Cambridge University Press.

Baddeley, A. (2007). *Working memory, thought, and action.* Oxford: Oxford University Press.

Bickel, W. K., & Marsch, L. A. (2000). The tyranny of small decisions: Origins, outcomes, and proposed solutions. In W. R. Bickel & R. E. Vuchinich (Eds.), *Reframing health behavioral change with behavioral economics* (pp. 341–391). Mahwah: Erlbaum.

Bickel, W. R., & Yi, R. (2008). Temporal discounting as a measure of executive function: Insights from the competing neuro-behavioral decisions systems hypothesis of addiction. *Advances in Health Economics and Health Services Research, 20,* 289–309.

Bickel, W. K., Jarmolowicz, D. P., Mueller, E. T., Gatchalian, K. M., & McClure, S. M. (2012). Are executive function and impulsivity antipodes? A conceptual reconstruction with special reference to addiction. *Psychopharmacology, 221,* 361–387.

Damasio, A. R. (1994). *Descartes' error: Emotion, reason and the human brain.* New York: Putnam.

Elster, J. (2015). *Explaining social behavior: More nuts and bolts for the social sciences.* Revised edition. Cambridge: Cambridge University Press.

Evans, J. S. B. (2010). *Thinking twice: Two minds in one brain.* Oxford: Oxford University Press.

Foxall, G. R. (2014a). Neurophilosophy of explanation in economic psychology: An exposition in terms of neuro-behavioral decision systems. In L. Moutinho et al. (Eds.), *Routledge companion to the future of marketing* (pp. 134–150). London/New York: Routledge.

Foxall, G. R. (2014b). Cognitive requirements of competing neuro-behavioral decision systems: Some implications of temporal horizon for managerial behavior in organizations. *Frontiers in Human Neuroscience, 8,* 184.

Foxall, G. R. (2016a). *Addiction as consumer choice: Exploring the cognitive dimension.* London/New York: Routledge.

Foxall, G. R. (2016b). Metacognitive control of categorial neurobehavioral decision systems. *Frontiers in Psychology, 7,* 170.

Kahneman, D. (2011). *Thinking, fast and slow.* London: Allen Lane.

Kirton, M. J. (2003). *Adaption-innovation: In the context of diversity and change.* London: Routledge.

Madden, G. J., & Bickel, W. K. (2010). *Impulsivity: The behavioral and neurological science of discounting.* Washington, DC: American Psychological Association.

McClure, S. M., Laibson, D. L., Loewenstein, G., & Cohen, J. D. (2004). Separate neural systems value immediate and delayed monetary rewards. *Science, 306*(5695), 503–507.

McKim, T. H., & Boettiger, C. A. (2015). Addiction as maladaptive learning, with a focus on habit learning. In T. S. Wilson (Ed.), *The Wiley handbook on the cognitive neuroscience of addiction* (pp. 1–xx). Chichester: Wiley.

Norman, D. A., & Shallice, T. (1986). Attention to action: Willed and automatic control of behaviour. In R. J. Davidson, G. E. Schwarts, & D. Shapiro (Eds.), *Consciousness and self-regulation: Advances in research and theory* (Vol. 4, pp. 1–18). New York: Plenum.

Redish, A. D. (2013). *The mind within the brain: How we make decisions and how those decisions go wrong.* New York: Oxford University Press.

Redish, A. D. (2015). Addiction as a symptom of failure modes in the machineries of decision making. In T. S. Wilson (Ed.), *The Wiley handbook on the cognitive neuroscience of addiction* (pp. xx–xx). Chichester: Wiley.

Rolls, E. T. (2014). *Emotion and decision-making explained.* Oxford: Oxford University Press.

Ross, D. (2012). The economic agent: Not human, but important. In U. Mäki (Ed.), *Philosophy of economics* (pp. 691–736). Amsterdam: Elsevier.

Shallice, T., & Cooper, R. P. (2011). *The organization of mind.* Oxford: Oxford University Press.

Shea, N., Boldt, A., Bang, D., Yeung, N., Heyes, C., & Frith, C. D. (2014). Supra-personal cognitive control and metacognition. *Trends in Cognitive Sciences, 18,* 186–193.

Stanovich, K. E. (2009a). Distinguishing the reflective, algorithmic, and autonomous minds: Is it time for a tri-process theory? In J. S. B. T. Evans & K. Frankish (Eds.), *In two minds: Dual processes and beyond* (pp. 55–88). Oxford: Oxford University Press.

Stanovich, K. E. (2009b). *What intelligence tests miss: The psychology of rational thought.* New Haven/London: Yale University Press.

Stanovich, K. E. (2011). *Rationality and the reflective mind.* Oxford: Oxford University Press.

9

Consumer Choice as Decision: Macro-Cognitive Psychology

Introduction

Cognitive interpretation is further explored in Chapter 9, this time from the standpoint of a macro-cognitive psychology (MaCP)which links the Intentional Interpretation to processes of collective intentionality in which consumers create the contingencies of reinforcement to which they will respond. Chapter 8 set forth the necessity to develop a cognitive psychology that could link the personal level of behavior and intentionality with the sub-personal level of neurophysiological functioning. This chapter is concerned to link the personal level with the super-personal domain of environment-behavior relationships. While Chapter 8 argued that the concerns of MiCP should not obscure the need for understanding at that level to reflect operancy, this chapter brings the behaviors and intentionality that constitute consumer choice at the personal level of exposition firmly into contact with the contingencies of reinforcement that influence them.

The following depiction of a macro-cognitive psychological framework has four elements. First, it traces the development of individual intentionality and collective intentionality as proposed by Tomasello (1999,

G.R. Foxall, *Perspectives on Consumer Choice*,
DOI 10.1057/978-1-137-50121-9_9

2014, 2016). Second, it examines Searle's (1995, 2010a, b) argument that social reality might be created via collective intentionality. Third, it expands these insights to deduce implications for the analysis of consumer choice, proposing that the decision perspective of the BPM must incorporate concepts of the symbolic consumer situation and the symbolic pattern of reinforcement. This means that the understanding of rule-governed behavior can be revised in light of these symbolic portrayals of the BPM. Finally, it turns to the evaluation of theories of collective intentionality as MaCP. This means outlining the requirements of metacognitive control proposed by Shea et al. (2014)—that is, distributing metacognitive representations for verbal communication, evaluating metacognitive representations to motivate appropriate action, and extricating metacognitive representations from weak metacognitive information—as they apply to MaCP and, in particular, collective intentionality theories.

Macro-Cognitive Psychology

Aims and Scope of Macro-Cognitive Psychology

If metacognitive processes such as those identified by Shea et al. (2014) are to promote supra-personal communication and cooperation, it is necessary that the organisms in which they exist be linked by social contingencies and communal means of enforcing them. Theories of collective intentionality seek understanding of how these super-personal patterns of contingency are formed and how they operate. They go beyond the kind of super-personal cognitive psychology embodied in conventional studies of operancy (i.e., by radical behaviorists) to suggest that the actors themselves exert control over what counts as a reinforcer and what the consequences of conforming to or breaching social rules are to be. The objective of macro-cognitive psychology is to show (i) how humans create contingencies of reinforcement through collective intentionality (ii) how a cognitive theory of decision making relates the constitutive rules that make up social reality and the personal-level representation, inference, and (iii) the role of self-monitoring in promoting conformity to rebellion against social expectations. These are the three components of the *shared intentionality hypothesis* that Tomasello (2014) puts forward to account for the social coordination, specifically with collaboration and communication, the building blocks of cooperation among individuals. Great apes other than ourselves engage in social behavior but we have to understand what is unique about human cooperation in order to emphasize that it can be understood only intentionally.

There is also an extensional way of viewing social groups. Sprott's (1958, p. 9) classic definition of a group in social psychological terms as "a plurality of persons who interact with one another in a given context more than they interact with anyone else" provides an intersubjective guide to the identification of groups and the measurement of such aspects of group behavior as cohesiveness. The behavioral sociologist, George Homans, stated that what made a relationship "social" was that "when a person acts in a certain way, he is at least rewarded or punished by the behavior of another person" (Homans 1951, p. 2). Skinner (1957) defined "verbal behavior" in almost identical terms as "behavior that is reinforced by the behavior of another person." These are all definitions that are amenable to observational confirmation or disconfirmation and which permit the use of extensional language in the scientific exploration of social relationships. Such an extensional approach is to be assessed on pragmatic grounds and accepted to the degree that it renders behavior predictable and, possibly, modifiable. However, it will not suffice as an account of how humans came to be social since this requires consideration of the cognitive aspects of interaction. This intentional conception of the nature of social groups entails each individual's recognizing that others are, like himself or herself, intentional beings capable of ascribing desires and beliefs to others, and interpreting their behavior in terms of this attributed phenomenology (Tomasello 1999).

From Individual to Collective Intentionality

The behaviorist doctrine that behavior is inexorably stimulus bound belies the fact that animals possess adaptive capacities which allow feedback control based on goal representations linked to action propensities.

Cognition evolves from these adaptive mechanisms, not through increasingly complex stimulus-response relationships but from the individual's (i) flexible decision-making capacities and related behavioral control and (ii) the facilities to represent and draw inferences from the intentional and causal relationships among events (Tomasello 2014, pp. 7–8).

Adaptations are specialized accommodations to circumstances, designed moreover in the course of natural selection to allow them to operate in relatively similar situations, those that are more or less like previously confronted conditions. Not only is no ingenuity required of the individual in such circumstances: the organism simply lacks the awareness of its environment that would enable it to make causal or intentional inferences. It has, in any case, no mental apparatus for responding purposefully or adaptively toward *new* situations. Novel situations demand the capacity to appreciate the causal texture of environments and to act accordingly. These are cognitive capacities which enable the organism to assess situations in light of its goals and to select those actions which promote its values. This cognitive approach, which Tomasello (2014) terms *individual intentionality*, requires more than the goal representation that an adaptive system relies on: it depends also on an epistemic relationship to the world that makes these judgments possible, rendering the individual capable of flexible self-regulation.

Crucially, in terms of the triprocess theory described above, individual intentionality includes the ability to think offline so that future experiences and their outcomes can be mentally simulated or rehearsed. Prebehavioral imagination of this kind entails the three cognitive capacities to which Tomasello draws attention: (i) to undertake the offline cognitive representation to oneself of hypothetical experiences; (ii) to simulate these representations' causal, intentional, and logical properties; and (iii) to self-monitor and evaluate how what has been simulated would contribute to behavioral effectiveness. These necessary capacities immediately suggest a link between MiCP and MaCP by recalling the facilitation of cognitive rehearsal by Algorithmic Mind in Stanovich's (2011) tripartite model.

In terms of the relevance of cognitive representation to the BPM, it is interesting that Tomasello argues that both the individual's internal goals and external direction (perception and attention) have content not in terms of individual stimuli but in response to *whole situations*. This view harmonizes with the emphasis the BPM places on the entire consumer behavior setting as the stimulus field relevant to the performance of a particular operant behavior. The pattern of reinforcement that controls such behavior is the result of simulations of future behaviors and their consequences on the basis of currently available stimuli. These are molded also by the patterns of reinforcement remembered as having influenced behavior in the past (the consumer's imagined learning history). The totality of those stimuli must be taken into consideration in order that the full range of utilitarian and informational reinforcement that may shape and maintain future behavior be brought to bear on current decision making, viewed as action selection. Situations that are *relevant* to the goals of the organism are the ones to which attention must be directed.

With regard to the simulation of a novel situation's causal and intentional texture it is important that experiences be represented not as single instances but as *types* if they are to be useful in future goal-achievement. This emphasizes that the behaviors under consideration at the decision-making stage are operant classes of behavior, governed by patterns of reinforcement. It is the entire setting and its representation that is responsible for action and its outcomes, and it is the *nature* of a situation that determines how it should be treated.

Coupled with the individual's ability to learn from experience is the necessity of its being able to watch its behavior in relation to its goals and assess its performance accordingly. Self-observation and judgment are essential for offline cognitive simulation. This is the central component of executive function and it is metacognitive "because the individual, in some sense, observes not just its actions and their results in the environment but also its own internal simulations" (Tomasello 2014, p. 14). Humans' capacity to draw on others' imagined evaluations in assessing their own behavioral performances is an indispensable part of the individual's knowing what he or she is doing.

Beyond the intentional activities of the individual lies the need to act cooperatively with others to pursue and achieve common goals. Activities like foraging and hunting require joint goals, joint roles, and above all joint understanding. They require inter-personal monitoring of performance, the identification of freeloaders, and their punishment or elimination from the group. This in turn entails self-monitoring according to group standards. The social communication on which all of these rely is predicated on the ability to think in new directions and to adopt new intellectual styles.

Tomasello (2016) hypothesizes that two stages in human development necessitated social cooperation. The first, some hundreds of thousands of years in the past, arose from the need to adopt joint foraging in order to survive. This meant extending sympathy to others than one's immediate family and friends, that is, to partners who were chosen because they could collaborate effectively. Coordination of this activity could only be achieved through the establishment of *joint intentionality* which involved a shared goal and various kinds of joint knowing. Each partner played a part in this joint enterprise and understandings of the ideal nature of the roles each played would be worked out in the course of hunting. Overriding needs were the avoidance of freeloading and the development of both inter-personal respect and the capacity to enforce the joint standards on which the operation depended. This entailed relinquishing some personal autonomy in favor of a commitment to "us." Thus humans created for themselves the means of self-regulation in order to attract collaborators and other-regulation in order to ensure attainment of group goals.

> And so was born a normatively constituted social order in which cooperatively rational agents focused not just on how individuals do act, or how I want them to act, but, rather, on how they *ought* to act if they are to be one of 'us.' In the end, the result of all these new ways of relating to a partner in joint intentional activity added up for early humans to a kind of *natural, second-personal morality*. (Tomasello 2016, p. 5)

Further development coincided with the emergence of *Homo sapiens* some 150,000 years ago and was instigated by demographic change as small hunting groups came to derive their overarching cultural identity from their belonging to a tribe which provided common cultural norms and institutions. Other members of this cultural group were those to whom one was sympathetic and loyal, while outsiders were considered freeloaders or competitors. The cognitive skills required to sustain social control eventuated in a *collective intentionality* which enabled the evolution of cultural norms and institutions.

> Conventional cultural practices had role ideals that were fully "objective" in the sense that everyone knew in cultural common ground how anyone who would be one of "us" had to play those roles for collective success. (Tomasello 2016, p. 5)

Tomasello's portrayal of early human social development can be read as an account of the emergence of informational reinforcement, performance feedback, the means by which individuals monitor and evaluate their own performance, leading to self-esteem or private shame, and that of others, leading to social esteem or public shame. These inter-personal processes are necessary for social control leading, for instance, to mutual cooperation or the expulsion of freeloaders. The joint determination of what is to count as a reinforcer or punisher for these purposes of social control establishes the institutions that, in turn, confirm the shared basis of the cultural group. What he calls common cultural ground is more than agreement on goals; it is a shared sense of what it means to work toward or against their attainment and on the suitable rewards and sanctions that *should* be provided to or exacted from group members. Informational reinforcement is relative to this kind of social understanding, not only in terms of the social esteem or shame that will reinforce or punish behavior, but in the personally felt emotions of self-honor and dishonor that follow adherence to or deviation from deontic rules that have acquired a moral force.

Constructing Social Reality

The purpose of pursuing MaCP is to show how the intentionality (desires, beliefs, emotions, and perceptions) ascribed to the idealized consumer in the course of Intentional Interpretation would be produced through decision making. In particular, it seeks to link the decision process to super-personal concerns, the level of operancy. Macro-cognitive psychology must link the contingencies of reinforcement and punishment with behavior via personal decision making that eventuates in the desires and beliefs that are consistent with the consumer's revealed behavioral choice.

A route to this connectivity is to be found in the concept of *collective intentionality*, a system of deontology, status ascription, role ascription, and of rewards and sanctions for behavior considered, respectively, prosocial and antisocial or asocial (e.g., Searle 1995, 2010a; Tomasello 2014). The deontology comprises a system of *rules* that describe a complex of contingencies that relate behavior to its rewards and sanctions. The behavior patterns whose frequency of enactment is explained by the collective intentionality based system of contingencies must also be related to a neurophysiological level of exposition that is consistent with the capacity of the rewards and sanctions to explain behavior. In this way, the super-personal, personal, and sub-personal levels of exposition are linked in the explanation of behavior.

Having accepted the imperatives of intentionality and shown how a philosophy of psychology based upon them, namely intentional behaviorism, adds to the explicative capacity of the BPM, our task is to inquire how intentional terms may be implemented in our emerging framework of conceptualization and analysis. That is, the components of the model must be intentionally construed and coherently related to form an appropriate explanation of consumer choice that transcends the limitations of extensional behavioral science. Some of the intellectual tools required for this task are found in Searle's (1995, 2010a, b) account of the construction of social reality. Searle's overall mission is to understand how we can speak of consciousness in a physical world, which he characterizes as "the single overriding question in contemporary philosophy" (Searle 2010a, p. 3).

One answer to this conundrum is suggested by the idea of *collective intentionality*, the view that the performance of many human behaviors relies on a collective acknowledgment of a particular social status (Searle 1995, 2010a). Collective intentionality requires that there be a sharing not only of actions but also of the beliefs, desires, and attitudes that make both the assignation of status function and the performance of the behavior in question possible. Hence, a couple is only married (and entitled to the legal benefits and obligations of marriage) because society invests them with this status. The pieces of paper in the consumer's wallet will only function as money because they are generally accepted as a means of the settlement of financial obligations. Searle's theory of human social reality comprises six components—denoted (i) to (vi) below.

The essence of his understanding of the *collective intentionality* (i) that has just been described is that humans can impose a *status function* (ii) on an object or a person over and above the physical capabilities of the object or person (Searle 2010a, b p. 7). The object or person can perform this function only by virtue of its being endowed with a status that is collectively invested in it by a verbal community. A piece of molded and stitched leather can thus become a brief case, a piece of sharpened metal embedded in a wooden handle can become a chisel, and a man or woman who has fulfilled certain socially imposed rules and regulations (including standing for office, being elected, swearing an oath of loyalty to the Head of State) can be regarded as the prime minister of the UK. Searle argues that this capacity of objects and people to be socially invested with a collective recognition of their status is such that it forms the essence of social reality in human communities.

Moreover, without such collective assent to the investment of the appropriate status function in an individual, that person lacks the capacity or authority to undertake or perform it. Once an individual is willingly ascribed a status function, he or she is entitled to certain considerations as of right. These might include deferential ways in which others react to him or her, the right to occupy certain residences as his or her home or working environment, a salary of a given magnitude, and the right to retain this office for a specified time period. However, his or her continuing in the office granted relies on the fulfillment of prescribed tasks: status functions carry *deontic powers* (iii), rights, permissions, and entitlements, on the one hand, obligations and requirements, on the other (Searle 2010a, b pp. 8–9). A positive deontic right is to work in the USA if one has a green card; a negative deontic right is the consequent necessity of filing an annual tax return in that country.

Deontic rights confer or impose reasons for the occupant of a status position's acting in a particular way that are independent of his or her desires; hence, I may recognize the legally conferred property rights of another person even though I would like to take his new sports car for the trip of its life. These *"desire-independent reasons for action"* (iv) as Searle refers to them are closely allied to the next component of his system, *constitutive rules* (v). There are two types of rule. Having to drive on the left in the UK does not create a new behavior—one *could* drive on the left even if this regulation did not exist; the rule, actually a law, that one must drive on the left or face sanctions, does not create driving or even driving on the left. Having to park your car only in a designated parking space is another example: you can park your car even without this rule; the rule does not create this style of parking behavior. Regulative rules of this kind, neither of which, it is worth repeating, creates a new behavior, typically take the form "Do this… and these rewards and/or those sanctions will follow": that is, they are *tracks* or *plys*.

By contrast, rules that lay down how to play tennis actually create the behaviors known as playing tennis. They not only determine how tennis will be played but *that* tennis will exist to be played. Tennis only exists because of the rules. *Constitutive rules* of this kind take the form "X counts as Y in C." The final component, *institutional facts* (vi), refers to the collectively derived social reality on which the whole system depends and which marks it off from the physical reality which is the mainstay of non-human animal reality. The "brute facts" that inhere in both human and nonhuman experience exist independently of human institutions. The facts that this is a mountain, grass is green, and mammals suckle their young are examples of brute facts. Brute facts are known by their physical consequences as in the paradigm case of Dr. Johnson's "refuting" idealism by resolutely kicking a large rock. Institutional facts, however, exist only because of human acceptance or approval; hence, the fact that this person is a minister of the church depends on certain people's agreement that she is, as does her being married and having a joint bank account. All are institutional facts because they are real only by virtue of inter-personal fiat.

The Symbolic Consumer Situation

In all its perspectives, the consumer situation foretells in some sense the nature of the consequences likely to follow the performance of particular behaviors. In the behavioral perspective, as we saw in Chapter 3, reinforcement is bifurcated into its utilitarian and informational components. The term "utilitarian reinforcement" is used there synonymously with "functional reinforcement" and that identity is also found in the action and decision perspectives, though in them this source of utility is understood in terms of the consumer's subjective valuation of product-mediated benefits. "Informational reinforcement" has sometimes been used in expositions of the BPM synonymously with "symbolic reinforcement" but it is now possible to refine this usage.

Informational reinforcement consists in physical stimuli, brute facts that take the form, principally, of auditory and visual stimuli. Insofar as these stimuli are interpreted by the individual as performance feedback, they can be regarded as intentional. Just like the paint that constitutes *The Fighting Temeraire*, they may acquire the property of aboutness, of secondary or derived intentionality, even though their import and effect on behavior derive from their physical characteristics. In sum, informational reinforcement, which inheres in physical S^D and S^r that govern the rate of emission of behavior, participates in the continuity of both contingency-shaped and rule-governed behavior by virtue of these stimuli being physical, principally auditory and visual, stimuli that regulate the performance of behavior. Both utilitarian and informational reinforcement rely on brute facts to strengthen behavior, on actually existing behavioral outcomes.

However, beyond the intentionality of informational reinforcement, *symbolic reinforcement* derives from what the individual thinks, believes, desires, or feels to be the case. All of these can be expressed in the form of propositional attitudes which open up their verbal expressions to the linguistic rules of intensionality. Symbolic reinforcement enters into the ascription of tracking, pliance, and augmenting in order to interpret complex behavior (that is not amenable to an experimental analysis) when these are conceived intentionally as constitutive rules. In the action perspectives of the BPM, that is, the action, decision, and as we shall see, the agential perspectives, reinforcement is understood as integral to the consumer situation where it exists symbolically. Having clarified the nature of reinforcement in the action perspectives we can define more accurately the nature of the symbolic consumer situation that is central to the decision perspective.

The symbolic consumer situation and the patterns of reinforcement it heralds can be most usefully understood as a complex of rules that govern behavior. We noted in Chapter 2 that two series of contingencies control rule-governed behavior: nonverbal consequences of contingency-shaped responding and verbal relationships that influence its taking a form that is socially acceptable. It is now apparent that our recognition of the intensionality of choice raises the possibility of an even more involved complex of contingencies stemming from the contemporaneous operation of utilitarian, informational, and symbolic reinforcement. Searle points out that the same item may be described in terms of brute facts or institutional facts. On the one hand, there is an object in front of me that I may describe as an intricate assemblage of metals and hydrocarbons; on the other hand, I may describe it as a television set. The first description comprises brute facts—it is about physical things that amount to objects that inhere in nature. The second is relative to the intentionality of humans. Tracking, pliance, and augmenting are behaviors that can be described in two ways: as responses to physical and social stimuli and as actions that are explicable in terms of intentional idioms. The first depiction is consistent with the extensional account that is the aim of radical behaviorism; the second goes beyond radical behaviorism to provide a more detailed interpretation of the behavior at the personal level of explanation.

It is useful to remember that, in understanding behavior as rule-governed, it can sometimes prove difficult to disentangle the possible effects of the contingencies at work, difficult to be sure that this or that behavior is an instance of tacting or pliance or augmenting. This task becomes even more complicated when we find that we must include intensionality as a set of explanatory variables. There is a further complexity. We are not making ontological pronouncements here. It is not the fact that some behaviors can be described in their entirety as extensional, contingency-shaped, based on brute facts while other behaviors are intensional, rule-governed, and based on institutional facts. We may wish to describe any behavior in either mode depending on whether our aim is to predict and control it or explain it at the personal level. Either mode has its limitations. The extensional approach encounters difficulties, as we have seen, accounting for behavioral continuity, the personal level, and delimiting its interpretations of behavior. But the intensional approach is limited when it comes to predicting and influencing the behavior. The recurring question raised by our investigation is that of how we use language to make sense of behavior. Hence, tracking is not something that a person does: it is a way of referring to what a person is observed doing that makes it more intelligible to the observer. Pliance and augmenting are similarly not instances of rule-governed behavior that exist in the world; they are styles of deploying words so that we can understand better what is apparently happening in behavioral space.

Tracking Revisited Tracking, viewed extensionally, is a matter of responding to sounds or signs previously associated with success in reaching a goal position—typically following instructions to get somewhere or to construct a model or bake a cake by following instructions. A track is a statement concerning how to navigate brute facts. We are dealing here with secondary stimulation, the power of which to influence behavior is derived entirely from pairing with primary stimuli that have acted as discriminative stimuli or USs. This could well meet the behaviorist's requirements that it makes behavior predictable and controllable. The behavior is guided by utilitarian reinforcement and is mediated by physical stimuli. But it may also be seen as influenced to a degree by performance feedback and therefore informational reinforcement. Each landmark specified by the speaker constitutes a socially mediated indicator of how close the rule-follower has come to reaching the goal.[1]

Even in this context, however, it is intentional behavior in that it is about something else—about reaching a goal which, at the time the instruction is given and received, exists only in the imagination of the speaker and the listener. The extensional account, therefore, raises questions that point toward taking an intentional perspective on tracking. In this perspective, tracking not only involves holding a goal in mind but in formulating a cognitive map of the means of reaching it. All of these

---

[1] Understood extensionally, tracking is contingency-shaped, reinforced by utilitarian reinforcement, and relies on brute facts. It is not, in this depiction, a matter of constitutive rules or institutional facts. It is behavior generated by the verbal behavior of another. We can only accord it the full status of verbal behavior in the sense that its reinforcement is socially mediated if we make the inference that, by acquiescing to the requirements of the rule, the rule-follower providing himself or herself with informational reinforcement, feedback on his or her own verbally directed performance. We may say this is verbal behavior on the basis that it originates in the words or gestures of another person but, even in a radical behaviorist framework, it can only be thought of as quasi-verbal.

stimuli exist only in imagination prior to the enactment of the behavior called tracking; the goal stimulus exerts control over the behavior since its fulfillment causes tracking to cease. The behavior on this perspective is intentional therefore because it is symbolic, relying for its achievement on the intrinsic intentionality that is the holding of images in mind and the derived intentionality with which the landmarks along the way (the physical stimuli encountered which were previously described by the rule-giver as indicative of progress toward the goal) are invested. They are not just road signs, say, but symbols that one is approaching one's goal location. Insofar as these are socially mediated they constitute performance feedback and are therefore akin to informational reinforcement, as we have noted. However, the explanation of why they influence behavior differs in an intentional account from that of an extensional explanation. In the extensional explanation they are simply visual stimuli that induce further travel. In an intentional account however they are also images with mental content that form part of a cognitive map. Although there is no topographical difference in the two accounts, the appearance of these indicative stimuli in the intentional account of behavior suggests that they ought to be classified as symbolic stimuli to differentiate the nature of the explanations. The mental counterparts of the physical signposts/indicators, their meanings in terms of their measuring the progress the place seeker is making means we should think of them as symbolic stimuli.

For example, suppose Ego asks Other how to get to such-and-such a supermarket. Other replies "Walk along High Street to the courthouse, turn left there, and walk 150 meters down Green Avenue. The supermarket will then be on your right." We could conjecture all sorts of mental operations on Ego's part but let us concentrate on the two most salient. In Fig. 9.1, S denotes a public stimulus and R a public response; r is a private (symbolic) response which also has a stimulus function to elicit s which is a private (symbolic) stimulus that leads to R. (a) Arriving at and recognizing the courthouse, Ego compares a mental image of this building with the word "courthouse" uttered by Other. This comparative image stimulates a further symbolic interaction, namely the comparison of the courthouse image, first with the remembered instruction to "turn left" on reaching the courthouse, and then with the image of the

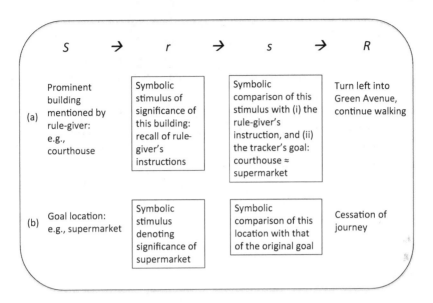

Fig. 9.1   *Symbolic portrayal of tracking.* ≈ indicates "compared with"

supermarket that is the final goal. These comparisons, all present only in imagination, in turn stimulate turning left and further walking on Green Avenue until the supermarket comes into view. At (b) in Fig. 9.1, Ego recognizes the supermarket on the right (S) which triggers a mental image of the significance of this building (r), namely that it is Ego's goal destination. The r leads to further symbolic stimulation, s which denotes a mental comparison of the present position with the goal location. The equivalence of these images leads to the cessation of instructed travel (R), subsequent to Ego's moving right and entering the store.

In this psychological explanation, the consumer is viewed not simply as responding to the brute facts provided by the physical environment as it provides utilitarian reinforcement. Following the contours of the physical environment in order to reach a specified destination can, as we have seen, be accounted for in terms of an extensional explanation and if instructions are provided this can extend to treating the sounds or sights of the verbal behavior of a speaker in auditory and/or visual terms. Take the case of getting to the supermarket on the basis of instructions provided by a rule-giver on how to navigate the physical environment to reach a particular goal. In extensional terms, such behavior may be described as tracking since it involves following signs posted along the way. The interpretation that is given in an extensional account is that the rule-follower is simply responding to stimuli, given a particular learning history. There is no reason why the sounds issued by a way-shower should not influence the subsequent behavior of the rule-follower in just the same way as would any other physical stimulus. Crucially, in an extensional explanation, while the instructions received by the rule-follower are mediated by another person, the consequences of following the rules are not. Tracking may be viewed as predominantly contingency-shaped behavior, therefore, subject to the brute facts and utilitarian reinforcement. Such rule-governed behavior would, therefore, result from the "acoustic blasts" that constitute physical stimuli (Searle 1969). The behavior cannot, therefore, be understood as symbolic: it is construed as though it were entirely explicable in terms of stimulus-response associations.

Viewed this way, the behavior of the rule-follower is social and verbal but not symbolic since no effort is being made in its interpretation by the behavioral scientist to invoke intentional idioms. Its verbal nature rests on its being mediated by the verbal behavior of another (and presumably a learning history of following the rules of similar persons in similar situations) and resulting in the behavior pattern shown by the rule-follower. Note that any informational reinforcement resulting from Ego's reaching the destination is self-conferred: no other person is involved in proffering informational reinforcement, though they have offered informational stimulation. If our aim is to predict and control behavior, this may be sufficient. The consumer situation he or she is enmeshed in is a simple interaction of the current stimuli defining the setting and the individual's learning history. We can predict that the rule-follower (the person who asked directions) will reach their destination if they have the appropriate learning history (they have found places before, sometimes by following directions) and respond to the physical sounds of words ("Turn left at the traffic lights") as though they were discriminative stimuli. We can control this behavior by making the sounds involved in the rules we provide this person more appropriate to his learning history (instead of saying "Turn left at the traffic lights," we can say, if necessary, "Turn left at the traffic lights outside the pharmacy.") The extent to which we can predict and influence the rule-followers' behavior by these means is an empirical question. We can refine the layout of the environment, the teaching of English sounds in relation to places, the signage of the shopping district, and so on. But the extensional approach is limited: there are several things we cannot accomplish in this way. We cannot, for instance, account for the continuity of the rule-follower's behavior when confronted by a new situation in which a destination is to be reached. We need a theory of perception and probably also a theory of beliefs and desires here; emotions may also need to enter our theoretical framework in order to account for the personal level of explanation. And in order to interpret the behavior of a stranger whom we are observing as he walks, map in hand, around our town, we need to incorporate the delimiting role of all of these intentional influences. That is, our account's use of extensional language has become exhausted; we turn to intentional idioms.

And we find that the situation is permeated with intentionality: the sounds are so obviously about something other than themselves. Moreover, any statement about the behavior of either speaker or listener couched in terms such as "He said that..." or "She thought that..." is intensional. Either we must understand that this stimulation, inherent in the instructions-as-sounds, imbues the physical environment (notably in this example the courthouse) with significance or we must argue that Ego carries out this task. This is, however, an intentional explanation.

Pliance Revisited Pliance draws upon an involved concatenation of contingencies: the behavior of the child instructed by a parent to put on boots before going out to play in the snow is governed by the deleterious consequences of getting wet when he does not comply (any subsequent change in behavior, namely wearing boots on similar occasions, amounts to contingency-shaping) and the punishment meted out by the parent as a result (behavior change is the result of rule-following). All of this, which constitutes an extensional interpretation of behavior, may help to predict and control the child's activities but it is an incomplete explanation of them. We rely, for such prediction and control, on the brute observable facts and, as long as these are available and the behavior can be predicted and controlled by the analysis and manipulation of these stimuli, we can provide an extensional account.

Once again, however, pliance suggests itself as intentional. The rule delivered by the speaker is inevitably about other things: patterns of behavior are specified, rewards and sanctions are laid out, the disapprobation of the speaker is threatened. The child's behavior is controlled only if he or she can imagine the outcomes thereof, only if the goal of behaving can be established in mind and compared with progress being made as the behavior unfolds. An intentional account requires that the behavior be reconstructed from the personal-level perspective of the actor; in this example, it must take account of the child's perception of what its parent is saying, the import thereof in terms of punishment, what the child has been led to believe on the basis of its experience of similar situations, and what it desires. It is only by positing these intentional idioms that we can have any honest account of the behavior, that is, one that does not invent a learning history and a stimulus setting in order to answer the problems posed by the imperatives of intentionality. The use of symbolic language requires however that we have grounds for the child's being able to form a conceptual framework in which the words of the parent correspond to a state of affairs (consisting in punishment) that has existed prior to the present and to project a similar state in the future contingent upon the performance of a particular form of behavior. The discriminations which we must attribute to the child in order to make this interpretation can only be made in intensional language.

The instruction to wear one's boots outdoors and the explanation that doing so will (a) keep your feet dry (utilitarian reinforcement) and (b) please the parent who is speaking (informational reinforcement) has a (possibly unspoken) corollary: not wearing one's boots will (a) lead to wet feet (utilitarian reinforcement) and (b) displease parent (informational reinforcement). An extensional explanation of this is feasible on the grounds that the child has a learning history of following parental instructions. Although this understanding of the situation may suffice if one's intellectual goal is restricted to the prediction and control of behavior, it hardly accounts for the fact that the child's behavior (wearing its boots) depends on consequences of behavior that at the time of its donning them are entirely imaginary. This is so whether the imagined consequences are the result of the parent's recently given instruction or the child's memories of behaving in a particular way and the outcomes

Fig. 9.2 *Symbolic portrayal of pliance.* The ply ("wear your boots!") leads to the child's imagining the consequences of wearing boots, contrasted with those of not doing so. These mental images result in the conclusion that it would be better all round to wear the boots and this is the response that follows

thereof in the past (see Fig. 9.2 in which *S* is a public verbal stimulus emitted by the speaker, *r* a private response of the listener which occasions his or her private stimulus *s*, which evokes the public response *R*).

Augmenting Revisited In extensionally depicted behavior, one setting stimulus can assume the function of another setting stimulus if they are frequently paired together when a reinforcer appears. This is the basis of classical conditioning as well as that under which behavior comes under stimulus control in operant conditioning. It is the basis as I have said of rule-governed behavior if this is understood in extensional terms: your shouting "Dinner time!" is an auditory stimulus that has become paired with the availability of food in an articular context and I will come to respond on the basis of the new auditory stimuli just as I would to seeing the food being prepared and served. In the case of symbolic behavior, one stimulus comes to stand for another at an intentional level: when I *realize* that "Dinner time!" means that the food is now available and I had better make my way to the dining room, then I am interpreting the announcement intentionally or symbolically. The topography of both the speaker's and the listener's behaviors remains the same; the difference in the second case is methodological insofar as a novel explanation is being entertained. Moreover, the behavior that is being described intentionally, in terms that is of recognizing, believing, and so on, can only be rendered intelligible via this kind of language.

Although it is not part of the official lore of behavior analysis, I consider augmentals to be a form of verbal motivating operation that enhances the relationship between the response and the reinforcer. Once again there must be an extensional interpretation of this effect, one which simply traces the relationship between the vocal stimulus and the response. This may suffice for prediction and control purposes, but it would leave the explanation of the behavior, even in operant terms, ambiguous. "Enhances the value of the reinforcer" has no observable content that delineates a stimulus effect. It is entirely a theoretical explanation for the behavior that relies on the idea that the augmental generates cognitive representations that show the reinforcer in a favorable light. To the extent that the behavioral response is explicable as operant this can be achieved in terms of the reinforcer. To say a rule has a motivating effect on the rate at which the behavior is performed is to assign to it either the discriminatory force of an antecedent stimulus or the symbolic status of an enhancing stimulus. The judgment that the additional antecedent stimulus called an augmental is enhancing the response-reinforcer relationship is pure interpretation, an inference from the strength of the behavior subsequently witnessed. It is an intentional explanation.

Metacognitive Requirements of MaCP

In moving from an extensional model of consumer choice to the Intentional and Cognitive Interpretations that constitute psychological explanation, we have not changed our subject matter per se; its topography is identical in each account. What has changed is our methodological perspective, our means of explaining the behavior. We turn next to the question of how this perspectival switch is to be evaluated and in particular how accounts of collective intentionality contribute to the capacity of a Cognitive Interpretation based on it justifies or undermines the Intentional Interpretation that portrayed modes of consumer choice as differing predominantly according to the degree of temporal discounting they encompassed.

The circulation of metacognitive representations to enable symbolic communication to take place requires the availability of common understandings of how the physical and social worlds are constituted and how they can be manipulated to achieve individual and social goals. The vehicle for this level of common understanding is the social rule, understood intentionally. Rules are metacognitive constructions that lay out the contingencies and their meanings among individuals for their perusal and inter-personal communication. In other words, they enable the distribution of metacognitive representations so that they can be verbally communicated among the members of a social system. They thereby provide a common currency for the depiction of situations and the contingencies of reinforcement that govern behavior directed toward the achievement of goals, whether these be individually held or joint. While there is an extensional understanding of rule-governed behavior, the range of applicability of this depiction is very limited. Radical behaviorist accounts of behavior that must "explain" its continuity or discontinuity, or take place at the personal level of exposition, or complete a behavioral interpretation, frequently resort to descriptions of it as supposedly rule-governed behavior; such accounts are highly speculative and their nontestability puts them beyond the realm of scientific investigation. The real problem with them is their being stated in extensional terminology which gives the spurious impression of reliable scientific knowledge. It is not possible to give a responsible account of the sharing of information involved in tracking, pliance, or augmenting without resorting to intentional language which at least has the advantage that it demarcates a different kind of explanation that does not purport to be supported or supportable by empirical research. This is surely a more intellectually honest approach to knowledge than conjecturing guesses at the nature of contingencies that are portrayed in the language of extensional behavioral science.

Rules present a unique format in which metacognitive representations, having been laid out for public consideration, can be evaluated against the evidence of their efficacy provided by the correspondence of the outcomes of following them with the contingencies of reinforcement and punishment they specify. In this way, the efficacy of metacognitive representations can be socially appraised in order that future actions will be appropriate. The trustworthiness of rules can be ascertained by experience as can the trustworthiness of the rule-giver. Rules thereby make available a gold standard for behavior that will be efficacious and a means of avoiding behavior that will have deleterious consequences. Their function is to act as templates by reference to which decisions can be made about what to do and, once it is done, about the level of success that it can be accorded.

The explicit statement of rules enables individuals who may have limited knowledge of the contingencies and limited experience of behaving within the framework of rewards and sanctions they provide to deduce the actual relationships between their behaviors and likely outcomes. In this way, weak metacognitive information can be assessed, edited, revised, and incorporated into a nexus of regulations that will effectively influence future choice.

Bibliography

Homans, G. (1951). *Social behavior: Its elementary forms.* New York: Harcourt, Brace and World.

Searle, J. R. (1969). *Speech acts: An essay in the philosophy of language.* Oxford: Oxford University Press.

Searle, J. R. (1995). *The construction of social reality.* New York: Free Press.

Searle, J. R. (2010a). *Making the social world: The structure of human civilization.* Oxford: Oxford University Press.

Searle, J. R. (2010b). Consciousness and the problem of free will. In R. F. Baumeister, A. R. Mele, & K. D. Vohs (Eds.), *Free will and consciousness: How might they work?* (pp. 121–134). Oxford: Oxford University Press.

Shea, N., Boldt, A., Bang, D., Yeung, N., Heyes, C., & Frith, C. D. (2014). Supra-personal cognitive control and metacognition. *Trends in Cognitive Sciences, 18,* 186–193.

Skinner, B. F. (1957). *Verbal behavior.* New York: Century.

Sprott, J. (1958). *Human groups.* London: Penguin.

Stanovich, K. E. (2011). *Rationality and the reflective mind*. Oxford: Oxford University Press.

Tomasello, M. (1999). *The cultural origins of human cognition*. Cambridge, MA: Harvard University Press.

Tomasello, M. (2014). *A natural history of human thinking*. Cambridge, MA: Harvard University Press.

Tomasello, M. (2016). *A natural history of human morality*. Cambridge, MA: Harvard University Press.

10

Consumer Choice as Decision: Meso-Cognitive Psychology

Introduction

This chapter continues to seek to link the micro- and macro-depictions of decision making by means of a meso-cognitive psychology (MeCP) that demonstrates the capacity of individual consumers to choose and even create the contingencies to which their behavior will be subject. It does this by tracing the ways in which reinforcement histories support short- and long-range interests which interact in order to dominate the behavioral strategy of the consumer. Picoeconomic analysis provides a means of not only linking MiCP and MaCP but of suggesting the form that the necessary account of intra-personal, inter-agent communication, and cooperation takes. The picoeconomic strategy of bundling may enable the consumer who habitually selects a sooner-appearing but inferior reward so as to arrange the contingencies that he or she is more likely to forgo this and to wait patiently for a later-appearing but superior reward. It is appropriate to derive the decision perspective of the BPM when these considerations have been discussed and this is the subject of the concluding part of the chapter.

© The Editor(s) (if applicable) and The Author(s) 2016

G.R. Foxall, *Perspectives on Consumer Choice*,

DOI 10.1057/978-1-137-50121-9_10

Meso-Cognitive Psychology

Linking MiCP and MaCP

MiCP, exemplified here by dual and tripartite modeling, the CNDS hypothesis, and other approaches founded on the interaction of impulsive and executive decision modes, entails cognitive theorizing that predominantly links decision making and action with neurophysiology, that is, the personal level of exposition with the sub-personal level of exposition. The central mechanisms are the operation of the impulsive and executive decision modes based, respectively, on limbic and prefrontal cortical functioning, the balance of these functions determining the rate at which the consumer discounts the future. However, this linkage of models that are concerned with competing systems neurophysiological processes, while they might be said to focus on intra-personal cognitive conflict and its resolution by describing events at the sub-personal level, should not be interpreted as a claim that they ignore operancy. The point being made is that these models show an emphasis on the sub-personal basis of cognition; they also take into consideration, to differing degrees, the influence of super-personal operancy on both cognitive functioning and neuronal plasticity.

MaCP, exemplified here by theories of collective intentionality, entails cognitive theorizing that links decision making and action with operancy, that is, the personal level of exposition with the super-personal level of exposition. This is also an emphasis rather than an absolute rule. Like the observation that theories at the MiCP level tend to be concerned with relationships between the personal and the sub-personal levels, it is a reflection made for analytical convenience and the division of intellectual labor rather than an absolute distinction. Theories of collective intentionality are concerned with the ways in which members of social systems jointly create contingencies of reinforcement over and above those which are imposed by the natural world.

Such mutually devised contingencies arrange the reward structure that is dependent on specific actions deemed prosocial or antisocial by the members of a social system. In other words, such contingencies constitute a scheme of socially devised and socially policed rules that define what the BPM calls informational reinforcement and punishment. Behaving according to these rules is behaving in ways that the social group reinforces; against them, in ways that it punishes. In general, societies will devise rules through collective intentionality that encourage its members to engage in the level of temporal discounting that their members approve.

It is necessary now to show not only how these theories can be brought together but also how we can understand the capacity of individuals as well as collectives to create contingencies for the control of their behavior. In approaching these issues, our focus shifts from the separate intra-personal and supra-personal concerns that impinged, respectively, on the discussions of MiCP and MaCP in Chapters 8 and 9. Our focus shifts to their interaction in the individual consumer. For this, we require a theory of cognitive functioning at the meso-level. Such a theory must permit exploration of how individuals are subject to neurophysiological pressures and operant contingencies imposed by nature and other people as well as how they may escape both by generating contingencies that will regulate their behavior so that it evinces their chosen level of temporal discounting.

In order to fulfill this role, this meso-cognitive psychology should ideally be closely linked to both neurophysiology and operancy and suggest a therapeutic route through which individuals can alter or create contingencies of reinforcement and punishment that permit them a degree of control over their valuation of future events. It is important also that it relate directly to *consumer* behavior, perhaps more so than do the micro- and macro-cognitive psychologies we have considered. It ought, for instance, to act not only as a mediator between these cognitive psychologies but as a close link with the contents of consumer choice as interpreted in the Intentional Interpretation. The cognitive rehearsal that is a feature of Analytic Mind and of the community that projects a novel social reality in the form of rules that specify contingencies of reinforcement must also have a counterpart in the mental life of the individual that links it to both neurophysiological operations and learning histories.

The construction of social reality relies broadly on the thinking that underlies radical behaviorism—the capacity of human behavior to be influenced by its consequences. However, the analysis of contingency-shaped and rule-governed behavior in light of the considerations raised by collective intentionality remove the notion that consumer choice, like human behavior in general, is the passive response to a controlling external environment. We require in view of this a mechanism by which the reciprocal interaction of the person, the environment, and behavior (Bandura 1986) can be conceptualized within the context of human economic and social decision making. On all these grounds, Ainslie's (1992) picoeconomics may be considered an exemplar of such a procedure.

The Interaction of Picoeconomic Interests

The focus of picoeconomic analysis is the self-defeating behaviors in which people engage, from drug consumption to compulsive shopping, from procrastination to failure to exercise sufficiently (Ainslie 1992). Ainslie (2001) proposes that it is concerned with the temporary preference for a less rewarding payoff simply because it is available sooner, rather than a greater payoff that takes time. The difficulty is the commonplace human tendency toward weakness of will or akrasia. The economic theory of utility maximization does a good job of predicting behavior when alternative rewards occur simultaneously but is unable to deal with the selection of the more immediate but objectively less valuable reward over a more valuable alternative whose realization requires patience. It is not as if people do not start out with conventionally rational expectations of themselves, resolving to wait for the later payoff; it is just that at the moment when the less rewarding alternative will become available, they change their minds. Utility theory, based on exponential discounting, does not explain this, either. Hyperbolic discounting represents value as "inversely proportional to delay," as is apparent from the curves shown in Box 6.2; that for hyperbolic discounting is more bowed than that for exponential. Ainslie (2001) argues that evidence is mounting that people's natural discounting curves are often not only nonexponential but specifically hyperbolic.

The interesting feature of picoeconomics from the point of view of its providing a macro-cognitive psychology, linking subjective valuations of future rewards to both the contingencies of reinforcement that have enforced previous choices and decision processes, is its depiction of the human self as a population of agents that engage in intertemporal bargaining as though the mind were an internal marketplace. Whereas economic theory standardly presents the consumer as motivated by a single preference, the maximization of utility, he or she is actually an arena in which distinct, incompatible, and contradictory preferences are at war. The salience of each preference is a function of its temporal appearance. "The orderly internal marketplace pictured by conventional utility theory becomes a complicated free-for-all, where to prevail an option not only has to promise more than its competitors, but also act strategically to keep the competitors from later turning the tables later on" (Ainslie 2001, p. 40).

So the consumer is not the felicitous calculator of economic theory who can rationally reach an optimal judgment about what to buy and when: rather, consumers judge and rejudge the value of this or that act of purchase or consumption, and in the course of time their conclusions surrender whatever unity they may once have exhibited in favor of a mass of contradictions. The subjective experience of this process is not akin to the chaos of a disorganized mob, however; it is felt as the choice of one option among several.

In a passage that seems to extend Skinner's (1981) idea of selection by consequences to the realm of cognition, Ainslie (2001, pp. 42–3) presents mental operations as being selected for by particular rewards. In our terms, the consumer's learning history, determined by the patterns of reinforcement that have come to influence his or her patterns of behavior, is embodied in the cognitive and metacognitive processing that leads to choice. The mental operations selected in the course of a consumption history constitute the consumer's *interest* in each of the rewards available. Identifying such interests only makes sense when they are in conflict. In the case of everyday consumption typified by making a familiar brand choice, there is no conflict between Brand A and Brand B of cream cakes, so neither is there any conflict of interest between them. The consumer has no "Brand A interest" to conflict with a "Brand B interest" because choices among them are simultaneous, the brands are functionally interchangeable, and making the "mistake" of buying one rather than the other has no discernable consequences. This resonates well with what we know of consumers' multibrand purchasing. By contrast, between a consumer's interest in consuming the cakes now and their longer-term interest in being slim and healthy, there is a huge and continuing conflict. Competing rewards develop peculiar interests, each of which strives to hinder the other. It is interesting that Ainslie suggests that "I" may seek to allay one interest in favor of another: say, to try to strengthen my longer-range interest in being healthy vis-à-vis my immediate desire for the fattening food.

In summary, akrasia and addiction on one hand and normal behavior on the other result from conflict between their respective short-range and long-range *interests* (SRIs and LRIs). A consumer's early morning resolve to spend the afternoon reading for her degree in Medieval Greek Music (which promises the LLR of a prestigious qualification and a sparkling research career) might be thwarted by the noontide opportunity to go to the cinema with friends (which brings the SSR of immediate pleasure). This everyday example of akrasia demonstrates a shift in preferences between the gentle discounting of the future in the morning (t_0), giving way to the steep discounting that comes about at midday (t_1) when the SSR becomes a possibility. In economic terms, we would describe her utility function as indicating a preference for study over cinema at t_0, while at t_1 her utility function indicates a preference for cinema over study (Ross 2009).

Ross (2012) variously models picoeconomic interests as acting, first, synchronously and, second, diachronically. In the synchronous case, they become subagents with *either* conflicting utility functions *or* divergent time preferences. Agents with conflicting utility functions may, he points out, be modeled in terms of a Nash equilibrium game among these agents. Modeling the behavior of subagents whose time preferences diverge adverts to the sub-personal level of neurophysiology in which a hyperbolic time preference emerges from "competition between steeply exponentially discounting 'limbic' regions and more patient (less steeply exponentially discounting) 'cognitive' regions" (Ross 2012, p. 720). Modeling the person as comprising diachronically acting multiple selves, each controlling the individual's behavior for a limited period of time, requires that they be thought of as facing distinct and conflicting utility functions and each possessing incomplete information about the other. An agent's utility in this case is dependent on the investments made by earlier agents (Ross 2012, p. 720). A third way of modeling the consumer's SRIs and LRIs (Ross 2012) is neurophysiologically based, portraying the consumer's brain as producing behavior which, although it is externally rewarded in the short term, may invite deleterious consequences in the longer term. The metacognitive implications of such modeling are almost boundless.

Picoeconomics and the Requirements of Metacognitive Control

It is necessary to understand the functions of metacognitive control in the context of meso-cognitive psychology as it has been for micro- and macro-cognition psychologies. There must be means by which the individual mind assumed by picoeconomic analysis distributes metacognitive representations for verbal communication, evaluates metacognitive representations to motivate appropriate action, and extricates metacognitive representations from weak metacognitive information.

Distributing metacognitive representations for verbal communication is necessary in order that the competing interests can be aware of one another. There can be no possibility of one interest forestalling another unless they can be arrayed in a common forum for purposes of comparison, assessment of feasibility, determination of the costs and benefits of each, and so on. These are also processes involved in *evaluating metacognitive representations to motivate appropriate action* which are essential if, within the arena of warring factions, each interest is to be able to take the other's tendencies and strengths into consideration. There is, additionally, a role for *extricating metacognitive representations from weak metacognitive information.* There is no guarantee that the motivations of each interest will be articulated sufficiently loudly and clearly for its objectives and strategic strengths to be taken seriously into account by a competing interest. This metacognitive function becomes, therefore, a matter of augmenting the signals coming from the cointerest and is necessary if the interests are not to be surprised by the motivating effect of one another on the individual's behavior.

It is difficult to appreciate how these functions could be fulfilled in the absence of an overarching forum in which the working out of conflicts, the readying for action, and, especially, the resolution of conflicts via the revaluation of alternative rewards available at different times could be accomplished. The import of Ainslie's "I" who arbitrates among competing interests, strengthening one at the expense of the other, becomes apparent when we consider the methods by which an individual can arrange the contingencies of reinforcement in order to promote behavior change. How could intertemporal cooperation be fostered without such a setting?

Ainslie's (1992) description of several strategies for changing one's valuation of future rewards and of manipulating one's behavior to avoid the temptation of the SSR and practice the patience and self-control necessary to attain the LLR reinforces this conclusion. Physical commitment, arranging social influence, restraining attention, exciting one emotion or downplaying another are all tactics he argues to be less adaptable than willpower. Willpower requires the consumer to reframe his or her situation by mentally viewing it as not a choice between two distinct rewards but a matter of selecting between more far-reaching categories of choice. The strategy of employing personal side bets concerned with whole swathes of future behaviors and their outcomes rather than single instances is central:

> *Public* side bets – of reputation, for instance, or good will – have long been known as ways you can commit yourself to behave… What I'm describing are *personal* side bets, commitments made in your mind, where the stake is nothing but your credibility with yourself. They wouldn't be possible without hyperbolic discount curves, nor would they be of any use. (Ainslie 2001, p. 94)

We have seen that akrasia is prevalent and addiction a strong possibility because the SSR is likely to be disproportionately valuable just prior to its becoming available to an extent that eclipses the value of the LLR. Picoeconomics raises the possibility that an individual who has habitually chosen the SSR over the LLR can exercise willpower by "bundling" together the sum total of the gains from patience (waiting for the LLR) and comparing them with those that will accrue, again in total, from protracted selection of the SSR (Ainslie 1992; Elster 2015).

The tempted individual can thereby forestall selection of the SSR on the next occasion of its availability, a factor that is crucial to the possibility of his or her continuing to evince self-control rather than impulsivity (Fig. 10.1) As Ainslie (2001) and Rachlin (2000a, b) forcefully point out, the most accurate predictor of future abstinence is current abstinence. If the individual can act on the basis of bundling in this way, it is as though he or she is making a personal side bet that selection of the LLR will be the norm. Bundling thus becomes a central component of metacognitive control of behavior. In the imagined future scenarios that bundling makes possible, the LLR is always of superior value to the SSR (Foxall 2016a).

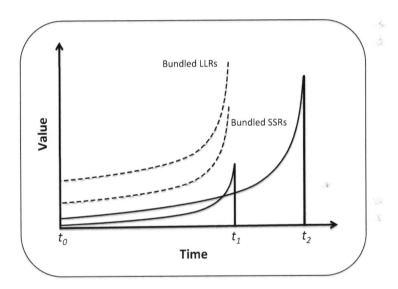

Fig. 10.1 *Bundling as a picoeconomic strategy.* The *solid lines* represent any of the individual members of the stream of paired SSR/LLR choices that will be available to the individual over time. (Hence, t_x is the time of any occurrence of an SSR which is paired with an LLR that occurs at t_{x+1}, and we are assuming a sequence of such SSR/LLR pairings over time.) The *dashed lines* represent the individual's imagined aggregation of these rewards if they were all brought forward to a point just prior to the appearance of the first SSR. In this case, LLR will always exceed SSR and a decision to select it exclusively on subsequent occasions can be more easily made. See also Foxall (2016a) (Adapted from Foxall (2016a). *Addiction as Consumer Choice: Exploring the Cognitive Dimension.* London and New York: Routledge)

Bundling and the personal side bets it incorporates are, moreover, consistent with an interpretation in terms of the maximization of utilitarian and informational reinforcement. What I lose if I do not keep to the terms of my bet with myself that my refraining from the SSR today that I will be able to avoid this choice on subsequent days is my self-esteem. This is the ultimate manifestation of my informational reinforcement consisting in being constantly true to myself. It is the emotional outcome of my seeking and gaining the performance feedback that accrues from keeping my promise to myself to manage my behavior in favor of long-range interests. The consideration of the behaviors enjoined by the short- and long-range interests, their evaluation and comparison, and the selection of one over the other requires a forum other than that in which each of the interests uniquely operates.

The requirements of metacognitive control are well-illustrated by bundling which involves not simply one representation of a unitary future but the interaction of imagined futures. Impulsiveness declines when decisions are made in clusters or bundles: if a series of SSRs is compared with a series of LLRs. Ainslie (2007, 2011), as we have noted, portrays this as the mechanism of self-control through willpower. The exercise of willpower consists in recognizing that resisting current temptation requires accessing the cooperation of one's future selves. This relies on interpretation of previous choices and of one's current prediction of those future selves' interpretation of one's current choice; this means that one's present choice cannot be predicted or causally dependent simply on the incentive value of the utilitarian reinforcement (incentives) currently on offer; it invokes issues of the informational reinforcement (status and self-esteem) that will be received from deviating from current decisions (i.e., to select a series of LLRs).

Any idea that the essence of willpower involves maintaining cooperation with future selves relies on being able to see oneself complying with internal or personal rules in the expectation of receiving entire bundles of LLRs. This strategy is a matter of metacognition: one cognition, in the form of personal rules based on expectations of future behaviors and their outcomes, is operating upon lower-level beliefs about the amount of reinforcement that will be forthcoming as a result of behaving now as opposed to behaving later. These beliefs refer not only to future behaviors but also to past behavior and its reinforcing and punishing consequences.

The essence of the metacognition being practiced here is that one has cognitive representations of (i) one's reinforcement history (past behavior), (ii) the LLRs to be gained in the future, (iii) the SSRs foregone, (iv) the perceptions and evaluations one's future selves will have of one's present behavior and of one's future behavior should one renege on the present decision, (v) the value of one's self-esteem in consistently choosing a series of LLRs in the future. These cognitive representations are acted upon by S2 metacognition which takes the form of decision making, choice, and willpower. The point of this S2 metacognition is to facilitate not inter-personal communication but communication between the current self and future selves, to allow future judgments made by self-agents yet to emerge to impinge on current decision making and commitment to a series of LLRs.

The three functions Shea et al. (2014) ascribe to S2 metacognition are instrumental in this recursive inter-agent communication: such intra-personal interaction requires the distribution of metacognitive representations for verbal communication, evaluation of metacognitive representations to motivate appropriate action, and the extrication of metacognitive representations from weak metacognitive information. The first involves making the cognitive control exerted by future selves available to the current self; the second, appraising the consequences of whole series of selecting SSRs and selecting LLRs; the third, transforming the vague outcomes of future choices (weak metacognitive information) into metacognitive information that facilitates decision and commitment to sustained action. The same process of S2-based metacognition for the cognitive control of agents is posited; however, the agents in our case are synchronously or diachronically occurring features of intra-personal experience. The S1 metacognitive information that Shea et al. (2014) posit to be the input to S2 metacognition in the individual is always disputable and indeed disputed—by the picoeconomic agents that compose the individual.

Conclusions

The Intentional Interpretation presented in Chapter 7 distinguished routine from extreme consumer choice by reference to the degree of temporal discounting they involve and the consequent tendency toward preference reversal. Both are encountered least of all in everyday consumption, especially when we recognize that the brands that compose a consumer's consideration set are functional substitutes that confer similar levels of utilitarian reinforcement. The preference reversals exhibited as most consumers' tendency toward multibrand purchasing over a sequence of shopping trips, if preference reversals is the correct term, reflect an important feature of informational reinforcement, namely the variety of selecting alternative versions of a product category which may differ in small degree in their flavors, colors, prestige values, and so on. Major preference reversal is reserved for more extreme consumer choices though even here the consumer's behavior may not be interpreted as irrational since he or she receives informational reinforcement in the form of pride or self-esteem (see Fig. 3.5) that accrues from a feeling of being in control of one's own behavior.

It is now possible to draw conclusions about the usefulness of the Intentional Behaviorism research strategy by evaluating how far the Cognitive Interpretation undertaken in this chapter justifies the Intentional Interpretation proposed in the preceding chapter. Any conclusions must be tentative given the exploratory nature of the exercise, the simplification of the consumer situations considered, and concentration on temporal discounting as the predominant source of intentionality. At the close of Chapter 7, I outlined the broad conclusions of the Intentional Interpretation. Chapters 8, 9, and 10 have attempted to specify what cognitive processes would be necessary to generate this intentionality, the mental activities it enjoins upon the consumer, and the pattern of choice to which it can be expected to lead. It is now time to assess how far the micro-, meso-, and macro-cognitive psychologies discussed above meet these requirements: in short, we must ask how far the cognitive theories proposed are capable of handling consumer choice as action.

The tripartite theory that has exemplified MiCP portrays how humans deal with the cognitive requirements identified by the Intentional

Interpretation: the overriding of impulsive tendencies toward rash choices, the decoupling of current mental preoccupations so that cognitive rehearsal can take place efficiently in a framework of "undisturbed" and nonconfusing contemplation of potential futures, the selection of a course of action that is in line with one's cognitive style, the learning necessary to ensure that future decision making and choice are increasingly efficient and effective. These cognitive functions are especially instructive in detailing how the immediate impulses of TASS, which is highly dependent on impulsive neurophysiological operations, can be overridden and replaced by Analytic Mind. The tripartite theory is thus an appropriate theory to fulfill the requirements of MiCP, though we must bear in mind that its strength also relates to its capacity to comprehend the super-personal level of exposition. The link with the BPM that this level of analysis opens up is the capacity of MiCP to show how alternative learning histories, each based on unique contingencies of reinforcement, severally strengthen the impulsive and executive decision modes. Operant behavior influences neuronal plasticity and with it the ability of alternative emotional and behavioral responses to influence patterns of behavior. The sub-personal level of exposition is rightly brought to the fore by the models that have been considered in the context of MiCP, particularly the CNDS model which explicitly links to the limbic and paralimbic system and the prefrontal cortex in explicating the operations of the impulsive and executive behavioral tendencies.

The construction of social reality through collective intentionality which we have considered in light of Tomasello's and Searle's theories indicates a capacity of humans acting in concert to fashion contingencies of reinforcement and to link them to the personal level of exposition via the formulation and enforcement of rules. These contingencies in addition to those that occur without intentional human intervention are a vital source of the behavior-environment relationships that determine learning histories and further behavior. Informational reinforcement is embedded in collective intentionality.

Picoeconomics, as the exemplar of the equally important MeCP, is particularly effective in identifying how the pattern of consumer choice can change in line with the expectations, desires, and beliefs of the individual consumer. The idea of bundling is of special significance in suggesting how the pattern of future reinforcements can be taken into consideration in decision making and brought to bear on the selection of a pattern of activity that has greater and more rewarding consequences than that previously selected. In short, picoeconomics links the contingencies of reinforcement of the symbolic consumer situation and the ultimate source of reinforcement of operant behavior namely the neurophysiologically instantiated emotional feelings that are the result of the receipt of reinforcers and punishers. Picoeconomics links the neurophysiology of the sub-personal level of exposition with the cognitive and behavioral strategies of the personal level, and the influencing environment of the super-personal level of operancy.

The Decision Perspective

What kinds of cognitive architecture and functioning would be necessary to originate and/or sustain the summary elements of the Intentional Interpretation set out at the beginning of this chapter? The first element is the formulation of a goal structure that maximizes the consumer's utility function (both utilitarian and informational reinforcement) within his or her budgetary constraints. The first requirement of a biological entity is a rapid response system which can ensure that immediate threats and opportunities are responded to in a timely and efficient manner These goals are set in the course of the phylogenetic evolution and ontogenetic development of the species and organism; hence, they are partly innate, partly learned. The need is for learning mechanisms capable of classical and operant conditioning. In the tripartite model these are taken care of by the S1 systems which we might identify with TASS.

There is also a need for the monitoring of the external environment and the assumption is that these are the responsibility of the sense modalities whether or not these are regarded as TASS in themselves. There is also a need for the monitoring of the internal environment via a mechanism that allows impulsive responses to be allayed in order that further information processing can occur before a response is selected and implemented. This requires a capacity to override, as necessary, the activities of the rapid response system. In the tripartite model this is the function of Reflective Mind via Algorithmic Mind. The specification that the individual will act within the compass of his or her cognitive style is also important as this sets the general "policy framework" within which his or her behavior will occur and the goals it will be expected to serve.

MiCP draws attention to the relationship between cognitive processing and neurophysiology, seeking to constrain personal-level theorizing by means of empirical knowledge gained through extensional methodologies practiced at the sub-personal. MaCP seeks to perform a similar task by relating cognitive processing to operancy, again with the objective of constraining the former, this time from the view point of extensional behavioral science. The dual and tripartite theories considered in regard to MiCP reach out to cover neurophysiology, behavior, and cognition; the theories of collective intentionality reach out to embrace operancy, behavior, and cognition. We have judged their success according to the extent to which they have fulfilled the requisite functions of metacognitive systems set out by Shea et al. (2014). They appear to meet these requirements with satisfactory rigor. There remains the task of showing how micro- and macro-approaches to cognitive psychology may be interrelated.

Picoeconomics answers the question of the kind of cognitive structure and functioning needed to set goals and motivate their achievement in a different but complementary fashion. Cast here in the role of the necessary meso-cognitive psychology presents a personal-level cognitive framework that reaches out to both the sub-personal and super-personal levels of exposition.[1] The goals of the separate short-range and long-range interests posited by picoeconomics are the result of alternative learning histories, principally manifesting in experience of the payoffs that typically follow particular behaviors. Such experience strengthens or weakens the probability of an excitatory or inhibitory response when similar situations to those previously encountered arise anew. Again, the relevant response to these situations is not only that of TASS but of the Reflective Mind and the ensuing operations of Algorithmic Mind. These operations are also necessary when the individual changes his or her goals, as when adopting picoeconomic strategies such as bundling.

---

[1] At the risk of repetition, I want to emphasize that I am not drawing the conclusion that the theories and models I have considered in the contexts of MiCP and MaCP are conceptually deficient in this regard. Rather, I have for analytical reasons regarded each type of theory as having a particular directional focus outwards from the personal level toward either the sub-personal or the super-personal.

Other elements of the Intentional Interpretation are the imagining of future choice scenarios that will likely be available, and undertaking the evaluation of imagined future contingencies. These operations require a mechanism through which the consumer can seek out information on future behaviors and their payoffs, and then evaluate it by means of active comparisons not only between these behavioral alternatives themselves but also of each with the organism's goals. The tripartite model casts this as the ultimate responsibility of Reflective Mind but it is primarily the task of Algorithmic Mind to engage in the cognitive rehearsal that fulfills these tasks having taken TASS offline and insulated its speculative program from interference by common-sense interruptions in favor of how things actually are.

The same S2 mechanisms are responsible for the function of evaluating the imagined scenarios and the comparison of these choice scenarios and their outcomes, followed by the selection of one particular goal, and the building of the intention to carry it out, plus working toward its achievement—all in a flexible manner. Bundling, or for that matter any other picoeconomic strategy or strategy for behavioral change, are tasks that similarly require a forum in which the interests can interact and decisions can be made.

It may be objected that the dual and tripartite models, theories of collective intentionality, and picoeconomics have been chosen deliberately to substantiate the Intentional Interpretation proposed in Chapter 7. All three approaches to theory have been subjected to critical examination prior to their use in the present context (Foxall 2013, 2014a, b, 2016a, b); moreover, the present account incorporates an additional means of specifying and evaluating the chosen theories according to an independent proposal for the functioning of metacognitive systems based on Shea et al.'s (2014) scheme, and the theories have been appraised in terms of its demands. However, there is nothing fixed about the use of these theories; they happen to be prominent examples of potential micro-, macro-, and meso-cognitive psychologies, but there is no reason why other cognitive theories could not be employed to ascertain the extent to which the Intentional Interpretation can be justified. Indeed, this is an essential part of the theory testing process that Chapter 6 laid out.

We can now derive the decision perspective on consumer choice, an elaboration of the intentional perspective, which is shown in Fig. 10.2 and the cognitive stance on which it rests in Box 10.1. This placing of decision

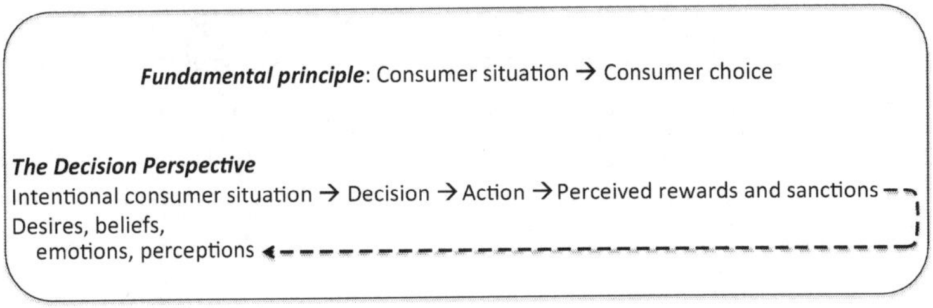

> *Fundamental principle*: Consumer situation → Consumer choice
>
> **The Decision Perspective**
> Intentional consumer situation → Decision → Action → Perceived rewards and sanctions
> Desires, beliefs,
>   emotions, perceptions ◄ ─

Fig. 10.2   Consumer choice: The decision perspective

Box 10.1 Summary of the Cognitive Stance

Philosophy of explanation:

Interprets the intentionality and the actions of the consumer in terms of cognitive structure and functioning. Determines whether the intentional interpretation of consumer choice is consistent with these and with neuro-scientific theories and findings with respect to cognition.

Method:

Given the intentionality ascribed to the consumer, assesses the extent to which this is consistent with theories of cognitive structure and functioning and its underlying neurophysiology and operancy.

Epistemology

The origins and nature of the consumer's intentionality are interpreted in cognitive terms.

Success criterion:

The generation of a convincing cognitive account of the origins and effects of the consumer's intentionality.

Scope:

Human action, and the actions of animals to which intentionality can be properly ascribed.

Agency:

Agency is attributed to the individual consumer.

---

making within the BPM framework raises several questions in view of the analysis contained in this chapter. Does the making of decisions determine behavior? In view of the capacity of individuals to select the patterns of contingency to which their behavior will be subject, as is apparent from pico-economic strategizing, and of communities to decide collectively the social realities to which their members will be subject and to enforce these via a system of constitutive and deontic rules, as is apparent from the discussion of collective intentionality, do we not require an agential perspective on consumer choice? These are the subjects of Chapter 11.

Bibliography

Ainslie, G. (1992). *Picoeconomics: The strategic interaction of successive motivational states within the person.* Cambridge: Cambridge University Press.

Ainslie, G. (2001). *Breakdown of will.* Cambridge: Cambridge University Press.

Ainslie, G. (2007). Emotion: The gaping hole in economic theory. In B. Montero & M. D. White (Eds.), *Economics and the mind* (pp. 11–28). London/New York: Routledge.

Ainslie, G. (2011). Free will as recursive self-prediction: Does a deterministic mechanism reduce responsibility? In J. Poland & G. Graham (Eds.), *Addiction and responsibility* (pp. 55–87). Cambridge, MA: MIT Press.

Bandura, A. (1986). *Social foundations of thought and action: A social cognitive theory.* Englewood Cliffs: Prentice Hall.

Elster, J. (2015). *Explaining social behavior: More nuts and bolts for the social sciences.* Revised edition. Cambridge: Cambridge University Press.

Foxall, G. R. (2013). Intentionality, symbol, and situation in the interpretation of consumer choice. *Marketing Theory, 13,* 105–127.

Foxall, G. R. (2014a). Neurophilosophy of explanation in economic psychology: An exposition in terms of neuro-behavioral decision systems. In L. Moutinho et al. (Eds.), *Routledge companion to the future of marketing* (pp. 134–150). London/New York: Routledge.

Foxall, G. R. (2016a). *Addiction as consumer choice: Exploring the cognitive dimension.* London/New York: Routledge.

Foxall, G. R. (2016b). Metacognitive control of categorial neurobehavioral decision systems. *Frontiers in Psychology, 7,* 170.

Rachlin, H. (2000a). *The science of self control.* Cambridge, MA: Harvard University Press.

Rachlin, H. (2000b). The lonely addict. In W. K. Bickel & R. E. Vuchinich (Eds.), *Reframing health behavior change with behavioral economics.* Mahwah: Erlbaum.

Ross, D. (2009). Economic models of procrastination. In C. Andreou & M. White (Eds.), *The thief of time* (pp. 28–50). New York: Oxford University Press.

Ross, D. (2012). The economic agent: Not human, but important. In U. Mäki (Ed.), *Philosophy of economics* (pp. 691–736). Amsterdam: Elsevier.

Shea, N., Boldt, A., Bang, D., Yeung, N., Heyes, C., & Frith, C. D. (2014). Supra-personal cognitive control and metacognition. *Trends in Cognitive Sciences, 18*, 186–193.

Skinner, B. F. (1981, July 31). Selection by consequences, *Science, 213*, 501–4.

11

Consumer Choice as Agency

Introduction

Thus far we have been concerned with consumer choice as behavior which we traced through the behavioral perspective of the BPM, and consumer choice as action, traced through the action perspective and the decision perspective. This concluding chapter offers a tentative view of consumer choice as agency, on the basis that actions are bodily movements for which the individual is responsible. The philosopher John Searle refers to the point we reach in our decision making when we can fail to be influenced by the desires and beliefs we have so carefully formulated and even the decisions we have firmly made as "the gap." The place of rationality in agency is discussed, and we conclude with coverage of consumer agency.

This concluding chapter briefly draws together the themes discussed earlier and proposes that only a multiperspectival consumer psychology can capture the subtleties and nuances of consumer choice. It contrasts the consumer behavior, which is explicable by reference to a controlling environment, with the consumer action which is brought about by the individual acting purposefully. Finally, it assimilates the implications of cognition and action for the understanding of consumer choice as agency.

© The Editor(s) (if applicable) and The Author(s) 2016   **279**
G.R. Foxall, *Perspectives on Consumer Choice*,
DOI 10.1057/978-1-137-50121-9_11

Cognition and Agency

Our investigation of economic and social choice has presented a picture of the consumer as a locus of causative influences, whether these originate in the external environment or in the desires, beliefs, and decision processes in terms of which we conceptualize the mainsprings of his or her activities. This concluding chapter explores the personal involvement of the consumer in the initiation of his or her choices. It does so by raising three questions. First, in what sense, if any, do agents' desires, beliefs, emotions, and perceptions provide an explanation of their behavior? Second, is intentionality determinative of choice? And, third, what are the essential characteristics of agency?

The last chapter explored two realms of consumer experience in which the environmental locus of control, though not irrelevant, was subordinated to the internal locus. In the bundling behavior which provided a focus for the discussion of macro-cognitive psychology, the individual consumer was depicted as capable of modifying his or her activities by effectively selecting the set of contingencies to which they would henceforth be subject. In the construction of social reality which featured in the discussion of macro-cognitive psychology, people are depicted as collectively capable of inaugurating novel contingencies of reinforcement by deciding that in a specific context, one artifact, for example, euro bills, or one status-defined office, for example, the president of France, would respectively *count as* a legal means of settling debts or as a person with particular authority and responsibilities. Both of these are a far cry from the strict determination of behavior by environmental contingencies.

These approaches to cognitive psychology suggest that the explanation of human behavior in intentional terms requires further consideration and clarification. The possibility of employing picoeconomic strategies to overcome addiction—a mode of consumer choice marked by economic irrationality, steep temporal discounting, preference reversal, and cognitive irrationality—inspires the ascription of agency to those responsible for effecting this change in themselves and their behavior. The capacity to engage in cognitive rehearsal and to change behavior on the basis of one's valuation of alternative projected courses of action is indicative not only of action but also of agency. Similarly, in the case of collective intentionality, we have a situation in which humans decide for themselves what will count as reinforcement and punishment. The contingencies of reinforcement are not therefore something to which they are subjected by their environment acting as an agent: they are modifiable by human action, human decision to behave in a particular manner, and to arrange the contingencies so as to encourage similar action among others. The pursuit of both MiCP and MaCP portrays consumer behavior in terms that are not caught by a mechanistic approach to the explanation of behavior, be it behavioristic or cognitive. The implications of being able to so arrange the contingencies as to change one's behavior by means of picoeconomic strategies or by collectively deciding what shall count as a reinforcer or punisher takes us beyond action to the possibility of agency. These are the themes of this concluding chapter. In it I shall not attempt to comprehensively debate agency, which would require a volume in itself, but will review key considerations that bear on the discussion.

Agency in the Gap

We can now begin to answer the questions posed at the head of this chapter. First: in what sense, if any, do agents' desires, beliefs, emotions, and perceptions provide an explanation of their behavior? Intentionality supplies an explanation but not the sort of causative account that an experimental/correlational analysis can provide. We do not seek a psychological explanation of behavior until the possibilities for explaining it by reference to a stimulus field that defines its learning history and current setting, including the extent to which these prefigure a pattern of reinforcement and punishment that will follow the performance of certain behaviors, have been exhausted. Having reached this point in seeking to understand behavior it becomes imperative to suggest an interpretation in terms of nonextensional language. This is the sole means now at our disposal to account for the behavior and it necessarily involves the use of intentional language. The other questions emerge from this point. Does intentionality provide a determinative explanation of behavior? (Conversely: does psychological explanation entail freewill?) And, what are the essential characteristics of agency? (In other words, to what sorts of entity does psychological explanation apply?)

In the case of extensional behavioral science we found it straightforward to show that some stimuli caused an increase in the rate of the consumer behavior they followed, while others caused a reduction in that rate. We could say that A causes B (or perhaps that A explains B, or that B is a function of A) and be easily understood. But I have argued that when no stimuli are apparent on which this sort of inference can be based, our only alternative is to provide an account based on the intentionality of the consumer. Discriminatory, reinforcing, and punishing stimuli are replaced in this analysis by desires, beliefs, emotions, and perceptions, and rather than speak of explanation it may be more accurate to think in terms of interpretation. It is natural to inquire whether desires and beliefs and other components of the consumer's intentionality cause their behavior and, if so, in what sense.

These theoretical entities are not directly amenable to scientific investigation but they can influence experimental and correlational studies through the careful devising of behavioral, especially verbal, and neurophysiological indices. The resulting measures are not infallible reproductions of the mental entities that are publicly unobservable and they are not unassailable predictors of behavior. Measures of intentionality, even when they reflect the individual's belief state immediately prior to an opportunity to behave accordingly (Foxall 2005) do not necessarily predict behavior accurately. This failure to act in consonance with our own intentionality is explored by Searle (2001) in terms of what he calls *the gap*, a hiatus between taking a decision and performing an action. This is a good place to begin the discussion of the import of intentional explanation.

Rational Explanation

One way of defining the gap alludes to the *experience* of decision making and acting in which we recognize that, whatever we have decided, we can choose to act differently. Desires and beliefs that resulted in earlier deliberations do not appear to us as causally sufficient conditions for deciding and acting. All of the mental operations in which we engaged to reach a decision—the examination of the reasons we have for acting in relation to our goals, the formation of intentions to do a particular thing—do not ultimately determine what we will do. We realize that we could do something else just as validly; so, whatever deeds our preceding deliberations, exercise of sensibility, and willpower led us to expect we would carry out as rational beings can be set aside in favor of alternative courses of action. And, even having commenced the execution of an action, we sometimes experience a gap in which we examine whether to continue with it, to see it through to completion. Our desires, beliefs, attitudes, and intentions are, we realize, not causally sufficient to bring about the actions to which they pointed. The gap arises then in three kinds of circumstance: first, between the deliberation that precedes a decision and the decision itself; second, between the formulation of a prior intention (reaching a decision) and the inauguration of action, that is, trying or intention-in-action; and third, once the intended sequence of action has been initiated, between the prior intention and the intention in action and the completion or continuance of the action (Searle 2001, pp. 62–3).

This conception of cognitive gaps, based upon the kinds of subjective experience that most of us would admit to having, is at odds with the notion that explanations of behavior couched in intentional terms (*rational* or *reason explanations*) are not causally sufficient to account for what we do. By contrast, statements of the form A causes B, which we have seen as characteristic of extensional science and to which Searle refers as *ordinary causal explanations*, allow us to conclude with confidence that the occurrence of A determined that of B, at least within the confines of experimental and correlational analyses. However, *rational explanations* do not take this form: they state, rather, that a person performed A by acting for reason R. This kind of explanation assumes the existence of an agent, self or ego: hence, "Agent S performed Act A because reason R" is a radically different kind of explanation from A caused B. A rational explanation like "a self S performed action A, and in the performance of A, S acted on reason R" (Searle 2007, p. 53) does not provide an account of the conditions that were sufficient to cause an individual's observed behavior. Rather, it alludes to reasons he or she acted upon. This would seem sufficient to justify redefining such behavior as action. But Searle goes further, seeing the actor as an agent.

The reason is that rational explanation rests upon the inference of "an irreducible self, a rational agent, in addition to the sequence of events." It is also part of Searle's argument that making some additional assumptions permits the derivation of this self. While reason explanations do not usually reference *causally sufficient* conditions, they can nevertheless explain actions *adequately*. Moreover, the adequacy of rational explanations is suggested by their naming conditions that, *in relation to the relevant context*, are generally accepted as causally sufficient. The import of this assumption is that for a causal statement to explain an event, it has to advert to some condition which, as far as that particular context is concerned, was enough to generate the focal event. If I say that I took the pills recommended by the pharmacist in the belief that they would assuage my indigestion, most people who know me would accept this as the cause of my purchasing and taking this medicine.

A reason explanation like this would be inadequate if it were presented to my friends as an ordinary causal explanation: reason explanations simply do not purport to be ordinary causal explanations. This raises an important question: How can we construe reason explanations as adequate if they would not be acceptable as standard causal explanations? Searle's response is that, although a rational explanation does not provide a sufficient cause of an event, it does set forth the manner in which "a conscious rational self" would have acted for a reason, how a rational and reasoning agent would have acted (Searle 2007, pp. 53–4).

The discussion of conceptual dualism in Chapter 6 is relevant to this move. Since an individual has knowledge by acquaintance of his or her reasons for having acted in a particular manner, he or she knows that those reasons and only those reasons were the mainspring of the action. The implication is that the ascription of agency is built in to psychological explanations because desires, beliefs, emotions, and perceptions and other forms of intentionality belong inexorably to conscious, rational beings who are, at least to a degree, in charge of their behavior: "the logical form of such explanations requires that we postulate an irreducible, non-Humean self" (Searle 2007, p. 55). Hume famously saw humans as "bundles of perceptions"; what Searle is saying is that rational explanations have the built-in assumption of a self that is more complicated than this, one that is something more than a composite of desires, beliefs, and other forms of intentionality. What justifies our seeing reason explanations as adequate is their capacity to explain why such a self would have acted in the observed manner. Their very function is to explain why such a self would have acted as it did by stipulating the reason that such an entity would have acted on. Reason explanations are, of course, precisely what we have considered under the rubric of Intentional Interpretations and for which we have sought support in the form of Cognitive Interpretations which are another kind of reason.

We return now to the idea of the gap, which thus far we have defined only as a hiatus between decision making and action. Searle notes two routes to such gaps, experiential and linguistic: we have the experience of ourselves acting in the gap and thereby expressing freedom; backing this up is the logical nature of the explanations we use to account for our actions.

The experiential aspect is simply our firsthand knowledge of our acting as rational agents and the fact that we can verbalize our explanations of our behavior provides the linguistic factor. Because our explanations do not identify causally sufficient conditions for our actions, however, there must be some other element over and above the desires and beliefs we so describe that accounts for our actions. If our explanations are to be comprehensible we must "recognize that there must be an entity – a rational agent, a self, or an ego – that acts in the gap (because a Humean bundle of perceptions would not be enough to account for the adequacy of the explanations)" (Searle 2007, p. 56). The imperative of recognizing such a self stems from our authentic feeling that we are acting voluntarily as well as our tendency to explain such actions by providing the reasons why we acted. In summary:

> We have first-person conscious experience of acting on reasons. We state these reasons for action in the form of explanations. The explanations are obviously quite adequate because we know in our case that, in their ideal form, nothing further is required. But they cannot be adequate if they are treated as ordinary causal explanations because they do not pass the causal sufficiency test. They are not deterministic in their logical form as stated,

and they are not deterministic in their interpretation. How can we account for these facts? To account for these explanations we must see that they are not of the form A caused B. They are of the form, a rational self S performed act A, and in performing A, S acted on reason R. That formulation requires the postulation of a self. (Searle 2007, p. 57)

Searle notes also that the grounds for concluding that reason explanations are adequate take the form of a Kantian "transcendental" argument in which, assuming the facts of the argument to be the case, we seek the conditions under which such facts are possible. Hence, the adequacy of rational explanations inheres in there being a self that has the properties of irreducibility, rational agency, and being able to act on the basis of reasons (Searle 2007, p. 57). The failure of what Searle calls the Classical Model of Rationality, which has no room for the gap, assuming simply that an action A is caused, tout court, by beliefs and desires, leads on to the third conclusion. As a result, rational explanations require the postulation of a self or agent not because of some intrinsic property they own but because of what they lack: their failure to acknowledge the experience of the gap between intentionality and action.

Causation, the Self, and the Gap

The import of "the gap" is that we have a sense, whatever we are currently doing, that we could be doing something else. Numerous alternatives are available to us. We have, that is, a sense of free will, a sense of being the authors of causation. This is accompanied by the awareness that the causes of our behavior, our reasons for doing it, are not sufficient to bring it about; they are not deterministic. Why should this convince us? The whole matter may be an illusion: like colors, which we seem to perceive but which have no physical basis. Searle admits that the gap could be an illusion but maintains that it is an experience we cannot ignore. Acceptance that there is a gap is borne out by our experience and underlies our very capacity to decide and choose. If an individual believed that desires and beliefs were causally sufficient he or she would not need to do anything: he or she could simply observe how the decision process was resolved and make a note of what his or her subsequent action turned out to be. But we do not do this. Having formulated desires and beliefs about what to have for dinner, the consumer still has something to do psychologically to bring it about, namely make a decision. The desires and beliefs themselves are not sufficient to bring the meal about. It is necessary to decide, to "plump for" one alternative. Much consumer behavior is like this. We have noted already that most consumers are multibrand purchasers and that their next specific brand choice, among the alternatives that make up their consideration set, is almost impossible to forecast. There are still matters to be settled when the consumer gets to the store and sees the brands that compose the consideration set. What brand is bought, how many packs are purchased, how the consumer pays for the items, and numerous other matters are settled on the spot.

We might explain the occurrence of such actions, knowing that the consumer's desires and beliefs are not causally sufficient to bring them about, in two ways. First, they might completely lack a sufficient explanation: we conclude that they are random happenings. Second, we could argue that these actions have an adequate psychological explanation even though they have no causally sufficient prior intentional conditions. They are undertaken for a *reason* even though the reason "does not fix an antecedently sufficient cause" (Searle 2007, p. 80). However, the first of these conclusions cannot be correct. Such actions are not random; even though they may be undetermined, they are not arbitrary. Hence, the second explanation must be adopted: in Searle's formulation, S performed A for reason R. But how can we entertain this as an adequate explanation if the reason does not determine the action?

In order to understand why reasons offer an explanation of behavior even though they are not causally sufficient in the ordinary sense, we need a special idea of agency: "Something is an agent in this sense if and only if it is a conscious entity that has the capacity to initiate and carry out actions under the presupposition of freedom" (Searle 2001, p. 83). An agent of this kind is not just a bundle of perceptions and other kinds of intentionality (as Hume proposes). If an agent can make decisions and act for reasons, it has also to be capable of "perception, belief, desire, memory and reasoning." An agent capable of volition must also be capable of conation and cognition:

The agent must in short be a self. Just as agency has to be added to the bundle to account for how embodied bundles can engage in free actions, so selfhood has to be added to agency to account for how agents can act rationally. *The reason that we can rationally accept explanations that do not cite sufficient conditions in these cases is that we understand that the explanations are about rational selves in their capacity as agents.* (Searle 2001, p. 84, emphasis in original)

Summing-Up

Searle's idea of the gap in which a self may act contrary to or despite its intentional deliberations is intuitively appealing for several reasons. It resonates with everyday subjective experience; it is consistent with a world view in which only a self that was not simply the inevitable outcome of a Humean bundle of perceptions (or other intentions); and the adequacy of rational explanations can only be possible on the assumption that such a self can behave as an agent, capable of bodily movements$_T$. However, an objection might be made that all of this relies too heavily on our intersubjective agreement that our individual phenomenologies are in agreement with Searle's. At the least, we require more understanding of the nature of agency before agreeing entirely with Searle's analysis. Steward's (2012) agency incompatibilism is a source of clarification.

We, therefore, have an answer to the second question posed at the head of this chapter: Is intentionality determinative? The answer in the negative is supported by Searle's analysis of the gap and Steward's argument that action settles matters that only it can settle. Some things are up-to-us. However, there is still room to consider further what kinds of entity can be thought of as agents, and this requires further clarification of the nature of agency. I should like to discuss this by examining the intentionality of a simple system, which is clearly not an agent, building toward consideration of the third question posed at the start of this chapter, in terms of whether consumers can be considered agents and on what grounds. We have some idea of the answer to this question from the work of Taylor, Hornsby, and Steward considered above, but it is instructive to consider it anew from a rather different standpoint. In particular, the following section discusses agency in terms suggested by List and Pettit (2011) which it extends by raising briefly the possibility that only entities to which we can adopt the intensional stance can be thought of as agential.[1]

Agency, Rationality, and Reasoning

Rationality

List and Pettit (2011) propose that an agent has three distinguishing characteristics: representative capacity ("beliefs"), motivation to act in an instrumental way ("desires"), and the capacity to so act. An agent is, therefore, necessarily an intentional entity: these requirements of agency are the beliefs, desires, and action tendencies which can be expressed in propositional format. These authors' illustration of an agent of this kind is a simple robot that returns cylinders on a table top to an upright position. Those that have toppled over are simply restored to their former state. This is a classic example of what Searle refers to as secondary intentionality. On the view I am putting forward, the primary intentionality is that of the designer of the robot: it is his or her intentionality that is expressed in the device he or she has created. Had the designer had access to an extensible wooden arm at the end of which was a device for picking up objects, he or she could well have used this instead of devising the robot. The robot differs from such a handheld device for picking up toppled-over items only in that it is remote. In intentional terms it differs not at all from an alarm clock that I set to wake me at an hour of my determination. The clock has an internal representation of the environment's current state (the time), the motivational representation to act when the

---

[1] List and Pettit (2011) present an extensive and sophisticated theory of agency and I am aware that in the following section I do no more than sketch their initial contribution. I look forward to incorporating further aspects of their work on group agency into a more substantial contribution on collective intentionality.

These comments are notable not only for the immediate point they make but for their confirmation of the observation that Skinner scrupulously sought to avoid intentional language and therefore intentional explanation.

time reaches a certain point, and the means of so acting. Neither robot nor clock has the capacity to reason, any more than does a paramecium. There is nothing that is up-to either of these artifacts, nothing they can do that is not programmed into them. Neither has the capacity to deviate from its pre-determined program (unless it malfunctions). It is not feasible therefore on Steward's reasoning to ascribe agency to either of them. In Searle's terms, there is no possibility of a gap. List and Pettit agree that the robot cannot reason; moreover, the scope of its intentionality is strictly limited. Complex intentional systems like humans can, especially, form long-range intentions. Intentional explanation is, they argue, both more difficult to accomplish (since the intentionality of humans is far more diverse and less amenable than that of a simpler system) and yet more essential since the alternatives also elude us.

A creature or other entity is usually ascribed agency not only by virtue of its behavior meeting specific standards but also its capacity to learn from its monitoring of these standards. Three "standards of rationality" are distinguished by List and Pettit: attitude-to-fact, attitude-to-action, and attitude-to-attitude. First, *attitude-to-fact* standards judge favorably those representations that accord with how things actually are and unfavorably those that do not. They are concerned with considerations of how one should react to evidence, how the environment should be monitored to gain this evidence, and how it should be judges when it becomes available. Attitude-to-fact failures generally result from inattention, *idées fixes*, or paranoia. Second, *attitude-to-action* standards judge favorably those actions that are called for by the agent's representations and motivations and unfavorably those that are not. Attitude-to-action failures often reflect weakness of will, compulsion, and obsession. Finally, *attitude-to-attitude* standards judge unfavorably those representations that are incompatible with others, excluding representations that assume propositions to be true even though they are not corealizable, or motivations that need such propositions to be true when they serve as bases for action. They, therefore, rule out failures of consistency, and motivations to act that do not take the agent's representations into consideration. For example, when desires are so compelling that they might override beliefs, the desires are ruled out. As a result, attitude-to-attitude rationality precludes means-ends failures.

The two possible sources of complication with respect to representations and motivations that List and Petit describe are noteworthy, partly because they suggest a third that is germane to the current argument. They argue that representations and motivations consist of two parts: an attitude (which is either representational or motivational) and the object of that attitude (which takes the form of a proposition). Both attitudes and propositions have subdivisions, however. Hence, representations and motivations may be *either* binary (on-off) *or* involve degrees. Propositions can be *either* simple *or* sophisticated.

Binary and Nonbinary Attitudes   In the case of a binary representational attitude, an agent may either judge that p or not judge that p. There is no intermediate position. For example, the radio set is either switched on or off. However with a nonbinary representational attitude is a degree of belief (or a "credence") that the agent shows with regard to p, and this may take any value between 0 and 1. An individual may opine that there is a .2 chance of Party X winning the election, for instance.

Motivational attitudes may also be binary or nonbinary. The former may take the form of a preference regarding p. The agent either prefers p or does not prefer p: there is again no intermediate choice. A nonbinary motivational attitude is a degree of satisfaction assigned by the agent to p. A carnivorous diner may obtain a degree of satisfaction (or a "utility") of 0.1 if served beef, of 0.3 if served lamb, and of 0.4 if served venison. In general we can say that representations (beliefs) take the form of judgments (in the case of binary representational attitudes) or credences (in the case of nonbinary representational attitudes). Motivations (desires) take the form of either preferences (in the case of binary motivational attitudes) or utilities (in the case of nonbinary motivational attitudes).

Simple and Sophisticated Propositions   Propositions may be open to being expressed in "sparse, single language" or they may need "a richer language or a combination of two languages: an 'object-language' or a metalanguage." The first type we term simple; the second, sophisticated. Simple propositions include atomic propositions such as that p, and also combinations of atomic propositions linked by logical connectives like "and";

"if then"; and "if and only if." Sophisticated propositions evoke expression in more complex language, for example, the use of quantifiers such as "some" and "all" or modal operators such as "it is necessary that" or "it is obligatory that." Or sophisticated propositions may involve metalanguage which expresses propositions that assign properties to other propositions which are known as "object-language" propositions. Hence, complex agents can form intentional attitudes toward p and q, *and* toward metalanguage propositions that assign properties or relations to p and q. Such agents can believe that p is true, that p and q are consistent, that p and q jointly entail r, that p is probable or unlikely, that p is an attractive scenario, or one that someone else desires, and so on.

Intensional Reasoning   I believe that we can add a further source of sophisticated propositions to those suggested by List and Pettit (2011), one based on intensionality as a linguistic phenomenon. More complex agents are not only intentional in the sense that they have representations and motivations that have the property of aboutness; they can, in addition, appreciate and use the linguistic conventions that allow them to distinguish extensional from intensional sentences. Indeed, if an agent is to be accorded the status of an intensional system, it must be able to do these things. Only a system that is so equipped linguistically can be called an intensional system that is explicable by means of an intensional stance. Before elaborating on this, let us briefly consider the nature of reasoning ability.

An entity can be considered an agent only if it is capable of reasoning. Possessing rationality, in the sense of having attitudes-to-facts, attitudes-to-actions, and attitudes-to-attitudes, is not enough, however, since it is possible to be rational without awareness of the demands of rationality or the ability to aspire to be rational (List and Pettit 2011). This would entail having no beliefs and desires *about* one's rationality. Creatures that do have beliefs about the properties of propositions, however, such as their truth or consistency, can reinforce their rationality by posing questions to themselves concerning its nature and efficacy. Humans can impose checks on the logic of the propositions they entertain, for example, by examining why they believe that p, and why believing p entails q. It then becomes possible for them to accept by deduction the belief that q as well as examining the logic of these moves. Humans ask questions like: Why do I believe that p? Is "If p then q" true, actually the case? Why does the truth of these propositions entail that q?

This deliberate pursuit of beliefs in a metalanguage designed to impose additional checks on rational processing is what reasoning itself consists in (List and Pettit 2011, p. 30). It seems clear that one aspect of this ability to reason abstractly (at a higher propositional level) would include the capacity to understand the principles of nonsubstitutability of codesignatives without loss of truth value, the necessary existence of extensional objects, intentional inexistence, and the nontranslatability of intentional into extensional sentences without alteration of the meaning of what is being said. Especially in understanding and predicting the behavior of others on the basis of ascriptions to them of realistic desires and beliefs, it is necessary to be able to discern what those others know and think. It is as important to be able to rule out what they do not or cannot know. Such knowing requires the ability to appreciate that "X believes p" is not equivalent to "X believes q," even though p and q are interchangeable in extensional sentences without loss of truth value.

Two conclusions may be drawn. First, an entity that has representational and motivational content in the sense List and Pettit attribute it to their simple robot is a secondary intentional system but the actual intentionality involved belongs to the designer of such systems. Humans and some animals possess primary intentionality, which is a prerequisite of agency. Robotic systems and other entities possessing secondary intentionality are not, therefore, agents. Their designer is. When we use Dennett's intentional stance to predict the behavior of such entities we are reverse engineering the intentionality of their designers. The entities themselves may have secondary rationality but they are not capable of reasoning. They are secondary intentional systems. This will not convince the Dennettian for whom all intentionality is secondary intentionality but Searle's distinction, for which I argued in Chapter 2, is supportive of this proposition.

Second, an entity that has the capacity to reason along the lines that List and Pettit outline, *and* in the sense which I have elaborated in terms of intensionality, can be thought of as a primary intentional system.

While such primary intentional systems are almost certainly agents, there is more to agency than reasoning ability. For, as we have seen, the behavior of agents is not necessarily caused by their proposition-based reasoning. Crucially, they are creatures who are capable of being aware of their beliefs and desires and can reason from them how they *ought* to act. But they are in addition agents, first because their behavior is subject to the gap for which Searle argues, and therefore open to a rational explanation, and second because their mental as well as physical actions are capable of settling matters as Steward points out, and therefore beyond universal deterministic causality. In short and at risk of repetition, such systems *are* agents but not on account of their capacity to reason: their behavior is not invariably *caused by* their intentionality but is in a degree up-to-them. These considerations are central to their being capable of behaving with the flexibility required for the achievement of adaptedness and for their ability to innovate with respect to both the physical world that provides utilitarian reinforcement and, especially, the social world which involves informational reinforcement. These competencies are necessary to confer primary intentionality and agency, and additionally they have the effect of confining these qualities to adult humans and some animals.

Once more, this is not to imply that the behavior of such agents is caused by their intentionality or intensionality, by their desires and beliefs, and additional reasoning about them. The gap is still there as is the fact that humans have the capacity to settle some matters, and it is these that undergird the ascription of agency. The ascription of rationality and reasoning ability are prerequisites of the designation of activity as action, however. If we interpret behavior as psychologically rational, in the sense of being consistent with a particular set of desires, beliefs, emotions, and perceptions, we are interpreting it as something other than activity that is shaped and maintained in its entirety by contingencies of reinforcement. Moreover, acceptance of the reality of the gap and of the settling of matters, does not remove intentionality of this kind from the causal path of behavior. In the case of an individual who develops a picoeconomic strategy for the modification of his or her behavior, the settling of matters is first accomplished through mental action and only then by physical action. Moreover, the first alters the probability of the second. A person may be swayed from the logic of this intentionality by dint of his or her choosing in the course of the gap to behave differently. But this is not to deny that the preceding intentionality was instrumental in bringing him or her to the point of decision. Failures to follow through on plans are part of the preference reversal that characterizes such behavior. Most lapses from intended behavior are followed by regret and reexamination of one's previous behavior plus resolutions to act differently in future. This is possible only through the exercise of intentional reasoning.

In the case of collectively intentional behavior that selects and in fact creates contingencies of reinforcement, the intentionality of the individual is instrumental in controlling his or her behavior and that of many others through the construction of rules that control what is to count as correct and incorrect behavior and what reinforcers and punishers are to be made contingent upon it. This is a matter of intentionality factors having a causal influence on behavior, even though the option to choose differently in the course of experiencing the gap is open to the individual actor.

Summing-Up

A simple robot, which in List and Pettit's example returns to the upright cylinders that have overturned on a table top, exhibits intentionality because it contains representations—of an overturned cylinder, of an upright cylinder, of how to change the status of cylinders, and stop trying to do so when they return to the upright. A degree of rationality can be ascribed also to such an entity but this is secondary rationality: it is a set of procedures programmed into the robot by its designer and could only do otherwise if its design was effected in a different manner by that person who is the locus of the primary rationality. The robot is not an agent: there is nothing that is up to the robot or that *it* settles by *its* own action. There is no sense in which it moves itself by undertaking activity$_T$. Its intentionality is derived—the primary intentionality involved is that of its designer. It is up to the designer how the cylinders will be disposed. How human consumers differ from robots is obvious from a more detailed consideration of the decision-action process.

The Consumer as Agent

The Decision-Action Process

The fact that we are positing an agential self that is responsible for acting in the gaps and for settling matters does not imply that a major part of the explanation of action lies in the desires and beliefs of the actor. Some of these may be abandoned as the decision-action process reaches one of the gaps depicted in Fig. 11.1, but either a competing intentionality comes to the fore to bring about another action or the self brings additional reasons at this point to bear on the nature of the action performed. The settling of matters is a function of the agent but that does not mean that it has no basis in his or her reasons for acting, in his or her reasoning procedures. The desires and beliefs shown in this are germane to a process of deliberation in which goals and strategies are weighed and evaluated, criteria confirmed, and conclusions reached about what is desirable, what is possible, what the consequences of each feasible course of action might be. There is the possibility of abandoning the project at this point if it is judged that no program of action can be implemented that will likely lead to the objective function that is necessary. This is an explanation of the aborting of the project in terms of a Humean self who is simply a bundle

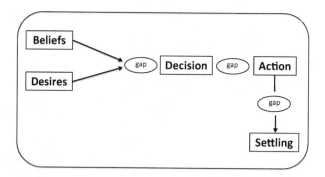

Fig. 11.1 *Action and settling.* There are gaps (Searle 2001) between the initial deliberation and the decision, between the decision and the initiation of action, and between the onset of the action and its completion by the settling of matters (Steward 2012)

of intentions. Both Searle's and Steward's thinking have moved our ideas of action beyond this notion, however. The agential self, irreducible, non-Humean, may simply withdraw from the venture in the gap. At the point of decision he or she may disregard the rational decision processes and fail to carry through the decision or do something else. Some actions of such a self may be *guided* by intentionality but they are not so *determined*.

At some later time, additional information may be sought (i.e., beliefs formulated) and desires (goals) may be adjusted. Deliberation will follow and a new gap may then ensue. If the stage of decision making is reached, then one set of the policies and strategies developed in the process of deliberation may be formally resolved upon. Many decisions are never implemented because new information and goals arise before they can be put into practice. This is another explanation in terms of the Humean self. But the possibility that an agential self will simply countermand the decision so rationally arrived at is also a possibility.

Humans differ from robots in having primary intentionality, a capacity for intensionality, primary rationality, and the ability to reason. All of these—let us call them *primary cognitive capacities* for short—are necessary for the exercise of agency. The explanation of matching requires this sort of cognitive operation. Viewed behavioristically, matching makes it possible to predict and control behavior: this achieves the behaviorist's aims. However, the extensional analysis of matching phenomena is incomplete because some of the required stimuli are not available. There must be stimuli that induce switching from one manipulandum to the other. Does the behaviorist assume that the animal has some kind of internal clock and, if so, are his or her explanations getting rather mentalistic? There must also be calculation of the returns from each of the manipulanda and a comparative evaluation of the two. If concurrent variable interval schedules are in operation, one could point to the passage of time as an environmental stimulus. But there must also be a perceptual mechanism in operation and this invites an intentional explanation. On concurrent vertical ratio schedules, where animals tend to opt exclusively for the more generous payoff, there must be a calculation of which is the richer schedule. Choice, or rather our explanation of it, has ceased to be extensional once we begin to reason in this way: intentionality has become the inevitable alternative.

Action and Reasoning

Agency does not mean the absence of reasoning; it only implies that reasoning is not causally sufficient of acting. The processes of deliberation and decision making shown in Fig. 9.1 are necessary to the exercise of agency even if they do not cause the agent's actions. Sometimes for instance the rejection of a reasoned course of action during the gap is simply the deliberate selection of an alternative reasoned course of action. The exercise of agency consists then in the selection of which of a number of competing reasoned alternatives is allowed to guide action: as in the case of the consumer who reverses preference at t_1 by selecting SSR over a LLR. Moreover the consumer with a learning history of choosing SSR and thereby precluding LLR can change this behavior through precommitment to the later alternative, overcoming the history of reinforcement and punishment that has guided his or her behavior thus far, and even overcoming a mental tendency to prefer SSR. This may still amount to behavior being determined by a set of reasons but it is the consumer who selects that set from among a number of alternatives. We may be unable to know whether an action is the result of reasoned deliberation and decision making since the set of reasons ultimately chosen might be one previously considered during the decision-action process or it might be a new concatenation of desires, beliefs, emotions, and perceptions that are unconscious processes and which only come to fruition at the point of the enactment of the action or its continuance. But it is the consumer acting as a self who is responsible for this course of action. It is he or she who settles matters thereby and is thus an agent. Ultimately it is up to him or her.

It is impossible to know if some set of reasoned plans is chosen when there is a change of direction in the course of the gap. Who can tell if the apparently spontaneous decision made by the consumer at this stage is free of all previously entertained considerations about possible goals, strategies, and their putative outcomes? By surmising what could be happening subconsciously we are encouraging the idea that there is some kind of extra magic at work over and above the rational processes of the consumer. It is always possible that the individual whose action does not embody his or her most recent plan is still acting on some earlier plan or other but doing so unconsciously.[2] Explaining behavior by appealing to unconscious intentionality, for which there is no evidence other than the apparently aberrant behavior pattern that is conveniently "explained" by the assumed unconscious decision making, is a dubious explanatory strategy, however. Who knows where such speculation may end? There remains the gap, and with it the possibility of a divergence from a course of actions resolutely decided upon. And it is still the consumer acting as a self, and not his or her intentionality that settles matters. This may be as close to freedom as we can approach but it is certainly a far cry from universal determinism.

The proviso that agency requires the primary cognitive capacities we have outlined is justified on the grounds that the operation of selfhood during the gap in acting so as to settle matters is not random, spontaneous, magical, or immaterial. The ultimate settling of matters at this stage in a manner apparently contrary to previous reasoning processes is neither random nor unaffected by the information processing that has occurred during the decision process. It is not irrational. It can be understood only by a knowledge of the desires, beliefs, emotions, and perceptions that guided the decision process. Even if what is known of it does not show why the consumer acted as he or she did we cannot assume it had no effect or that the consumer simply ignored all the deliberations to which he or she was a party and acted autonomously or in spite of them. The consumer is still the settler of matters. It is still up to the consumer what he or she does, but his or her cognitive processing is still germane.

The fact that the consumer as self acts consistently with a particular set of desires and beliefs that would be reasonably ascribed to him or her on the basis of his or her learning history and current situation does not override the view that he or she is an agent. His or her task as an agent is

---

[2] Nanay (2013, pp. 69–70) discusses the context of another aspect of Searle's work. Searle (1983) argues that the intentionality that explains an action may be of one or other of two kinds. In the first case, "prior intentionality," an intention exists in the mind of the actor which is deliberatively formed by the actor before the action takes place. The other, "intention-in-action," does not involve any previously existing intention before the action is performed. A consumer who suddenly leaves off browsing in the food aisles of a supermarket and slowly walks up and down the clothing aisles, apparently absent-mindedly, before returning to the food aisles and recommencing shopping, exhibits intention-in-action according to this view. It is not necessary, on Searle's view, to appeal to prior beliefs or intentions to account for this activity (see also Malafouris 2013, pp. 137–140).

to go through the deliberative processes involved in the decision-action sequence. It is still up to him or her to settle matters by the selection of a specific action.

While Fig. 11.1 presents a first approximation of the process in which gaps and settlings/actions feature in an individual's decision sequence, the reality is more complicated. Figure 11.2 suggests how this complexity may be portrayed but even this is a simplification. What it is important to stress is that every gap eventuates in a settling, which is brought about by an action, be it mental or physical. In the gap between deliberation and decisions and between decision and action, these are primarily mental actions but they may be accompanied by physical actions that are necessary to bring about the next stage in the decision-action sequence. Even the final settling may be in the form of a mental action (say a resolution

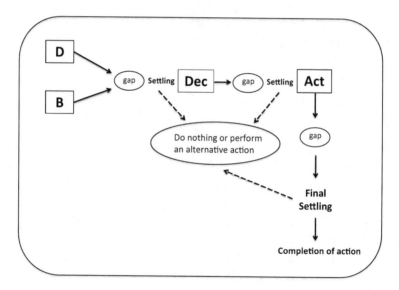

Fig. 11.2 *The decision-action sequence.* Gaps between the marshaling of desires (*D*) and beliefs (*B*) and the making of a decision (*Dec*), and between decision (*Dec*) and the initiation of an action (*Act*), eventuate in mental actions that are a settling of matters. The initiation of this final action is followed by a gap which eventuates in a final settling which may be a mental or a physical action. Any of the settlings may be actions that advance the decision-action sequence or that lead to the individual doing nothing or performing an alternative action

to seek a new job), and this may or may not lead to physical actions, but often this stage will of itself be principally a physical action.

Settling on the Grand Scale

Steward's (2012) instances of settling matters, her examples of concerns that are up-to an agent, such as picking *this* shirt to iron next, exercising the left leg first, and so on, are almost incidental properties of behavior, virtual side effects. They are nonetheless important for illustrating the case against universal determinism. However, while much routine consumer choice, as we have noted, is also commonplace but still constitutes a settling of matters, an action, the doing of an agent, so also are many examples of larger patterns of consumer activity.

If many routine consumer choices can be characterized as noninvolving, it is certain that the execution of a picoeconomic strategy such as bundling is a highly involving pattern of behaviors. And yet it takes place as the culmination of a series of selections of SSRs to the point where the consumer can be considered compulsive or even an addict. His or her behavior is habitual and reinforced in a manner that is likely to increase the frequency of its repetition or the magnitude of its indulgence. The decision to weigh the benefits of an entire sequence of novel future activity, cumulating them so that they can be compared with the alternative sequence of unaltered activity and its outcomes, entails mental activity that is cognitively expensive. The making of side bets with oneself on the understanding that a selection of LLR on this occasion will enhance the probability of executing a sequence of similar choices over time is a highly structured cognitive operation. Putting this strategy into operation, however, is not certain no matter how firmly one is resolved on the divergent pattern of choice. There is a gap from which will emerge an action, a settling of matters one way or the other. In the case that the settling resulting from the gap is in favor of bundling, the prior resolve to change one's behavior, reached on the basis of considerable mental deliberation, is confirmed in action. However, the fact that the mental deliberation, the concatenation of a matrix of desires, beliefs, emotions, and perceptions was always subject to rejection in the course of the gap should not obscure its efficacy as part of the causal texture of the action that ensued. Without it, there would have been no modification in the consumer's activity, no switch from the pattern of continuously choosing the SSR to even a single instance of selecting the LLR, let alone a fresh sequence of activity of which it is the characteristic mode of choice.

Should the settling that follows from the gap be the abandonment of the resolve to change, and the subsequent return to a pattern of choosing SSR, then the pattern of intentionality that explains it is that built up on the course of the preceding sequence of impatient choices. Again there would have been no resumption of the earlier behavior pattern without the expectations engendered by this process and their capacity to win out over the novel resolution to exercise self-control. Either way, what is important is that the action formulated in the gap settles the matter. The consumer is acting not robotically, as though he or she were a simple stimulus-response mechanism, even one that was sensitive to the generalization of stimuli and responses, the inter-stimulus transfer of function, or other environment-behavior regularity. Nor even is the consumer acting as though his or her behavior were entirely explicable by reference to the desires, beliefs, emotions, and perceptions that led to the mental resolve to change, guided by a set of advanced primary cognitive capacities. The fact that the post-gap pattern of action could be either in accord with his or her resolution or diametrically opposed to it demonstrates that the Classical Model of Rationality is not sufficient to account for the consumer's action.

An even more auspicious example of consumer action is the devising of contingencies of reinforcement and punishment for the explanation of which we must turn to the idea of collective intentionality. In this case, the community decides for itself what kinds of behavior, defined by rules based on an understanding of two concurrently operating and intertwined sets of contingencies, will be reinforced and which punished, not by naturally occurring primary contingencies but by secondary contingencies purposely devised and enforced by the social system.

Especially in her Chapter 5, Steward (2012) seeks to establish the range of animals to which agency can be ascribed. If we were to confine psychological explanation to the Intentional Interpretation, we might include almost all creatures in this, earthworms as well as primates, since, in Ross's (2005) view, agency is to be attributed wherever a utility function can be established. However, the second phase of psychological explanation, namely the Cognitive Interpretation, is also relevant to what counts as an agent. An agent must be able to undertake certain cognitive operations which are the province, respectively, of MiCP and MaCP. The first is psychological rationality in the sense of the lateral thinking involved in Analytical Mind's overcoming the promptings of Automatic Mind: that is, the entity must display Reflective Mind and the capacity to operate intelligently as in the functioning of Algorithmic Mind. The second is to show signs of participating in a symbolic consumer situation which is both a mainspring of individual action and the basis of collective intentionality.

The central question becomes: what does an agent's setting things translate into in a theory of consumer choice? Settling can be conceptualized extensionally within a particular set of contingencies: we have seen that the consumer settles questions of when, where, what, and so on when making a purchase or consuming a product or service. But a more demanding criterion would be to ask what creatures can free themselves from the contingencies, especially those that are immediately acting, or even create their own contingencies. The requirements of such ascription would be to transcend the immediate contingencies of reinforcement, even to construct contingencies. Each of these actions settles things that could not have been pre-determined. The actions$_T$ that this involves are mental movements rather than physical but are no less actions for that. They still settle things by acting as novel interventions. They might be amenable to explanation as caused events in one sense (just as physical movements are attributable to neurophysiological events) but they lie outside the determination process insofar as they settle matters that would not otherwise be settled in the fashion that transpires. Some aspects of consumer choice entail breaking with one's learning history in ways that settle a course of behavior that is decided upon by the individual's imagination of future contingencies to which he or she might not have been previously subjected; this is illustrated by the various pre-behavioral valuations of the outcomes of future behavior that were discussed in the Intentional Interpretation in Chapter 7. Other aspects of consumer choice involve the creation or modification of the contingencies of reinforcement in ways that settle what will count as a reinforcer or punisher; this is apparent in the devising of novel contingencies of reinforcement as a result of collective intentionality and such picoeconomic strategies as bundling in which the consumer either formulates new patterns of contingency or decides which patterns of reinforcement his or her actions will be influenced by.

It becomes possible, therefore, to distinguish two levels of agency: individual and collective (Fig. 11.3). A creature's capacity to transcend the contingencies of reinforcement in which it is currently embedded is an index of its ability to act as an agent whose patterns of behavior constitute actions$_T$ which settle matters. Individual settling occurs when a creature's current mental actions enable it to settle the outcomes of its future behavior patterns. The contingencies to which it subjects its behavior by means of this settling already exist but the individual's behavior has not previously come under their influence. The imagining of how these future contingencies would function to generate particular outcomes for the individual and the comparison of these outcomes with those that would obtain if the present contingencies proceeded unhindered are mental actions$_T$ which mark the creature in question as an agent. Collective settling entails the settling by a social group of what action or usage (A) will symbolize (count as) an established behavior or reinforcer (B) in specified contexts (C). The collective intentionality which creates such novel contingencies is a joint action$_T$ which indicates that the social group is acting as an agent.

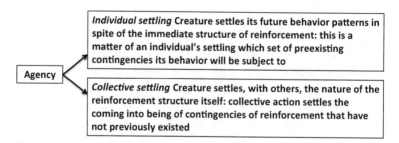

Fig. 11.3   Individual and collective settling and agency

These styles of agency, individual settling and collective settling, correspond, respectively, to the explanations of behavior in terms of picoeconomic strategizing and collective intentionality.

Conclusion

We now arrive at a final perspective on consumer choice within the BPM framework of conceptualization and analysis, the agential perspective (Fig. 11.4.)

The topography of consumer choice is the same whether we view it from the perspective of the contextual stance as we seek to understand it as behavior or from that of the intentional or cognitive stance in order that we may perceive it as action or agency. What changes as we switch perspectives is our objective in studying consumption. Each objective we may pursue—the prediction of consumer behavior, reconstructing consumer intentionality, or laying out the cognitive and agential processes that verify it—throws a different light on the economic and social activities involved in consumption.

Consumer choice is in all cases a function of consumer situation. This fundamental principle of the Behavioral Perspective Model recognizes that the idea of consumer situation, and indeed of consumer choice or activity itself, varies depending on the perspective we adopt toward its understanding (Fig. 11.5). Consumer situation in the case of the extensional perspective comprises the consumer's learning history in interaction with the independent variables that compose the consumer behavior

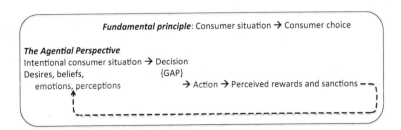

Fig. 11.4 Consumer choice: The agential perspective

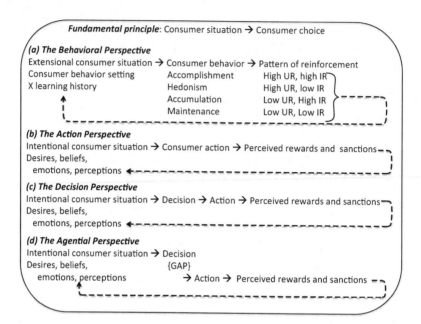

Fig. 11.5 Behavior, action, decision, and agency: Summary of the perspectives

setting. These are the physical and social discriminative stimuli and motivating operations that predict particular patterns of contingency and operant classes of consumer behavior. Discriminative stimuli do not elicit responses, as do UCSs and CSs in Pavlovian conditioning; rather, they are said to "set the occasion" for responding. Motivating operations work by enhancing the relationship between behavior and the reinforcing or punishing stimuli that follow it. There is a neurophysiological connection here too. Discriminative stimuli may occasion the release of the neurotransmitter dopamine which readies the individual for behavior; and motivating operations may be stimuli that have acquired incentive salience: they too occasion the release of dopamine which has the effect of conferring desirability on any reinforcing stimuli that follow (Berridge and Robinson 1993; for discussion of both effects in the context of consumer choice, see Foxall 2016a).

The consumer *behavior* that is predicted by the extensional BPM is conceived as resulting from these elements of the consumer situation, and its operant class is determined by the pattern of utilitarian and informational reinforcement it has tended to generate in the course of the consumer's consumption history. This behavior is defined by the pattern of reinforcement that has generated its recurrence in the past; this pattern of utilitarian and informational reinforcement is responsible for the understanding of the behavior in question as belonging to the operant class of Accomplishment, Hedonism, Accumulation, or Maintenance. The consequences of each of these classes of consumer behavior are fed back into the learning history of the consumer, shown by the dotted line.

The consumer situation portrayed by the intentional perspective comprises the intentionality of the consumer that comprises his or her consumer behavior setting in interaction with his or her learning history. In this case, the consumer behavior setting consists of whatever desires, beliefs, emotions, and perceptions influence choice: that is, the goals the consumer is seeking and conceptions of the means of attaining them. The discussion of this perspective in Chapter 7 took as its vehicle of exposition the subjective evaluation of future rewards appearing at different times. This is not the sole aspect of consumer intentionality but it is particularly apposite because it applies, in varying degree, to the whole spectrum of consumption that composes the Continuum of Consumer Choice.

The cognitive model portrays the action of the consumer as the outcome of a decision process comprising not only the desires, beliefs, emotions, and perceptions that compose the consumer behavior setting and the memories that make up the learning history but the additional mental procedures inherent in the comparison of the alternatives they present and the selection among them. The agential model goes further than this by suggesting that the Classical Model of Rationality that it assumes may not be causally sufficient to explain action.

These perspectives are complementary rather than competitive. Only someone who wished to confine the study of human choice within an unnaturally artificial frame would seek to build a study of consumption within just one of them. All three are necessary for what it adds to intellectual comprehension. It is not simply that ideas from one perspective fire off insights in the pursuit of another; it is that each perspective *requires* the others if it is to succeed even on its own terms.

The basis of consumer choice provided by the extensional model is not sufficient to understand consumer choice in its entirety but it is fundamental nonetheless to the construction of the Intentional Interpretation; its demonstration, for instance, that what consumers maximize is a combination of utilitarian and informational reinforcement is a vital starting point for the intentionality portrayal of consumer choice. It is necessary to ground the Cognitive Interpretation which contextualizes and justifies the intentional account. The Intentional Interpretation and Cognitive Interpretation are particularly interactive as was suggested in Chapter 7 and, I hope, demonstrated in Chapters 8, 9, and 10. Cognition is not an external force, like the contingencies of reinforcement, that act unidirectionally to compel a particular pattern of behavior: the cognitive control that manifests itself in the *creation* of contingencies through the enactment of picoeconomic strategies is a source of agency, of settling, of our deciding things that are up-to-*us*. Furthermore, the intentional and cognitive viewpoints can critically challenge the extensional understanding. They draw attention for instance to the subtleties of a behavioral theory that deals in a learning history that is not usually empirically available and a stimulus field consisting of discriminative stimuli and motivating operations that are supposed only to set the occasion for responding but which must thereby be about something other than themselves. They point, for example, to the reinforcing and punishing consequences that responding generates.

The idea that we should imagine the facts we do not have, the learning histories that prove elusive once we leave the closed-setting confines of the operant laboratory, for instance, is inimical to this view of intellectual pursuit. There is surely no reason not to engage in such envisaging as a first approximation of additional explanation. But it is scarcely the endpoint of the endeavor to understand. "Every way of seeing is also a way of not seeing," as Kenneth Burke (1935, p. 70) has so aptly put it. The realization that the perspective in which we have been working has revealed its boundaries so that further enlightenment within its confines is impossible is the invitation to a new manner of comprehending, a novel perspective. Not instead of, but as a vital complement. I have frequently quoted John Stuart Mill's discernment that "He who knows only his own side of the story knows little of that" and I make no apology for appealing again to its embrace of intellectual expansiveness.

There are those who maintain that only performance theories have a place in science, who would constrain the study of choice by opening it up to no purview other than extensional behavioral science. I have the highest regard for the extensional sciences, believing that they alone can give rise to the generation and empirical testing of performance theories. But alternative perspectives are fully justified when those sciences can no longer deliver. Moreover, the Cognitive Interpretation component of psychological explanation is a competence theory as much as the Intentional Interpretation and I believe this is as far as the intrinsically theoretical psychological explanation can take us. There is no reason to restrict the perspectival range of our approaches to explaining human activity; equally, who can say that the pursuit of action and agency may not enhance our knowledge and understanding of consumer behavior?

The fundamental shift in perspective that this book has sought to make clear is between behavior and action: all else follows from this distinction. The explanation of consumer choice in intentional terms is not something we choose to undertake on a whim. It is enjoined upon us by the limitations of the extensional behaviorism from which we made two kinds of discovery: first, that many aspects of consumer choice are made available to us only by pursuing an extensional model to its furthest capacity; second, that that capacity has limitations which make inevitable the imperatives of intentionality. However, the research effort that follows the imperatives of intentionality also has two lessons: first, that there is much that can be understood by the consideration of the consumer's desires, beliefs, emotions, and perceptions; second, that this style of explanation is appropriate only if we posit a self, an agent, a personality which not only might be predictable on the basis of an assumed and attributed intentionality but which actually thinks and feels and decides.

Bibliography

Berridge, K. C., & Robinson, T. E. (1993). The neural basis of drug craving: An incentive-sensitization theory of addiction. *Brain Research Reviews, 18,* 247–291.

Burke, K. (1935). *Permanence and change: An anatomy of purpose.* Los Angeles: University of California Press. (Third edition, 1984).

Foxall, G. R. (2005). *Understanding consumer choice*. London/New York: Palgrave Macmillan.

Foxall, G. R. (2016a). *Addiction as consumer choice: Exploring the cognitive dimension*. London/New York: Routledge.

List, C., & Pettit, P. (2011). *Group agency: The possibility, design, and status of corporate agents*. Oxford: Oxford University Press.

Malfouris, L. (2013). *How things shape the mind: A theory of material engagement*. Cambridge, MA: MIT Press.

Nanay, B. (2013). *Between perception and action*. Oxford: Oxford University Press.

Ross, D. (2005). *Economic theory and cognitive science: Microexplanation*. Cambridge, MA: MIT Press.

Searle, J. R. (1983). *Intentionality: An essay in the philosophy of mind*. Cambridge: Cambridge University Press.

Searle, J. R. (2001). *Rationality in action*. Cambridge, MA: MIT Press.

Searle, J. R. (2007). *Freedom and neurobiology: Reflections on free will, language, and political power*. New York: Columbia University Press.

Steward, H. (2012). *A metaphysics for freedom*. Oxford: Oxford University Press.

Bibliography

Banich, M. T. (2004). *Cognitive neuroscience and neuropsychology* (2nd ed.). Boston: Houghton Mifflin.

Barrett, L. F. (2005). Feeling is perceiving: Core affect and conceptualization in the experience of emotion. In L. F. Barrett, P. M. Niedenthal, & P. Winkielman (Eds.), *Emotion and consciousness* (pp. 255–285). New York: Guilford.

Barrett, L. F., Mesquita, B., Ochsner, K. N., & Gross, J. J. (2007). The experience of emotion. *Annual Review of Psychology, 38*, 173–401.

Bennett, M. R., & Hacker, P. M. S. (2007). The conceptual presuppositions of cognitive neuroscience: A reply to critics. In M. Bennett, D. Dennett, P. Hacker, & J. Searle (Eds.), *Neuroscience and philosophy: Brain, mind, and language* (pp. 127–170). NY: Columbia University Press.

Bermúdez, J. L. (2005). *Philosophy of psychology: A contemporary introduction.* New York/London: Routledge.

Boden, M. A. (1978). *Purposive explanation in psychology.* Hassocks: The Harvester Press.

Brentano, F. (1874). *Psychology from an empirical standpoint.* Leipzig: Meiner.

Buss, D. M. (2004). *Evolutionary psychology: The new science of the mind.* Boston: Pearson.

Campbell, A. (2007). Sex differences in aggression. In R. I. M. Dunbar & L. Barrett (Eds.), *The Oxford handbook of evolutionary psychology* (pp. 365–382). Oxford: Oxford University Press.

© The Editor(s) (if applicable) and The Author(s) 2016   **311**
G.R. Foxall, *Perspectives on Consumer Choice,*
DOI 10.1057/978-1-137-50121-9

Crane, T. (1998). Intentionality as the mark of the mental. *Royal Institute of Philosophy Supplement, 43*, 229–251.

Crane, T. (2009). Intentionalsim. In B. P. McLaughlin, A. Beckerman, & S. Walter (Eds.), *The Oxford handbook of philosophy of mind* (pp. 474–493). Oxford: Oxford University Press.

Cummins, D. D. (2005). Dominance, status, and social hierarchies. In D. M. Buss (Ed.), *The handbook of evolutionary psychology* (pp. 676–697). Hoboken: Wiley.

Demaree, H. A., Everhart, D. E., Youngstrom, E. A., & Harrison, D. W. (2008). Brain lateralization of emotional processing: Historical roots and a future incorporating "dominance,". *Behavioral and Cognitive Neuroscience Reviews, 4*, 3–20.

Dennett, D. C. (2006). *Sweet dreams: Philosophical obstacles to a science of consciousness*. Cambridge, MA: MIT Press.

Dennett, D. C. (2007). Philosophy as naïve anthropology. In M. Bennett, D. C. Dennett, P. Hacker, & J. Searle (Eds.), *Neuroscience and philosophy: Brain, mind & language* (pp. 73–95). NY: Columbia University Press.

Dennett, D. C. (2009). Intentional systems theory. In B. P. McLaughlin, A. Beckerman, & S. Walter (Eds.), *The Oxford handbook of philosophy of mind* (pp. 339–350). Oxford: Oxford University Press.

DeYoung, C. G. (2013). Impulsivity as a personality trait. In K. D. Vohs & R. F. Baumeister (Eds.), *Handbook of self-regulation: Research, theory, and applications* (2nd ed., pp. 485–502). New York: The Guilford Press.

Dickinson, A. (1989). Expectancy theory in animal conditioning. In S. B. Klein & R. R. Mowrer (Eds.), *Contemporary learning theories: Pavlovian conditioning and the status of traditional learning theory* (pp. 279–308). Hillsdale: Erlbaum.

Dunbar, R. I. M. (2004). *The human story*. London: Faber and Faber.

Fodor, J. A. (1968). *Psychological explanation: An introduction to the philosophy of psychology*. New York: Random House.

Fodor, J. A. (1975). *The language of thought*. New York: Crowell.

Fodor, J. A. (2008). *LOT2: The language of thought revisited*. Oxford: Clarendon Press.

Foxall, G. R. (1997). Explaining consumer behaviour: From social cognition to environmental control. *International Review of Industrial and Organizational Psychology, 12*, 229–287.

Foxall, G. R. (2008). Reward, emotion and consumer choice: From neuroeconomics to neurophilosophy. *Journal of Consumer Behaviour, 7*, 368–396.

Foxall, G. R. (2016). Consumer behavior analysis comes of age. In G. R. Foxall (Ed.), *The Routledge companion to consumer behavior analysis* (pp. 3–22). London/New York: Routledge.

Foxall, G. R., & Sigurdsson, V. (2012). When loss rewards: The near-miss effect in slot machine gambling. *Analysis of Gambling Behavior, 6,* 5–22.

Foxall, G. R., & Sigurdsson, V. (2013). Consumer behavior analysis: Behavioral economics meets the marketplace. *The Psychological Record, 62,* 231–237.

Foxall, G. R., James, V. K., Oliveira-Castro, J. M., & Ribier, S. (2010a). Product substitutability and the matching law. *The Psychological Record, 60,* 185–216.

Foxall, G. R., James, V. K., Chang, J., & Oliveira-Castro, J. M. (2010b). Substitutability and complementarity: Matching analyses of brands and products. *Journal of Organizational Behavior Management, 30*(2), 145–160.

Frankish, K., & Evans, J. S. B. T. (2009). The duality of mind: An historical perspective. In J. S. B. T. Evans & K. Frankish (Eds.), *In two minds: Dual processes and beyond* (pp. 1–29). Oxford: Oxford University Press.

Gilbert, M. (1989). *On social facts.* London: Routledge.

Herrnstein, R. J. (1982). Melioration as behavioral dynamism. In M. L. Commons, R. J. Herrnstein, & H. Rachlin (Eds.), *Quantitative analyses of behavior* (Matching and maximizing accounts, Vol. II, pp. 433–458). Cambridge, MA: Ballinger.

Herrnstein, R. J., & Vaughan, W., Jr. (1980). Melioration and behavioral allocation. In J. E. R. Staddon (Ed.), *Limits to action: The allocation of individual behavior.* New York: Academic.

Higley, J. D., Mehlman, P. T., Poland, R. E., Taub, D. M., Vickers, J., Suomi, S. J., & Linnoila, M. (1996). CSF testosterone and 5-HlAA correlate with different types of aggressive behaviors. *Biological Psychiatry, 40,* 1067–1082.

Hurley, S. L. (1998). *Consciousness in action.* Cambridge, MA: Harvard University Press.

Juarrero, A. (1999). *Dynamics in action: Intentional behavior as a complex system.* Cambridge, MA: MIT Press.

Kagan, J. (2006). *An argument for mind.* New Haven: Yale University Press.

Kendrick, D. T., Sadalla, E. K., & O'Keefe, R. C. (1998). Evolutionary cognitive psychology: The missing heart of modern cognitive science. In C. Crawford & D. L. Krebs (Eds.), *Handbook of evolutionary psychology: Ideas, issues, and applications* (pp. 485–514). Mahawa: Lawrence Erlbaum.

Knutson, B., Wolkowitz, O., Cole, S. W., Chan, T., Moore, E., Johnson, R., et al. (1998). Selective alteration of personality and social behavior by serotonergic intervention. *American Journal of Psychiatry, 155*, 373–379.

Lindquist, K. A., Wager, T. D., Kober, H., Bliss-Moreau, E., & Barrett, L. F. (2012). The brain basis of emotion: A meta-analytic review. *Behavioral and Brain Sciences, 35*, 121–202.

Marques dos Santos, J. P., & Moutinho, L. (2016). Decision-"making" or how decisions emerge in a cyclic automatic process, parsimoniously modulated by reason. In G. R. Foxall (Ed.), *The Routledge companion to consumer behavior analysis* (pp. 328–349). London/New York: Routledge.

Müller, A., & Mitchell, J. E. (Eds.) (2010). *Compulsive buying: Clinical foundations and treatment*. London/New York: Routledge.

Oliveira-Castro, J. M., Foxall, G. R., Yan, J., & Wells, V. K. (2011). A behavioural-economic analysis of the essential value of brands. *Behavioural Processes, 87*, 106–114.

Oliveira-Castro, J. M., Cavalcanti, P., & Foxall, G. R. (2015). What consumers maximize: Brand choice as a function of utilitarian and informational reinforcement. *Managerial and Decision Economics DOI.* doi:10.1002/mde.2722 (Published online May 2015).

Over, D. E. (2003). *Evolution and the psychology of thinking: The debate*. Hove/New York: Psychology Press.

Panksepp, J. (1998). *Affective neuroscience: The foundations of human and animal emotions*. New York: Oxford University Press.

Panksepp, J. (2007). The neuroevolutionary and neuroaffective psychobiology of the prosocial brain. In R. I. M. Dunbar & L. Barrett (Eds.), *The Oxford handbook of evolutionary psychology* (pp. 145–62). Oxford: Oxford University Press.

Rey, G. (1993). Sensational sentences. In M. Davies & G. Humphreys (Eds.), *Consciousness*. Oxford: Blackwell.

Sober, E., & Wilson, D. S. (1998). *Unto others: He evolution and psychology of unselfish behavior*. Cambridge, MA: Harvard University Press.

Strawson, G. (2010). *Mental reality* (2nd ed.). Cambridge, MA: MIT Press.

Sulloway, F. J. (2007). Birth order and sibling competition. In R. I. M. Dunbar & L. Barrett (Eds.), *The Oxford handbook of evolutionary psychology* (pp. 297–310). Oxford: Oxford University Press.

Taylor, S. E., Klein, L. C., Lewis, B. P., Gruenewald, T. L., Gurung, R. A. R., & Updegraff, J. A. (2000). Biobehavioral responses to stress in females: Tend-and-befriend, not fight-or-flight. *Psychological Review, 107*, 411–429.

White, G. M. (1980). Conceptual universals in interpersonal language. *American Anthropologist, 82,* 759–781.

Wiggins, J. S., & Broughton, R. (1985). The interpersonal circle: A structural model for integration of personality research. In R. Hogan & W. H. Jones (Eds.), *Perspectives in personality* (Vol. 1, pp. 1–48). Greenwich: JAI Press.

Zuriff, G. E. (1979). Ten inner causes. *Behaviorism, 7,* 1–8.

Index

Note: Page number followed by 'n' refers to footnotes